We Are Not Manslaughterers

The Epsom Riot and the Murder of Station Sergeant Thomas Green

If you enjoy this book, please pass on & send an email to info @ london-books.co.uk.

Best wishes
Martin Knight

or leave a review on Amazon.
xx

This book is dedicated to Thomas Green and
Frederick Bruns – casualties of peace.

We Are Not Manslaughterers

The Epsom Riot and the Murder of Station Sergeant Thomas Green

Martin Knight

www.tontobooks.co.uk

Published in 2010 by Tonto Books Limited

Copyright © Martin Knight
All rights reserved

ISBN-13:
9781907183140

British Library Cataloguing-in-Publication Data:
A catalogue record for this book is available from
the British Library

Cover design & photo section by Elliot Thomson at
www.preamptive.com

Printed and bound in the UK by
CPI Mackays, Chatham ME5 8TD

Tonto Books Ltd
Produced Up North
United Kingdom

www.tontobooks.co.uk

Our men, living in holes in the earth like ape-men, were taught the ancient code of the jungle law, to track down human beasts in No Man's Land, to jump upon their bodies in the trenches, to kill quickly, silently, in a raid, to drop a hand-grenade down a dugout crowded with men, blowing their bodies to bits, to lie patiently for hours in a shell-hole for a sniping shot at any head which showed, to bludgeon their enemy to death or spit him on a bit of steel, to get at his throat if need be with nails and teeth. The code of the ape-man is bad for some temperaments. It is apt to become a habit of mind. It may surge up again when there are no Germans present, but some old woman behind an open till, or some policeman with a bull's-eye lantern and a truncheon, or in a street riot where fellow-citizens are for the time being 'the enemy'.

Death, their own or other people's, does not mean very much to some who, in the trenches, sat within a few yards of stinking corpses, knowing that the next shell might make such of them. Life was cheap in war. Is it not cheap in peace?

Now It Can Be Told, Sir Philip Gibbs, 1920

CONTENTS

FOREWORD

In *We Are Not Manslaughterers* Martin Knight describes the events surrounding the death of Station Sergeant Thomas Green at Epsom Police Station in 1919. He writes with passion, with great attention to detail and with a determination that the story of Green and the small group of officers who courageously confronted 400 furious Canadian soldiers should never be forgotten.

There is a common, often unspoken, assumption that the end of a war brings an end to the social, political and economic upheavals wrought by the conflict. A cursory glance at the evidence proves this to be wishful thinking. Restructuring an economy for peace time can be as traumatic and troublesome as restructuring for war. When Nelson's seamen returned from the Napoleonic Wars they found merchant ship owners who wanted to continue with the skeleton crews they had been forced to employ during wartime. Jack Tar promptly went on strike and brought coastal shipping to a standstill. Men have always returned to hear gossip about their wives or sweethearts flirting, and worse, with others in their absence. And since the early modern period at least, there were fears that men trained in the use of arms and brutalised by the violence of the battlefield would return home and, unable to find work or unable to settle back in to their peacetime trades, would engage in violent crime. The end of the First World War was no different.

Throughout the war, as well as at its end, men had come back from the Western Front to hear stories or to find evidence that their womenfolk had been unfaithful. Some men took violent action, usually against the woman, but sometimes against the man, and the courts often dealt leniently with them. If a man made a pass at someone's girl or wife, or simply appeared a rival, it could be the cue for a fight. If the offender was from a different national army, or even from a different regiment, the violence might spread to supporters. In the estaminets and streets behind the lines in France and Belgium, as well as in the pubs and streets of Blighty, English Tommies were fully prepared to take on Australians, Canadians, New Zealanders, Scots and Irish, and vice versa: infantry fought cavalry, sappers fought gunners – and the police, sometimes military, sometimes civilian, endeavoured to sort things out. At times the interfering police officer found himself rounded on by both sides, and sometimes by civilians too.

A punch-up in or outside a pub involving soldiers, or sailors, was generally seen by the participants as having some justifying cause. Justifying causes also commonly underpinned what the army called 'mutiny' and the other forms of noisy demonstration that could slip into violence, and what the civilian authorities defined as 'riot'. Occasionally the civic celebrations of peace in 1919 became violent when veterans believed that they were being ostracised from the junketing arranged by, and for, the great and the good. In Luton the trouble resulted in the destruction of the Town Hall. Earlier in the year soldiers, who could not understand why they remained in khaki and subject to harsh military discipline when the war was over, mutinied on both sides of the English Channel. Some among the mutineers ran up red flags and the authorities, nervously eyeing events in disintegrating Russia and defeated

Germany, were concerned about the likelihood of Bolsheviks in the British ranks.

The violent events at Epsom were thus part of a much wider context. In Epsom Tommies resented Canadians and anyone else who had turned their womenfolk's heads while they were away. The Canadians wanted to go home: after all, the war had been over for six months when the initial trouble flared in The Rifleman pub on 17 June 1919.

Both historians and police detectives have to sift their evidence carefully, construct their narratives to the best of their abilities, and to persuade their audiences to accept their version of events as the most plausible account. Unlike the police in 1919, Martin Knight has what appears to be the confession of Sergeant Green's murderer. He moves also to make a forceful argument about an official cover-up designed to keep the lid on further trouble both between the British populace, especially that of Epsom, and Canadian soldiers, but also on the potential for diplomatic and political friction between Britain and her North American Dominion. Lloyd George was certainly Machiavellian. The police did a poor job in investigating the death of one of their own, and the coroner's enquiry into the death of Private Bruns was conducted with unseemly haste. But coroners' courts were not as efficient and well-regulated at the beginning of the twentieth century as they are today. Even today the police can make major mistakes in serious investigations, and in spite of the aura that often surrounded them, at the beginning of the twentieth century detection by English police forces seems to have rated poorly in comparison with that of their contemporaries elsewhere. And if, having had time to think, a policeman decides that he cannot make a positive identification, does that not fit with the work of contemporary forensic psychologists who have shown the problems of what people can actually remember in a moment or dim light and high adrenalin?

Today we are much more prepared to accept and to look for conspiracies. They are more satisfying than mere cock-up or confusion. Moreover, modern politicians have given us good cause. At the end of the twentieth and beginning of the twenty-first century the British public saw a prime minister forced to admit that an enemy warship was attacked and sunk as it was leaving the area where it could have been a threat, it has seen its young men sent to war on the strength of a 'dodgy dossier' and another prime minister investigated for selling honours. Martin Knight marshals his evidence impressively and presents his case forcefully.

Clive Emsley
May 2010

LEADING CHARACTERS

The Green Family

Thomas
Lilian
Lily
Nellie

The Canadian Defendants

James Connors, identified as assaulting Sergeant Green
Alphonse Masse
Robert McAllan, military policeman
Allan MacMaster, the murderer
Gervase Poirier
Herbert Tait
Robert Todd, the bugler
David Wilkie
David Yerex

The Other Canadian Soldiers

Private Frederick Bruns, soldier found dead
Eddie Lapointe
William Lloyd
Private John McDonald, imprisoned in Epsom Police Station
Major James Ross, the officer who tried to quell the riot

Sir Richard Turner, head of Canadian forces in the UK
Driver Alexander Veinot, imprisoned in Epsom Police Station

The Epsom Policemen

PC Harry Hinton
Sergeant Bill Kersey
Inspector Pawley, head of Epsom's police force
PC James Rose, identified James Connors as assailant
PC Joe Weeding
Sergeant Fred Blaydon

The Medics

Gilbert White, the coroner
Dr Thornely, the police doctor

The Legals

Edward Abinger, defence counsel
Harold Benjamin, defence counsel
Justice Darling, the judge
Sir Richard Muir, prosecution counsel
Sir Ernest Wild, prosecution counsel
Cecil Whiteley, prosecution counsel

The Politicians

Sir Rowland Blades, MP for Epsom
Winston Churchill, Secretary of State for War
James Chuter Ede, foreman of inquest jury
David Lloyd George, British Prime Minister

The Royals

Edward, Prince of Wales, heir and oldest son of George V and
Queen Mary
George V, King of the United Kingdom and the British
Dominions, and Emperor of India, 1910–1936

Scotland Yard

Inspector Ferrier, detective assigned to Sergeant Green's case
Major Edgar Lafone, Chief Constable 'V' Division
Sir Nevil Macready, Commissioner of the Metropolitan Police

INTRODUCTION

'Of course, there was a lot more to it ...'

The cemetery climbs up Ashley Road on the edge of Epsom town towards Epsom Downs. Slowly it is edging nearer and nearer to the iconic Grandstand as the local deceased demand more space. My father is in the latest bit of requisitioned land and if you stand with your back to his stone you have a perfect view of the new, pearly white Grandstand – the prime vantage point for well-heeled Derby spectators. I don't think my mum could have found a better place for him. He's in good company: my childhood pals John, Dave, Eamon and Mickey rest there, along with Frank Kidwell, the genial milkman who was murdered in an armed raid on his depot, which so disturbed our childhood innocence. So does former Trades Union Congress leader George Woodcock, and Phyllis Dixey, the world-famous stripper (although not in the same grave). Further back, near the Victorian chapel, lies Lieutenant Colonel Northey, killed in 1879 by Zulu warriors. I can lose hours of my life meandering around, reading the memorials and guessing at the stories behind them. Being Epsom, there are a large amount of gypsies buried in the cemetery, and it is not an unusual sight to see whole families picnicking around the tomb of a grandparent or great grandparent who died fifty years earlier. In keeping the memories of their forebears alive and their graves colourful and vibrant, they put the rest of us to shame. The Council has not, so far, bowed completely to the ridiculous politically correct practice of pulling down stones that fail the notorious 'wobble-test' and are therefore deemed a health and safety risk, though there are some contenders. It is likely that the servile wobble-tester himself did cast a jobsworth eye over the grave of one Thomas Green, because it stands as one of the tallest, at eight feet, in the whole graveyard, a row or three in front of the little Victorian chapel. But even he would have decided against securing the stone from the hundred-million-to-one chance that it might fall and land on a passerby. He would have decided against it because Thomas Green is an Epsom hero, and the inscription on his gravestone would have told him why. Almost.

As a child of the 1960s and 1970s growing up in Epsom in Surrey I was vaguely aware of the events that took place at Epsom Police Station in June of 1919. I realise now that when I first heard about Station Sergeant Green in the 1960s those events were only as far away then as the England football team not retaining the World Cup in Mexico in 1970 is to me now. Yet at the time black and white photographs of Sergeant Green, with his high collar and pantomime moustache, that on anniversaries of the Epsom Riot of 1919 appeared in our local papers seemed to me to be from a distant almost Napoleonic past.

Nobody outside of Epsom appeared to know anything of the riot by Canadian soldiers that led to Thomas Green's murder, which always surprised me. Angry mobs in quiet rural towns besieging the police station and putting to death an officer of the law was surely mouth-watering fare for a book, film, play or documentary, yet besides the aforementioned Epsom newspapers and the occasional mini-exhibition in the local museum it was as if it had never happened. I assumed that I was missing something – a reason why the sergeant's killing was historically unimportant or not newsworthy.

2

When Harry Roberts shot and killed three policemen in Shepherd's Bush, London in 1966 the outrage was national, prolonged and loud. Football crowds even made up chants about him. The ensuing manhunt consumed the media and public alike and when he was finally captured the pressure to restore the death penalty by hanging was intense. A few years later a man called Frederick Sewell shot and killed a Blackpool superintendent and again there was national shock and public anger, because the killing of police officers during the course of their duty was extremely rare. If it was rare in 1972 imagine how big such a story would have been in 1919. Indeed, looking at the Metropolitan Police Roll of Honour, Thomas Green was only the third Met officer to be murdered directly in the line of duty that century and the only one I can discover that has been killed while defending a Metropolitan police station *ever*. When PC Keith Blakelock was trapped and savagely hacked to death by a rabid mob on the Broadwater Farm Estate in Tottenham in 1985 the media stated he was the first Met officer to die at the hands of rioters for sixty-five years. They did not elaborate on who that previous officer was, but it was Thomas Green to whom they referred.

Still, it wasn't my problem or mystery to resolve. I was looking forward to being wayward in my youth and had other things on my mind, yet every now and then I'd be reminded of the case. One such time was in the early 1980s. I was drinking in The Marquis of Granby in Epsom (a public house that figures briefly in this book) when my friend and I fell into conversation with an elderly gentleman at the bar who told us proudly that he was eighty-five years of age. We talked about old Epsom and how the town had changed and I asked him if he remembered the siege of the old police station.

'Of course I do,' he said. 'You couldn't forget that, could you?'

3

'Did you know Sergeant Green?' I asked.

'No, can't say I did. I never had any trouble with the law so I doubt if I ever met him.'

My face may have betrayed a slight loss of interest at this, so he added, 'But I knew the man who it all started over.'

At a stroke the gap between the old black and white photographs and me, now, pint of Kronenberg lager in hand, had been bridged. The old man lowered his voice and looked conspiratorially around the bar, presumably in case there were any surviving relatives or friends in the vicinity, and proceeded to tell us how the aforementioned Epsom man (and to my eternal regret he told us a name that I cannot now remember) had returned from the First World War to discover his wife or girlfriend had been consorting with a Canadian soldier in his absence.

'He bowled up in The Rifleman and found this matey and went up and smashed him full-on in the face,' he told us. 'All hell let loose and the Canadians and the locals had a proper old tear-up until the old Bill turned up and carted off some soldiers and that was what gave them the hump and made them go down the cop shop mob-handed and spring their mates out. Because, they felt it should have been the Epsom boy in the nick.'

The old gent had my full attention now.

Encouraged, he went on. 'Of course, there was a lot more to it.'

'Like what?'

'Well, the Canadians, you know, bit careless ...You know ...'

I didn't know. He winked and he frowned. I tipped my head back as if I understood. I think I understand now.

I could relate to the old man's story, and I see no reason why he would make it up. Being an Epsom boy myself I could

4

imagine how I would have felt, having survived the war and arrived home from France to discover my girl hob-knobbing, or worse, with crop-haired, gum-chewing Canadian soldiers (I'd recently seen the film *Yanks*). Of course, the more I learned the more I realised that the situation was far less clear-cut. Official accounts about the reason for the fight in The Rifleman differ from the old man's story, but there may have been reasons for this, as we shall see. Sadly, there is unlikely now to be anyone left alive with direct experiences of the incendiary summer of 1919, and if there are he or she may not be able to impart them, so one has to piece the jigsaw together through official records, second-hand memories and educated guesswork.

One man who did this was former policeman Edward Shortland and most importantly he has almost certainly solved the mystery of why the case of Sergeant Green had stayed below the radar for so long. It was his booklet *The Murder of Station Sergeant Thomas Green at Epsom Police Station 17th June, 1919* that reignited my interest most recently. Mr Shortland contended that the murder was covered up to avoid embarrassment or worse to the Royal Family and for high-level diplomatic reasons. Edward, the Prince of Wales, was to tour Canada and the dominions in 1919 and 1920 to thank them for their support, efforts and sacrifices in the First World War, and for him to do this whilst back in England we were hanging one or more of their soldiers could have caused much more than a diplomatic incident. The speed with which the Epsom case was 'solved', tried, punished and buried defies belief and is testament to the true power and political skills of the senior figures involved. At a minimum the Prime Minister, David Lloyd George, the Secretary of State for War, Winston Churchill, the Commissioner of the Metropolitan Police, Sir Nevil Macready, and a significant handful of senior policemen and Epsom politicians and dignitaries must have been aware of

5

the desired outcomes and therefore complicit. However, it is this author's opinion that unlike the cover-ups and media manipulation that we endure today, this conspiracy and blatant engineering of the legal system and establishment was perpetrated for the best possible reasons given the time and the unique circumstances. National and international interests demanded some fast and tough decisions.

Mr Shortland's further investigations subsequent to the publication of his booklet, which I was able to follow up and build on, reveal that, in all probability, the fall-out from the Canadian riot was greater than previously believed and that an escalation of the situation was suppressed at source and has remained unknown to the public at large until now. This book details another violent death in Epsom only days later and this time the victim was not only a Canadian soldier, but an American citizen. Thomas Green's death could not be easily erased from the public's conscience and history (although a pretty good fist of it has been made), but the second man's case was rubbed out almost completely. The fact that these undoubted manipulations and machinations took place and were executed so well has caused me to think twice about being so quickly dismissive of famous conspiracy theories of the past and present.

I believe the story of Sergeant Green and the Epsom Riot is an important one. It deserves to be told fully for all those involved, and thus far it has not been. There were reasons behind the ill-feeling between the Canadian soldiers and the Epsom men that have not been previously explored for fear of offending Victorian sensibilities. The whole affair is a small but telling piece of the modern historical jigsaw. Thomas Green was a victim of fatal violence in his life and a victim of international, national and local politics in his death.

Besides the Derby, the Epsom Riot is the most significant historical event to take place in my home town. Until recently I had always believed the most significant event to be the marriage of a Beatle, George Harrison, to Patti Boyd at Epsom Registry Office in January 1966. What Beatle George, his model wife, their best man Paul McCartney and their manager Brian Epstein would not have known that afternoon was that where they stood as vows were exchanged was within a few feet of the spot where Sergeant Green fell nearly half a century earlier.

I was finally inspired to research and write a book on the subject when in the summer of 2009 a plaque was erected commemorating that spot. Chris Grayling, the Shadow Home Secretary and local MP, did the honours. He said Green was a local hero. If so, why had it taken ninety years for the town's officials to acknowledge the fact? Why is Thomas Green just about the only Metropolitan Police Officer to be murdered in the line of duty who did *not* receive a posthumous award for gallantry? What did the old man mean about the Canadians being careless? As I started to dig and delve more and more questions presented themselves. In this book I have endeavoured to present the facts as I know them and the questions that those facts beg, and I attempt to answer those questions rationally without resorting to flights of fancy. At the same time I hope I have transmitted something of the mood of the era and provided background and colour to the key players in this most extraordinary real-life drama.

Martin Knight
Spring 2010

7

CHAPTER 1

THE BUILD-UP

The Quiet Before the Storm

For the 20,000 people of Epsom, Surrey, 4 June 1919 was a special day. It was the day that the Derby was coming home to them after four years away at Newmarket whilst a tumultuous and terrible world war had raged. In at least one way the classic horse race defined Epsomians, for when they met people from other parts of the country and said from where they hailed, they would often add 'Where the Derby is run.' Then the people they were conversing with would know. Even in 1919 Epsom and the Derby had been for a long time indelibly connected in the national consciousness.

Horse racing on Epsom Downs actually had its beginnings in the great Epsom Salts rush of the 1660s. The aristocrats who had flocked to Epsom to partake in the health-giving properties of the Salts would become bored merely drinking and bathing in spa water and would take their servants and footmen up on to the Downs and race them against each other, having side-bets to heighten the interest. Soon, though, and possibly at the suggestion of the servants themselves, their masters were persuaded to start running horses instead. By the 1730s horse racing was an established sport on Epsom Downs. In 1779, The Oaks – the premier race for fillies – was first run and the following year the first ever Derby Stakes took place, named after the Earl of Derby and won by a horse called Diomed. These two classic races have underpinned the horse racing industry that has characterised Epsom to the present day. In 1830 the first whitewashed Grandstand was erected, giving Epsom racecourse its own distinctive character.

For the British people generally, though, the Derby back at Epsom signalled that the Great War was truly over and things really were getting back to normal. Although the conflict had ended officially the previous November, for many it did not seem so. The misery and hardships continued. Many loved ones had still not arrived back despite surviving the war and in Epsom, for example, hundreds of convalescing Canadian soldiers were still restlessly waiting for their passages home. Families who had lost members, and there were few anywhere in the country who were unscathed, wondered whether the war that most had enthusiastically signed up for had been worth it after all. Those who had returned home often found their circumstances had changed. Relationships may have been dislocated and in need of repair, and jobs and homes were scarce. To rub salt into these open wounds there was a flu epidemic spreading across the world like a bush fire and everyone now knew someone who had succumbed.

Despite the downpours that punctuated the afternoon the hordes descended on to Epsom Downs from near and far, and most had dressed for the clement weather that normally warms the Downs on Derby Day. Excitement at what was being dubbed 'The Peace Derby' was such that men in shirtsleeves and women in light dresses did not seem to notice the grey, angry skies and the intermittent rain. Derby Day was the day more than any other when the country came together and came out to play. Kings rubbed shoulders with costermongers, northerners and southerners bought each other warm beer, and the poor and the prosperous united behind their chosen rides. It was the Londoner's unofficial bank holiday and such was the keenness to get there that men would start walking the ten to twenty miles from wherever they lived in London, following the A24 route from Elephant and Castle and through Clapham, Tooting and Streatham. They hoped they'd back a winner or two and afford the luxury of taking the train back in the evening.

Swarthy gypsy ladies moved among the throng selling their lucky heather whilst their husbands offered to share their alleged mystical insights into the outcome of a race for the price of a pint. A funfair whirled away in the dip and stuttered towards Tattenham Corner. Here punters were invited to spectate or even try their luck in the boxing booths, or have their palm read by an ancient Romany lady in a darkened wagon. Omnibuses scattered the crowds as they made their way to a berth near the rails. A man stood on an upturned crate and shouted at nobody in particular to repent sins whilst shysters produced packs of cards and tried to draw a crowd to shake down whilst playing 'Find the Lady', and furtive pickpockets loitered, waiting to seize their moment. A very young Prince Monolulu stood out in the crowd as a solitary black face exclaiming: 'I gotta horse!'

All the time the trains coming into Tattenham Corner, Epsom Downs and Epsom stations disgorged more and more revellers. Nobody really knows how many people the Derby has attracted. There was no entrance fee with the meeting being held on common land, and no capacity. There was space rolling back to Headley Heath if necessary. Newspapers estimate between half a million and a million people attend and on this day the crowd was swollen by large numbers of soldiers sporting British, American and Canadian uniforms. Among them are small clusters of men wearing the convalescence 'blues' of the nearby Woodcote Park Convalescent Hospital for Canadian soldiers. From the Royal Box Edward, the Prince of Wales, there with his parents, the King and Queen, and his siblings Prince Albert and Princess Mary, looked down at his father, George V's, subjects – a floating, chattering sea of flat caps and straw boaters, He could not have known that within a matter of days events in this normally quiet town would come to concern him.

Grand Parade, ridden by Fred Templeman, was the 33–1 winner, which made the bookmakers very happy and the punters, who had piled in on a horse called The Panther, less so. It was especially sweet for Templeman, as he had finished second by a neck in the previous two Derbies, and he was continuing a family tradition, his grandfather having won the race three times in the previous century. Perhaps it was a combination of the weather and the fact that many people were banking on The Panther paying out that shortly after the Derby was run the crowds started to drain away steadily, rather than by the mass exodus that normally took place after the last race on the card.

At the town end of Ashley Road, the route that meanders down from the Grandstand on the course to the centre of Epsom town, Station Sergeant Thomas Green waited in his police station expectantly. There was always activity on Derby Day, but bearing in mind the size of the crowds and the pressure on rural Epsom's infrastructure, surprisingly little trouble. The large force assembled by the Metropolitan Police on the Downs dealt with the bulk of the problems there and then, but it was now that the race-goers were packing into the town that his colleagues were most likely to be bringing in drunks, trouble-makers and criminals.

Sergeant Green was a largely contented man. At fifty-one years old he had filled out from the ten-and-a-half stone he had weighed when he had joined the force nearly a quarter of a century before. He possessed striking blue eyes and what hair remained on his head was still brown. He compensated for going bald by sporting a fine, bristling Edwardian moustache. Green had been the station sergeant at Epsom for almost eight years, having transferred from Putney in London. He preferred the bucolic surroundings of the countryside to the capital where he had worked as a constable, before being promoted to sergeant, for nearly twenty years. Epsom was geographically nearer to and reminded him of Billingshurst, the small village in West Sussex where he had been born and raised.

In 1868, when Thomas Green was born, Billingshurst was a bustling, rural village that lay seven miles south west of the busier and bigger town of Horsham, Sussex, and was home to 1,500 people: around 300 families and houses. Situated on the old Roman road, it boasted its own new railway station from where villagers could travel up to London Victoria or down to the coast to Bognor Regis. The Arun and Wye Canal ran by the village and the River Arun itself formed one of its borders. Fairs were held on Whit Monday and 8 November each year. The small village church, St Mary's, was well patronised, but perhaps not as much so as the King's Arms and The Station Inn, the two more popular public houses. A horse-drawn coach passed through the village on a Saturday morning taking goods or passengers to Pulborough, returning later in the afternoon. One of the gentry, Mr Carnsew, had demonstrated his philanthropy by paying for the construction of the National School and it had recently opened with Mr Henry Wright as the master. The young Thomas Green was one of the early pupils.

During the best part of the nineteenth century the Green family had lived in various working men's cottages in the Frenches Lane area of the village, where the Newbridge Road starts today. In 1851 Robert Green, Thomas Green's grandfather, who had just lost his wife Rhoda to cancer, lived at Black Cottage, which survives to this day as Black and White Cottage. Robert was a sawyer, which put him at a level above an agricultural labourer, having the tools and the knowledge to cut timber accurately, probably to be used as beams in house building, or to make veneers to be made into saleable products by furniture and cabinet makers. By 1871, when Robert Green was in his eighth decade, the census has him down as a farmer employing one man, which suggests that late in life he got hold of a small bit of land. By then he was living just with his daughter, Emily.

His eldest son, George, Thomas Green's father, had been born in 1829 and he too became a sawyer. In 1853 he married Emily Venn and they raised a family of four girls, Rhoda, Emily, Louisa and Alice, and five boys, George, William, Thomas, Francis Albert and Edgar. Like his father, George and his family lived in the same area around Newbridge Road in cottages called Three Houses and in Black Cottage, but also, later, in neighbouring Pulborough and Horsham. As the family grew up employment opportunities were limited and although among the boys the eldest, George, born in 1854, stayed in the area and married a local girl, the others sought their fortunes or sustenance elsewhere. William, born in 1860, initially continued the family tradition by becoming a sawyer and he too married a Billingshurt lady and had six surviving children, but in 1911, at the relatively late age of fifty-one he, his wife and the younger children emigrated, to Canada, for a new life. Thomas Green's sisters went into domestic service, some locally, some in London, and Thomas, at the age of nineteen, after labouring locally decided on a military career and joined up in 1887 with the Royal Horse Artillery.

He served for eight years and spent time in India, his last station being in Umballa, now Ambala. He was officially

14

discharged on 9 May 1895, having already signed on the dotted line for the Metropolitan Police. It was commonplace at the time for the police to take their recruits directly from the military. His joining papers describe Green as being 5'9½'' inches tall with dark hair and blue eyes and bearing a scar under his left ear. At this time he was a single man and living with a Mrs Carr in Hartfield, Sussex. This picturesque village would later become famous for being the home of the author AA Milne, its environs immortalised in his *Winnie the Pooh* stories, most notably the small bridge from where Pooh and his friends dropped 'pooh sticks' into the river below. Milne's home, Cotchford Farm, would later still become notorious as the final home of Brian Jones, the founder of the Rolling Stones rock band, who in 1969 was found drowned in his own swimming pool. (The death was judged accidental, but has been the subject of much speculation and mystery ever since.)

When Thomas Green was lodging with Mrs Carr he was already betrothed to a village girl, Lilian Elizabeth Sands Card, and they were married in St Mary's, the village church, on 18 May 1895. The union was witnessed by Lilian's brother William Bowers Card and her sister Louisa Mercy. The Cards were a Sussex family stretching back generations and populating the Hartfield, Rotherfield and Billingshurst areas. Lilian's father, Stephen, was an agricultural labourer born in 1831 who had married Anna Maria Sands, also in St Mary's Parish Church in Hartfield, in 1861. At least eight children had followed, including William Bowers, born in 1867, and Lilian born two years later. The family were raised in The Gallipots in the village, a charmingly named group of cottages that were so called because at one time they produced gallipots, which were small ceramic pots used for medicines. Today a pub called The Gallipot Inn survives and commemorates this genuine cottage industry.

After living in St Pancras and Putney Thomas and Lilian were happy in Epsom and felt it a pleasant and healthy place to raise their two daughters, Lilian and Nellie, who had been born in 1901 and 1902 respectively. The girls had attended the Pound Lane School around the corner from their house at 92 Lower Court Road and the family was very content. In less than a year Thomas would be able to retire and his police pension would be enough for him to maintain his simple but happy lifestyle. Whilst he felt very satisfied with his career he looked forward to tending his garden and riding his bike to the local stew ponds, or taking a train to the River Mole, where he could fish to his heart's content, as he had on the River Arun when he was a boy.

Most of all he wished for retirement so he could care for his wife, Lilian. Next year Thomas and Lilian would be celebrating their silver wedding anniversary, but his wife had collapsed with a stroke in the Wesleyan Chapel, across the road from the police station and where they both worshipped, some months earlier and she did not seem to be recovering well. The stroke had rendered her paralysed down one side of her body. She was at this point being treated in a hospital in Bloomsbury, London and Thomas and young Lily and Nellie visited, between them, daily. Thomas believed that if he could get the time he would be able to have his wife home and nurse her back to health. He might even move the family back to Sussex if that would help, he thought. Just a few days ago the doctors had cautiously advised they were hopeful that she would be able to leave hospital fairly soon and this had cheered him up enormously.

The police station was a two-storey, double-fronted, detached Victorian house with shrubs and small trees at the front behind a fence of spiked iron railings about four feet high. The gardens at the back and the front were well tended by Inspector

Pawley, Sergeant Green's superior, and a prettier more inoffensive police station would be hard to find. The Inspector lived upstairs with his family. Charlie Pawley was similar to his station sergeant in many ways, being fifty-one years old and counting down the days to his retirement, having also spent much of his police career in London and being a country boy. Charlie and his wife Kate were both born in Millbrook, Cornwall and had been married for thirty years. He had originally worked in the Devonport naval dockyard. The marriage had produced nine children, six of whom were living at home. Harry, his son, had only recently returned from his First World War service.

Pawley had joined the force in 1892, was promoted to Sergeant in 1901 and then again to Station Sergeant in 1906. Only two years later he was elevated to the rank of Inspector. The family had originally lived in nearby Hook Road in a red-bricked, semi-detached cottage and when Pawley got his promotion they were all delighted to move to the spacious rooms above the shop. The police court and the Wesleyan Church were opposite and almost next door were the manicured lawns, flowerbeds and ornamental ponds of Rosebery Park. The cells were directly below the girls' bedroom and many a night they could hear local drunks being locked up and their protestations being silenced by a gruff Sergeant Green: 'Sssh! There are nippers sleeping upstairs.'

Sometimes when young Freda Pawley would come in from school Sergeant Green would tease her.

'You been a good girl at school today, young Freda?'

'Yes, Sergeant Green.'

'You sure?' said Green his eyes narrowing, but smiling.

'Yes, Sergeant Green.'

'Well, that's not what I hears from Mrs Chittenden.'

He would wink and pat the little girl on the crown of her head. Mrs Chittenden was the headmistress of Pound Lane School. She had taught his two girls and he knew her well.

Less than a mile away, up at Woodcote Park, a military training camp had been set up by the University and Public Schools Brigade (UPS) – who later became the Royal Fusiliers – after procuring the land from the Royal Automobile Club (RAC) at the beginning of the war. It had been handed over to the Canadian Army as their main convalescence hospital in England. Post-Derby the soldiers, some in uniform, most in the 'blues', ambled back into the camp, having no money to spend in the town. They would while away yet another evening as they awaited news of their departure back to their homeland. Men stood in clusters outside their tin huts playing Crown and Anchor, a dice game they would place money on that very often they did not have. In each group stood a man with a book calculating and re-calculating who owed who what. Invisible debts and profits were transferred from man to man and ledger to ledger as they battled to keep boredom at bay. Other than the Derby, the main conversation centred on when they were going home. Rumour fed rumour. They'd heard about a riot at the Kinmel camp in Rhyl and cussed at the fact that some Canadians had died. Someone said it was close to 'blowing up' at the Witley camp in nearby Guildford, where more Canadians were queued for ships home. Others complained bitterly about the Epsom men coming back from France and being hostile towards them, and one man, a tall man, said he was fed up with the 'fucking police' who were always harassing them when they went to town.

18

'Bastard Tommies, they think we haven't fought too?' spat the tall man, shaking his head and moving on to the subject of the Epsom lads.

'They think we *want* to be here? They're all bleeding midgets. Jockeys. I just swipe 'em.' This was from a boy called Connors, who demonstrated with a back-handed slap through the air.

None of the Canadians could understand it. Tens of thousands of their number had died in the war doing what they had to do for Britain. And now she was penning them in half a year after the conflict had ended with no information, no news. They were being treated badly and their patience was exhausted.

Major James Ross was sympathetic. Many of his men had suffered enough and he was unable to give them the answers and pledges they wanted. Keeping a lid on their frustrations and anger was becoming harder by the day. He turned a blind eye to the gambling, drinking and carousing with local women, which were about the only diversions open to the men, but now the Epsom soldiers were returning home incidents of violence and aggression were becoming commonplace and polite phone calls from old Sergeant Green and others at the town police station asking him to fetch 'prisoners' from the cells were no longer a rarity.

As he surveyed his men the only one who seemed to smile all the time and be oblivious to it all was young Todd. You could barely call him a man as he looked no more than fourteen with his tiny stature and boyish looks. Life was one big adventure and so far the horrors of war had not damaged him. As a recent recruit and arrival in England he had not been sent to France. He had had a tough lot, though, what with being a Barnardo boy in Belfast and then immigrating to Canada for a better life before enlisting. As the Major looked over at him, enthusiastically polishing his prized bugle and totally immersed, he truly hoped he could get him home soon. Perhaps, mused Major Ross, he was unlike the others because he did not have a family to return to. This *was* his family.

David Lloyd George, the Prime Minister of Britain, had not gone to Chequers this weekend. Being a Prime Minister without inherited wealth, this country house at the foot of the Chiltern hills had been made available to him as a country retreat. He had stayed at 10 Downing Street because these were strained times and he felt he needed to be in the capital to deal with situations as they arose. The world war had been won, but the peace was proving to be brittle, especially at home. The euphoria of victory had subsided and Lloyd George was finding his popularity waning. Industrial unrest and influenza were paralysing the workforces and whispers of revolution and civil disobedience were becoming more audible. Even the police were agitating to strike and soldiers were disobeying orders. And then there was this problem with the Canadian soldiers still awaiting passage home. With all of the labour problems it was proving hard to get them away quickly, and now they were playing up. There had been riots at Guildford and Rhyl. People had died. The Prime Minister fretted over relations with Canada and the other Commonwealth countries, many of whom had come to our side during the war and may be now contemplating the nature of their relationship with the 'Mother Country'. The wily politician had a plan to strengthen and renew those ties. He had engineered a Royal Tour of thanks across the dominions. He just needed to ensure that nothing went amiss in the meanwhile …

'All who can, must prepare to fight or the nation will go under'

In the summer of 1919 Epsom was trying very hard to recapture its pre-war tranquil, semi-rural state. Five years earlier in the dying days of summer a great recruiting meeting had been held in the public hall there to encourage volunteers for Kitchener's Army. The Territorials had already enlisted and were on their way to Europe to check Germany, who had by now invaded Belgium. More and more men were needed and such meetings, which infused men with a mixture of patriotism, euphoria, duty and fear, were being staged up and down the country. In Epsom, Basil Braithwaite, the Justice of the Peace who lived in the grand Hookfield house on the edge of the Common, addressed the packed hall first. His niece was the theatre (and later silent film) actress Lilian Braithwaite, and this slight connection to stardom afforded him some extra celebrity in the town. He beseeched Epsom's men to come forward and enlist and warned solemnly: 'All who can must prepare to fight, or the nation will go under.'

A Captain Clay followed with some hard facts about the numbers of men that were going to be needed and ended his speech by quoting Captain Scott, of South Pole fame, with words that one would have thought would have sent a deep chill down many spines: 'Englishmen can endure hardships and help one another and meet death with as great fortitude as ever in the past.' 'God Save the King' was then enthusiastically sung by the audience and twenty-seven men came forward there and then and put pen to paper.

On Monday 1 September 1914 the first recruits were set to leave for active service. Crowds thronged the High Street to see

21

them off and cheered, applauded and waved handkerchiefs as Mr Braithwaite, again, addressed the new soldiers. 'It may seem hard to leave wives, mothers, sisters and sweethearts, but it is better to fight for them rather than see them butchered or treated in some other terrible way. Goodbye and God Bless You.' Wives, mothers, sisters and sweethearts of that first batch of young men and boys were not so jingoistic. Instinct told them that some of those boys would not be coming home. Even they, though, could not have guessed just how high a toll the war would take.

The fact that there was now a major conflict on was very evident in Epsom. A 'Dad's Army' force of special constables was formed under the command of Inspector Wootten. These older men were issued with a truncheon, a whistle and a badge and they each undertook one four-hour duty in every twenty-four hours, patrolling the town and paying extra vigilance to places where they believed the enemy might attack. Soldiers were all around. Battalions were camped out on the Downs, where they were undertaking rigorous training; families were encouraged to take in individual soldiers where they could and in short time the local hospitals for the mentally ill would be adapted to house and treat the casualties of war. The Public Schools Brigade, now ensconced in Woodcote Park, had attracted 2,000 to 3,000 men aged between 30 and 35 and who had a public school or university background, but had failed to secure a commission at the outbreak of war. These civilians, who desperately wanted to be soldiers but had been rejected, went about building a huge hutted camp in the grounds of the estate. By January 1915 they had knocked the camp and themselves into shape and Lord Kitchener himself paid a visit to them and nearly 20,000 other troops, who paraded before him on Epsom Downs in the snow.

In March 1915 the 2,143 inmates of Horton Hospital were gathered up and sent to neighbouring Long Grove Hospital and Horton was turned over completely to the military to provide 'the best treatment and doctoring that exists in the country' for injured soldiers. Wounded men from the much smaller Grandstand Hospital up on Epsom Downs were also moved there and the town was soon swelling with a growing influx of maimed and traumatised young men.

Built around the turn of the century, the hospitals for the mentally ill had become as important a part of Epsom's fabric as the horse racing industry. Five huge asylums were constructed in an area on the edge of the Common that became known as the 'Epsom cluster'. They were the Manor Hospital that opened in 1899, St Ebba's in 1902, Horton in 1903, Long Grove in 1907 and West Park in 1916. Almost identical in design and decoration, they became communities within a community, boasting their own chapels and churches, football teams, social clubs and living amenities. Their arrival triggered a programme of residential house building nearby and the red-bricked, solid, semi-detached cottages of Hook Road and Thomas Green's Lower Court Road were constructed with new hospital workers in mind. By the summer of 1919 the Horton, Long Grove and Manor hospitals were home for 5,000 of the 'feeble-minded' people of London. 'Patients', many of whom had qualified as such for merely suffering from epilepsy or having a bastard child, became institutionalised and introverted and were often glimpsed by the locals through the barrier fences as they traipsed aimlessly around the hospital grounds.

War or no war, the Epsom police were making few concessions. PC Joe Weeding, who lived at 54 Middle Lane with his wife, Annie, was especially industrious. In a short space of time he arrested three members of the Public Schools Brigade, one for having too powerful a light on a motorcycle, one for not displaying a rear red light on a motor car and another for having too bright a headlamp. The English, and especially members of the Public Schools Brigade, would have been used to this sort of petty, unbending small-town policing and taken it in their stride, but when soldiers from Australia and then Canada arrived in Epsom it would rankle. Weeding is a constant presence in the court reports of the time and his arrests seem to be more frequent than all of his colleagues' arrests put together. The arrival of the motor car, especially, appears to have enraged him and despite the offences listed above there are many more examples of unfortunate drivers who happened to be passing through Epsom being flagged down and summonsed because their motor cars were too noisy or considered by Weeding to breach some bye-law or other.

The local press gives a flavour of the type of crimes the police were dealing with up to this point. Men from London coming down to net songbirds presented a regular problem. They used lime sticks to entrap linnets, yellowhammers and goldfinches up on Walton Heath and Epsom Downs and then attempted to take them home under their coats, by train, for eventual sale at the Club Row market in London. Children were warned about the perils of blackberrying, as one poor lad had died after being poisoned by consuming some. One thirteen-year-old boy who was sentenced to be birched for house-breaking provoked some debate in the newspaper columns, but the punishment went ahead. Another wretched man was prosecuted for attempting to commit suicide. Now and then the police had a domestic or a drunken brawl to break up. It wasn't quite Will Hay *Ask a Policeman* territory, but other than when race meetings were on it was generally quiet and relatively serene.

24

Every now and then a soldier would return home from France as an injured or homecoming hero and the townspeople would turn out to cheer and sing 'For He's a Jolly Good Fellow'. One such homecoming was Sydney Martin's. Epsom born and bred, he was a groom at Richard Wootton's stables. A large crowd waited outside the 'Brighton Station' (from where trains went into Victoria and down to Brighton) on Station Road, now Upper High Street, and when he appeared enveloped him and chaired him across the road to his modest cottage in Pikes Hill. Sydney, a down-to-earth country man, had rescued two wounded soldiers from a crater that was being shelled by Germans. Later, this man, a humble stable lad certainly not accustomed to public speaking, was asked to address a public ceremony after a dinner in his honour. His short, unvarnished speech probably brought home the terror, squalor and misery of war more than a thousand press reports.

> I am not much of a speaker. You must take what I say in the rough. I done my duty at the word of command, the same as every man should do. When you see these poor fellows being knocked about with their limbs knocked off, perhaps their heads; men torn to pieces, and horses lying about everywhere, it makes you do something.

Besides such interludes as this and when the town hosted a military funeral when a soldier in one of the hospitals died, Epsom went about its business as usual. The Council continued its pedestrian civil administrative business, the courts dealt with local miscreants (and, later in the war, a succession of workers who put their case as to why they should *not* be conscripted) and the people got on with their lives. They went to the cinema, attended fetes, tended their gardens and drank in the pubs and clubs. However, in 1915, when the Woodcote convalescence camp started to take Australian, New Zealander and then Canadian soldiers recovering from their injuries (shortly afterwards it was given over completely to the Canadian military), Epsom's equilibrium began to be tested.

In 1916 when conscription was first introduced the war suddenly became a bit more real to those people who were now going to be *compelled* to fight. Ironically it was the jingoistic Justice of the Peace Basil Braithwaite's gardener who was one of the first to claim his job was indispensable and that he should not be forced to go to the Front. His claims were rejected. Elphick's, the High Street butcher who would later employ one of Inspector Pawley's daughters, similarly pleaded on behalf of one of their employees, Thomas Choules. Mr Elphick claimed that Choules was the only man on his staff who could kill a bullock. Perhaps that did not help his case in asking *not* to go to France.

Food prices shot up and many items became scarce or unavailable. The news from the Front was bad. A war that many thought was going to be over by Christmas 1914 was still in full, terrible flow by Christmas 1916 and hundreds of thousands of young men were dying. The prospect of a long-drawn-out conflict was now being publicly contemplated and the spectre of defeat privately contemplated. Two brothers from Epsom, Arthur and Sidney Randall, died within a few weeks of each other – one killed in action and the other from wounds. It was news like this that brought the disaster into every street. By the end of the war about 360 men from the borough had perished and many more suffered injuries, some visible, some not. No family could have remained entirely untouched. As each month of the war went by life became harder and bleaker and in 1918 the influenza epidemic struck. A local gravedigger was granted exemption from conscription such did his workload increase in 1918.

One morning in November of 1918 a telegram arrived at Epsom Police Station and was passed immediately to Inspector Pawley. It announced that Germany had signed the Armistice at 5.00am and hostilities had ceased at 11.00am. Pawley took the missive across the road to the Magistrates' Court, where a tedious planning permission case was in session. Mr West, the Chairman of the Bench, read the telegram aloud and magistrates, police, press and plaintiffs alike forgot the issues in front of them and burst into applause and cheering. The *Epsom Advertiser* describes how the following hours unfolded:

The good tidings were proclaimed by the raid system. Immediately all business, domestic or otherwise, was suspended, or practically so, the flags of the Allies were thrust into prominence from windows and balconies, and uninspiring streets became avenues of animation. Civilians and convalescent soldiers mingled with yelling, prancing schoolboys equipped with whistles, tin drums and flags. Epsom had begun to mobilise. A distant booming of barrage guns, heard for the first time without a shudder, convinced a doubting few that the news this time was not too good to be true.

Within a very short time the excitement and jubilation began to organise itself. First a procession of college boys, wondrously arrayed, paraded the streets, halloing and creating a din by every means that suggests itself to boys who are rejoicing. Later the band from Woodcote Park camp, marching about the town, varied the hullabaloo with martial music. Soldiers – thousands of them – joined in the procession. The fun – dancing and demonstrating in a mad-cap fashion – was maintained till late in the evening. A huge bonfire near the college, consuming an effigy of the Kaiser, frantically excited the youth of the district. During the afternoon thanksgiving services were held at the Christ Church, the Congregational Church and nearly all other places of worship.

Charlie Pawley must have been honoured that he was the man in Epsom that received the news of the peace first and it was he that then relayed it through the appropriate channels. In that small way he was now part of Epsom's history. He may also have breathed a sigh of relief that the war was over and that the worst was past. Regretfully, for him and for Epsom, it was not. The sight of the celebrating Canadian soldiers pouring into the town later that night and taking over the pubs, and in some instances raiding the bars and helping themselves to drinks whilst powerless landlords looked on, did not bode well.

'There is a little bit of feeling between the Imperials and the Canadians'

Having up to 4,000 members of colonial armies in a town with a population of around 20,000 was always going to require some finesse. Granted, they were Allies fighting for the same cause, but Epsom people could have been forgiven, at first, for feeling like they had been invaded and the frictions that soon came to the surface would have to be contained by a small-town police force some twenty-four men strong at most. The difficulty was that the Australians, New Zealanders and then the Canadians had little respect for, or fear of, English bobbies riding bicycles, blowing whistles and secreting truncheons. The colonials felt they were engaged in an altogether bigger conflict and obeying parochial rules and observing old English protocols was an annoyance. The police, on the other hand, were accustomed to receiving respect from the town's folk and were not happy about their authority being undermined. They believed that the soldiers should be policed by their own military force, especially with such a large contingent, and could not understand why they were not. On the previously quiet streets of Epsom and Ewell relations were strained right from the beginning.

One of the first serious clashes between police and convalescents took place in January 1916 and was splashed across the local newspapers, which artfully recognised the subtext. Two Australians, both veterans of Gallipoli, were charged with assaulting police officers and one of them was kept in custody for some days awaiting the hearing of his case. Trooper Frank Maynard had arranged to meet his Epsom girlfriend (to whom he said he was engaged to be married, although this could have been a white lie intended to preserve her honour) at the gates of the Manor Hospital and from there they walked through to the privacy of the Christ Church yard. At a quiet spot Maynard spread his greatcoat on the grass and the couple sat down and, no doubt, canoodled. After half an hour PC Weeding, dressed in plain clothes, stumbled over Trooper Maynard's foot. Weeding ordered them both to stand up and demanded the girl's name and address. She gave her name, but refused her address. Maynard maintained later that at no point up to then had Weeding declared himself a police officer. He asked what the girl's address had to do with him and in true Australian style punched him on the nose. Another Australian, Private Pinson, was also in the churchyard with a girl he had been seeing and ran over towards where he heard the commotion and joined the struggle between Maynard and Weeding. Only when Weeding blew his whistle and Inspector Pawley, also in plain clothes, popped up and struck Pinson did the two soldiers realise they were dealing with policemen. They ceased to resist.

'Are you special constables?' asked Pinson.

'No, we are regulars,' Inspector Pawley replied.

'Why didn't you say that in the first place?' protested Pinson.

Pawley told the court that he had announced he was a police officer when Pinson was about thirty yards away, but he could not swear that the Australian had heard it. Pinson also asked whether he could see Pawley's badge and the Inspector replied that he would show it to him down at the station. At this point Pinson decided his best course of action was to streak across the Common and back to camp and was not arrested until hours later. Maynard was taken into immediate custody.

In the court the defence lawyer pleaded on behalf of the prisoners, both of whom had pleaded guilty:

> These two men had come from the far ends of the world in response to the earliest appeal made by the old country when she was in great need. They were among the earliest to land on that hell upon earth – Gallipoli. They were men who had given up their lives to give assistance to the old country when many of our own young men had been hanging in the background.

Basil Braithwaite, the lead magistrate, appeared to take this on board and fined Maynard and Pinson £10 and £5 respectively when a prison sentence seemed likely and was clearly expected by the police, who had been keeping Trooper Maynard in custody.

One has to wonder why Inspector Pawley and PC Weeding took it upon themselves to hang around in plain clothes in a sheltered churchyard. Presumably it was known that colonial soldiers took Epsom girls here for liaisons: why else would they be there? But what criminal offence was being committed? Why was it given such importance that the most senior Epsom policeman and his enthusiastic underling mounted their own covert operation? The obvious conclusion to be drawn is that the officers were emotionally involved and did not approve of Epsom ladies forming relationships with the colonial soldiers, and they approved even less of the colonial soldiers taking advantage of the easily led Epsom females whilst many of the good Epsom men were away fighting, and in some cases laying down their lives. Inspector Pawley may have received a jolt when he saw the magistrates did not necessarily see it the same way.

Touchstone, pen name of Rowland Hedges, respected leader writer for the *Epsom & Ewell Advertiser*, had the following to say, hinting heavily at the town's general unease over the soldiers and their relations with local girls:

> 'Disgraceful' is hardly the word to use in connection with the scenes that have been witnessed around the town in the last few months and the intervention of the police will not be deemed premature.
>
> The police were right in taking action, but they did not go about in the right way. They should have gone with reinforcements.
>
> One can imagine the supercilious manner adopted by members of the force in asking for the names of certain persons and perhaps they exceeded their duties in threatening to take them to the police station on their refusal. Such a statement by men in civilian garb would arouse the ire of anyone, although extenuations cannot be made on behalf of the soldier who – no doubt in the heat of the moment – dealt the policeman a severe blow.
>
> Everybody is sorry that the police constable and the police inspector were given such a warm reception, but it will teach them the importance of being prepared to meet emergencies.

More evidence of how the dominion presence was seen to be corrupting the town came only a few weeks later when a Mrs Monk was hauled before the court charged with permitting her house to be used for immoral purposes. Mrs Monk, who was forty-one years of age and said that her husband was serving at

31

the Front, blamed all of her problems on a married woman to whom she had let one of her rooms. Inspector Pawley, in court, said there was no inference that Mrs Monk herself was committing immoral acts and added that on inspection her house was 'very clean'. Yet he and PC Shuttleworth had been watching the house for a week and had seen the married woman take in soldiers on numerous occasions and seen Mrs Monk usher them out again some time later. Basil Braithwaite, magistrate, found the case proved and fined Mrs Monk £2.

Again, one wonders about the motives of Inspector Pawley and the deliciously named Inspector Race Hooper of Kingston Police who prosecuted this case. To devote a week of PC Shuttleworth's time in observing the comings and goings seems extreme and one would have thought that Pawley would have been relieved if Australians and Canadians were sating their sexual needs in a low-key brothel rather than tempting the flowers of Epsom into alfresco unions in sacred churchyards. In their defence, though, overt prostitution would have come as a shock to genteel Epsom and the police would have felt legally and morally bound to stamp it out. At the Canadian camp in nearby Witley, close to Guildford, the soldiers had become a magnet for local prostitutes as well as ladies travelling down from London and it had become a major headache for the Surrey Constabulary.

Later, in February 1917, Inspector Pawley went to the court to oppose the licence of the proprietor of The Plough Inn in West Ewell. Pawley had been 'undercover' in this country public house and seen the barman serve beer to some Canadian convalescents. They were dressed in the blues uniform of the hospitals and as such, strictly speaking, they should not have been served. The magistrates declined Pawley's request. The Plough Inn stood at least two miles away from Epsom town centre in a sparsely populated area among farms and fields, and it was probably for this reason that these soldiers went there in the first place, yet Pawley tracked them down and made their life difficult.

It has to be said that the Epsom police's zealous pursuit of 'criminals' was not confined to just Canadian soldiers. Inspector Pawley and PC Weeding, again, saw fit to climb a tree in plain clothes with field glasses and gather evidence on a group of local men playing pitch and toss. Gambling was illegal and the group that ranged from boys to men, off the Epsom Common, were prosecuted and tried. Times have changed, but this seems extreme. At the same time they saw fit to arrest and prosecute Bertha Neville and Rose Ellis, from Meadow Walk and Heatherside Road respectively, for pulling the blossoms off shrubs in Rosebery Park. The two young girls, now criminalised, were fined five shillings each.

Public opinion towards the Canadians shifted considerably in the summer of 1917 when a private was accused of the attempted rape of an Epsom girl and the case was played out in court and in the local newspapers. At the same time local consternation about relations between the Canadians and the town's women provoked a leader in the *Epsom & Ewell Advertiser*. The sight of groups of women at Epsom railway station, from where trains went into Waterloo, bidding affectionate and tearful farewells to Canadian soldiers returning to the Front hit a nerve. The leader writer, Touchstone, attempted to dampen down the resentment.

In September there was a case reported of a Canadian soldier who had been robbed by a prostitute after a night out at The Maple Leaf Club in London and another where a Leatherhead police constable was threatened with a razor. Another case of assault of a woman reached the courts in November. This time Thomas Vicaire was accused of an unspecified serious assault on an Epsom lady. Vicaire was a native Canadian who had been born in Restigouche County, New Brunswick in 1892. He had arrived at Woodcote camp only a couple of months earlier following being wounded at Vimy Ridge, where the Canadians had lost many men and fought so valiantly. Vicaire had form for being AWOL and drunk whilst in France, and also for begging at Victoria Station in London, but this time the case against him was unproven.

The following summer, in 1918, a Private Archie McDonald was charged with assaulting Inspector Pawley when he and PC Greenfield were called to a pub where fighting had broken out. By this time it seems that Pawley was becoming aware of the dangers of relations breaking down completely between the convalescents and the police and he pleaded for leniency for McDonald, who was facing imprisonment.

'We want to be on the best possible terms with these boys,' he said.

The magistrates concurred and Private McDonald received a lenient fine.

In September a Japanese Canadian soldier with the unlikely name of Frank Barwell was charged with assaulting a woman. The newspapers described him as 'a Japanese'. The following month two soldiers, possibly brothers, Privates Fred and William Doyle, both from the Canadian Army Medical Corp (CAMC), were up in front of the justices for quite a serious fight outside The Marquis of Granby at the top end of the High Street. George Greenfield, now a sergeant, was in the thick of this one too and when the case came to court he was unable to attend as he was too badly injured. One of the Doyles stood before the magistrates with a bloody bandage wrapped around his head. Inspector Pawley, now even keener to put a lid on the escalating violence, resentment and lawlessness around the town, asked the court to reduce the charges from Grievous Bodily Harm to Common Assault. He did this even when his sergeant was apparently on his sickbed nursing grievous bodily injuries.

The first case to make the court of a returning Epsom Tommy getting into an altercation with the Canadians was in the January of 1919. Private Arthur Jones and Canadians Franklin Brown and Conrad Deacon were all arrested for fighting in the High Street. Acting Sergeant Shirley was the arresting officer and he testified that Jones persisted in trying to fight the two Canadians, who he said had used insulting language. Other witnesses said that Brown and Deacon had verbally abused some women.

The fuse for an explosion of violence was lit and with each day the likelihood of that explosion increased. Canadian relations with the police were at an all-time low, and every week brought the return of more Epsom men from the war who, for whatever reason, were immediately resentful of the colonial presence. The Canadians themselves, meanwhile, became more embittered about the failure of the authorities to return them home months after the war had ended.

These latter sentiments were being felt even more keenly at other Canadian camps in England and on 4 March 1919 at the Kinmel camp near Rhyl in North Wales a full-scale riot broke out. The disturbance raged over two days as the disaffected men wrecked and looted their own camp, taking on officers and defenders of the 'Tin Town', as the camp complex was known, in the process. By the time the rioters surrendered on 5 March six soldiers lay dead and twenty-five others were injured, shot by their own officers. That evening the Military Police herded thirteen handcuffed prisoners by special train to the Tower of London. The historical imagery of being imprisoned overnight here must have verged on the surreal. Twelve others were

35

shipped to Walton Gaol in Liverpool. Fifty-nine soldiers in all would later face court martial in Liverpool. Despite efforts to suppress news of the riot reaching the national media, it did, and inevitably the occupants of Woodcote convalescence centre would have heard lurid accounts. Significantly, they would have known that within days of the riot ending the remaining soldiers from Kinmel camp were on ships heading back to Canada.

Private Clifford Duby was up before the magistrates just a week before the fated Tuesday in June 1919 over a row in the High Street. He was charged with being drunk and disorderly, using obscene language and with assaulting PC Barltrop. His colleague PC Dan Stanford gave evidence to the effect that he was in the High Street with PCs Barton and Barltrop when he saw Duby drunk and shouting and swearing. The fact that three officers were patrolling together in a relatively small town like Epsom speaks volumes about the police's perception of the threat to public order (and themselves) posed by the Canadians by this time. Duby had thrown his coat to the floor and had his fists up, challenging civilians to fight. When Stanford asked him to put his coat back on and move along the street he did this at first, but further down the road threw the coat off once more and resumed his threatening demeanour. The officers then decided to arrest and take him into custody. Duby, only 5'3", put up a fight and threw Stanford to the ground and another Canadian hit Barltrop across the head from behind with a stick.

Inspector Pawley also gave evidence and complained of the military not providing police in the town to keep their soldiers in order. An officer from the camp said on that occasion it was not the duty of the camp authorities to do that, although he promised to make a representation to his superior in the matter. The Chairman of the Court, Magistrate Dorset, made the comment that if there was no one to look after the soldiers they should not be allowed into town. The same Canadian officer declined to give the prisoner a reference of previous good character and the bench fined Duby £5 and ordered that if the payment was not made he should be sentenced to one month's hard labour. The reason that the officer could not give Duby a good character reference was that he was trouble. He could not read or write and he signed statements with a scrawled X. Of French descent, he was the son of a painter born in 1899. He had enlisted twice, both times being underage, but ghosted through on the second occasion. He had been confined to barracks recently for being absent without leave. Duby did not, or could not, pay his fine and was duly imprisoned at Wandsworth. This may have been the best thing that could have happened to him as all the signs are that he could have been an enthusiastic participant in the riot that lay just a week ahead.

On the weekend before the Epsom disturbance Canadian tempers at the Witley camp in nearby Guildford in Surrey reached boiling point. As in Epsom, there had been trouble between returning British soldiers and Canadians, and a military presence on the streets of Guildford had been keeping a fragile order. On Saturday 14 June some soldiers were arrested for organising gambling and were placed in a guardroom to await some form of discipline. Gambling, especially the game Crown and Anchor, was about all these directionless and idle soldiers had to do and they did not take kindly to this imposition and the perceived heavy-handed tactics of the Military Police. Word spread of the arrests and a large crowd soon surrounded the guardroom, which began to threaten the guards to release the prisoners. When they refused some men smashed through the doors and did it themselves. By now the crowd was 2,000 strong and a mob mentality took over. All the frustrations, bitterness and anger boiled over into a seething human mass intent on violence and destruction.

The rioters battered a hole in the wire mesh fence that penned in the soldiers, who were patients in the attached venereal disease hospital, and rolled in barrels of beer to them. They then flowed across the London–Portsmouth road and rampaged through the 'Tin Town' that existed for the camp as its very own retail, leisure and facilities centre. Shops were looted and gutted and the big Garrison Theatre set alight. This time, fortunately, there were no fatalities, but the damage was extensive and expensive. With Witley being only twenty miles down the road from Epsom (and within days many Witley soldiers were transferred to Epsom) it was inevitable that the Woodcote men would have quickly absorbed news of the rioting and this would have been very much in their minds when two of their own men found themselves in a civil prison cell a couple of days later.

On the very morning of the riot, the Tuesday, the magistrates sat again with Mr Dorset in the chair and with Henry Banks Longley, leader of Epsom Urban Council, alongside. This time an Epsom man, twenty-four-year-old Walter Terry of Linton's Lane, was facing them. He was charged with using insulting words and behaviour whereby a breach of the peace may have been occasioned. PC Percy Taylor was giving evidence and described how there was a large crowd of civilians and soldiers in the High Street on the previous night, Monday. Terry was challenging the soldiers to fight and he and others had their coats off in preparation. Taylor said he asked Terry to move on, but the defendant refused, so he arrested him. Terry was asked if he had any questions of the constable, but all Terry said was, 'No, sir. I think he did his best for me.'

The court report does not throw light on what actually sparked the trouble between Terry, his friends and the Canadians. Terry's older brother Alfred had been killed two years earlier, near Ypres, but this would not necessarily explain the hostility felt towards the Canadians. Alfred, though, had left a young widow, Lily, and if a relationship had been attempted between a Canadian soldier and her, then that would. If such a scenario is on the right track then Walter Terry would have been unlikely to explain his motives to the court or the police in order to protect family dignity and privacy.

Taylor went on to explain that there had been trouble in the High Street nearly every night during the previous week and it looked like there would be more this week. His prediction would come true more rapidly and much more seriously than he could have ever imagined.

'What is the cause of this?' questioned Magistrate Dorset.

'I can't say.' Taylor replied. 'Like the soldiers at Witley camp, the Canadians seem bent on trouble.'

Sergeant Fred Blaydon, who was also present, gave the magistrates a more rounded view. 'The young men demobilised come into contact with the Canadians. That is the origin of it. They get drinking and quarrels start.'

'But, I don't understand the cause,' pressed Dorset.

'There is a little bit of feeling between the Imperials and the Canadians.'

'I should have thought there ought to be comradeship.'

'I'm afraid that is not so.'

PC Dan Stanford elaborated on the actual trouble. He thought there were up to 100 soldiers and civilians standing in the High Street in groups and openly hostile to each other. It was clear to him that feelings between the groups were running high. Percy Taylor offered further insight, revealing that a group of stable lads from the many horse training establishments on the Downs had banded together to come down town to give the Canadians a hiding. Epsom people will testify that what many of the stable lads lacked in inches (as at one time, at least, they had nearly all been aspiring jockeys) they made up for in spirit. They were nobody's mugs and were generally adept with their fists, often staging boxing matches in the London hotels. Stanford said that this time the Epsom boys and the stable lads aligned and were ready to fight the soldiers together. Walter Terry claimed he had only waded in to protect his brother [his other brother was present at the fight], but Mr Dorset told him he should have kept out of it and fined him £1. Sergeant Fred Blaydon reiterated the point that these disturbances were now occurring every night and two, and three or even four extra police officers were being employed to try and keep a lid on it.

Within hours every available Epsom police officer would be marshaled to defend their police station from an onslaught by 400 angry, frustrated and some murderous soldiers and Percy Taylor and Dan Stanford's trusted station sergeant would be dead, with his head literally caved in.

CHAPTER 2

THE RIOT

'We have some trouble here, right now'

Today The Rifleman public house still stands, largely unaltered over the last century, at the corner of Hook Road in Epsom and East Street, on the edge of the town centre. It is a small pub with a single entrance leading into a narrow lounge bar with a counter on the right-hand side. Remarkably, it is one of the few Epsom pubs to have survived the modern era of closures, name changes, branding and gimmicks. It unashamedly and almost uniquely courts an older clientele and recent landlords have varied their opening hours to accommodate those whose thirsts emerge earlier in the day than most. In these unforgiving commercial times, needs must.

On Tuesday 17 June 1919 an incident in this modest public house would provide the catalyst for events that would shock the country and demand the attention of a past, an incumbent and a future Prime Minister.

It had been another hot, balmy day and it felt like it would never get dark. Across the road a transfixed audience sat inside the new, swanky Electric Theatre cinema in a darkened room. They were glued to the big screen, watching Douglas Fairbanks in *Mr Fixit*, unaware that across the road real-life events were about to unfold that would be far more worthy of film treatment. Around 9.00pm Canadian soldiers Private McDonald and a sergeant accompanied by his wife were confronted by a local

41

man in the public bar of the beer house. The soldiers were both from the Woodcote camp. The man struck McDonald in the mouth. As the argument escalated and turned to general fighting between locals and soldiers the landlord, William Herbert, was unable to contain them and stepped out of his pub to seek help. In the High Street, just around the corner, he located Sergeant Shuttleworth and PC Orchard, who were patrolling together, and the three men returned to the pub where PCs Hinton and Monk, who had also been on the beat together, were already in the bar, having seen the disturbance.

John Allan Harding McDonald was born at Dartmouth, Nova Scotia in 1879. He had enlisted with the Canadian Expeditionary Force firstly in 1916 and was promptly rejected for having varicose veins. He re-presented himself ten days later and was this time successful. He arrived in England in March 1916. In July he was taken on strength to the 4th Divisional Train as a teamster, but was very soon after hospitalised with bronchitis. Throughout the remainder of 1916 and most of 1917, McDonald was in and out of hospital because of poor hearing and other complaints, and finally in December 1917 he was transferred to the CAMC Depot. As a member of the Medical Corps he was assigned to the Woodcote Park Convalescent Hospital, Epsom in June 1918.

Faced with four officers, McDonald screamed: 'I will fucking well fight him and give him a good hiding,' referring to the local man who was named in one statement as 'Williams'. He would not calm down, proceeded to challenge the police to fight, and was then overpowered and arrested. Shuttleworth and Orchard marched him into the road and up the High Street for the half-mile walk to the police station, unfortunately for them in full view of other Canadians. Hinton and Monk stayed around the pub to ensure there were no further disturbances. Another Canadian soldier, Driver Veinot, witnessed the scene in the High Street and approached the officers and began to remonstrate with them. Not wanting an incident to ignite in the centre of the town, he was promptly arrested too, by PCs Weeding and Bewick who had arrived in the High Street, and the party continued their journey to the station in Ashley Road. PC George Barton was outside the police station and he followed Shuttleworth and Orchard into the building with the first prisoner. There was now a minimum of seven police officers in the street in the short distance between The Rifleman and the police station.

Alexander Veinot was born in 1897, at Hemford, Lunenburg County, Nova Scotia. The family were Lutherans of German origin. By the age of fifteen he was working in the woods with his father, but in 1915 he volunteered with the 64th Battalion at Sussex, New Brunswick, but was rejected. Like McDonald he tried again and was successful. He departed from Halifax, Nova Scotia in July 1916 and docked at Liverpool two weeks later. By 1917 he was with the 3rd Entrenching Battalion, Canadian Engineers and in the field in France, but Veinot was inclined to illness and suffered from scabies, bronchitis, laryngitis and catarrh. He was returned to England in February 1918, but when he recovered his fitness was transferred in May 1918 to the Canadian Machine Gun Corps (CMGC) Reinforcement Pool. From there he was posted to the 3rd Battalion, CMGC, in August 1918, and was wounded in the October with gunshot directly into his arm and face. He was returned to England again and after spending some time in hospital in Basingstoke he arrived at Woodcote Park on 10 April 1919.

Sergeant George Greenfield was on station duty and received the two prisoners and promptly booked them into the cells at the side of the station building. Meanwhile, the remaining Canadians in The Rifleman and thereabouts had spread the word about the arrests on the High Street and pockets of men emerged from the Plough and Harrow, The Railway Hotel, The Marquis of Granby, The Wellington, The Spread Eagle and The White Hart public houses. The forming crowd became increasingly angry that two of their men had been unjustly (in their view) taken in to custody and by 10.15pm a small but vociferous group of Canadians were milling about outside the police station demanding that their two comrades be released.

Inspector Pawley came down from his living quarters and immediately took control of the situation, and with a handful of officers he went outside the station and dispersed the soldiers with reasoning backed up by the threat of arrest. Pawley, at this point, wanted the men away from the area because not only were they belligerent, but there was a dance turning out around the corner in The Parish Rooms in The Parade, and there would undoubtedly be more of the clashes with the local men, which had been going on all week. The promises to come back mob-handed as the men walked away shouting and swearing were not lost on Charlie Pawley, who was now well attuned to the festering and dangerous resentments of the soldiers. He knew too that it was not a good idea to keep McDonald and Veinot on the premises too long. On Pawley's instruction Sergeant Greenfield rang the Woodcote camp and requested a military escort to take the two prisoners away.

'It's all quiet up here … but there is some trouble down the road,' was the vague but ominous reply George Greenfield received.

At this point, around 11.00pm, Inspector Pawley set about calling all his off-duty officers into the police station to provide reinforcements. Sensing the trouble ahead, he had kept the evening shift on, and if everyone made it in he would have a complement of some twenty to twenty-five officers manning the station. At 92 Lower Court Road Thomas Green knew that a knock on his door as his fire was burning out and he was preparing for his bed could only be an emergency. His first thought was for his wife, Lilian, who was still in the National Hospital for Paralysis at Queen's Square, Bloomsbury, following her stroke. It was, at first, a relief when the messenger said he was needed urgently at the police station because the Canadians were threatening to break out a couple of their men in the cells. Shouting to his daughters that he was wanted up at the station, he decided against throwing on his uniform because he thought that if the Canadians were flooding the town in angry mood then he might not even make the station. He knew it was serious because his colleague George Greenfield had told him to come through the back entrance. Slapping his cap on to his balding head, he hurried out of the house.

'Look after yourself,' Nellie called after him. She and her sister Lily would never see their father alive again.

Inspector Pawley's worst fears were realised when he stepped outside of the station into the still, close night air and could hear clearly a climbing cacophony of noise in the distance. In 1919 the hum of technology was absent; there were few motor cars to speak of and no jet engines in the sky. From where he stood he would have been able to hear clearly a blackbird's alarm call in Rosebery Park and sometimes, depending on the wind, the church bells from Headley Village on the other side of Epsom Downs were audible. But instead he heard men's voices clamouring above one another, banging, and, alarmingly, the sound of a bugle calling Assembly. The noise was becoming louder. Getting nearer. Something in the pit of the veteran policeman's stomach plunged downward.

Up at the camp events had been moving fast. News of the arrests had been loudly announced by the Canadians returning from the town and as facts became blurred and exaggerated the whole camp rapidly worked itself into a frenzy of anger and hysteria. A few of the men were addressing the others, demanding they march on Epsom and free their boys and smash up the town for good measure. These men, some full of drink, took sticks and ran them along the corrugated iron walls of the huts, calling into them and purposely waking up as many soldiers as they could.

Major Ross witnessed *his* worst fears being realised. He stood before the men and pleaded with them to see sense, knowing that his regimental authority alone would not be enough to quell this mutinous explosion of ire. He shouted about the reputation of Canada and how the great sacrifices they had made and bravery they had shown at places like Vimy Ridge would be undermined by one night of madness. The soldiers, especially those with liquor inside them, were not listening. Now was the time. The big man, the blacksmith, shouted to young Todd to sound the bugle. Todd looked around. He was scared and he hesitated, hoping for a second opinion, but the big man, who was ten years older and ten inches taller, roared again and the boy put the bugle to his mouth and sounded the 'fall in'.

'Let's go, boys!' commanded Allan MacMaster, the black-smith, the big man.

46

'We will have to charge them'

Three to four hundred soldiers noisily fell in and the men marched out of the camp shouting and hollering. Young Todd, excited and urged on by his elders, intermittently sounded his bugle to add to the din. Along the route the animated men broke down walls and snapped railings from fences of local gardens. House owners quickly turned down gas lights, grasping quickly that a riot was forming, wishing to become invisible. The Ladas public house was the first trading establishment in their path and although the last of the customers had left for the night the landlord, Frederick Baxter, was busying himself inside and a barmaid was clearing the tables. When they heard the commotion they stood quite still. The window was smashed and the doors kicked in, but with the determination to free their comrades uppermost the Canadians did not linger. The landlord would later assess his damage at £15 (some £500 in today's money) and the barmaid claimed for a torn blouse and shock.

Major James Ross had hurried to the police station, hoping to get the two prisoners out before the mob arrived in an attempt to defuse the escalating and frightening situation. He had barely had first breathless words with Inspector Pawley when the men streamed out of Rosebery Park and into Ashley Road behind him. They were running and brandishing posts and clutching bricks and stones. Spreading across the width of the road, they kept on coming and coming. Like an army. They *were* an army. Mr Dorset, the magistrate, whose house, Hawthorn Dene, was next door to the police station building, came out into his garden and watched helplessly as the soldiers tore his fence down with their bare hands. 'Don't fret Dad, you won't get hurt, we ain't got no business with you,' reassured one Canadian.

Outside the station they pushed up against the gate and fence shouting raucously, but stopped short of entering police property as Major Ross and Inspector Pawley tried to reason with them. The policeman told the officer that if he could get his men to discontinue the rioting he would release the prisoners and Ross conveyed this offer as best he could to the baying mob. The men at the front of the crowd heard clearly and agreed to this, but as Ross and Pawley entered the police station door to effect the release, oaths, bile, threats and missiles flew over their heads as the men at the back of the crowd decided either there would be no compromise or, as was claimed later, they misinterpreted what was happening and thought Ross himself was being placed under arrest.

Upstairs Mrs Pawley gingerly pulled the children's bedroom curtain to one side, surveyed the situation outside and was horrified. She looked down on a seething mass of soldiers, both in khaki and blues, screaming and breathing as one, some pushing others forward, some holding others back, all wide-eyed and swearing and waving their fists and sticks and posts. There were soldiers as far as she could see and she knew that they were going to storm the station. A normal domestic evening had turned into a nightmare in seconds. Instinct kicked in and she hurriedly gathered the younger children together and put them in the pantry at the back of the house. For added protection she placed saucepans on their heads. Within seconds of doing this bricks sailed through the upstairs windows, spraying shattered glass all over the room and debris on to the warm depressions in the beds where the children had been sleeping seconds earlier. As the situation worsened, and Mrs Pawley feared that the crazed Canadians could well overrun the station, she and elder daughter Freda gathered the children up

48

and bundled them out the back door into the garden and over other fences to safety.

Outside, when Major Ross did not re-appear immediately, the mob was incensed further and surged forward, the men's cumulative power collapsing the double gates and bending the iron rails like they were rubber. Men charging with extraordinary strength had loosened them. They pulled them free from their footings and were now armed with spears. Marauding soldiers flooded the garden and courtyard and the windows of the charge room were promptly put in. The delicate floral archway over the rose-lined path that Inspector Pawley had carefully constructed and nurtured was tugged down and trampled over, as were his prized roses. The policemen inside were chilled to hear the cry: 'Let's burn the fucking show to the ground!' To underline this ominous threat, lighted paper was pushed through the letterbox.

Although help had now been urgently requested from New Malden, Wimbledon, Surbiton, Kingston and Wandsworth police stations, the Epsom officers briefly surveyed one another, eyes bulging and throats dry, trembling hands fingering their truncheons. When Canadians with contorted faces appeared at the now paneless windows, larger than life and struggling to push their bodies through, but with the wrought iron frames remaining thankfully secure, survival adrenaline surged through the police officers as one and they sprung into action, repelling the rioters with telling truncheon blows aimed at the head, hands, testicles or face. They were in no doubt they were now fighting for their lives.

The soldiers hesitated and were taken aback by this first sign of spirited resistance and the policemen, equally boosted by their own reaction, stepped out into the yard and attempted to drive back the mob. Policemen using truncheon, fist and foot waded into the crowd and soldiers replied likewise, backed up

49

with a continual shower of masonry, stones and wood from behind the front lines. The cumulative strength and ferocity of the colonials eventually told and the police retreated back into the station, some of them putting their weight up against the front door as it became the main focus of the rioters' attention. The soldiers battered the door with flagstones wrenched from the garden and charged it with logs, and eventually the door buckled, but did not give way. The police knew that only one or two Canadians could enter the doorway at any one time if they did gain access and were ready to deliver a severe pummelling to any who managed it.

Meanwhile, a large body of soldiers were at the side of the building where the cells were located, bent on freeing the prisoners. Sergeant Green and Inspector Pawley listened to the roaring, malevolent throng and exchanged knowing looks and unsaid, worried thoughts. Both men knew that if the Canadians gained entry, here and now, disaster would follow. Green was clasping a poker from the house, not his police truncheon. A truncheon, whilst capable of inflicting serious damage and even death, may not have provided the psychological comfort that an iron poker offered. Policemen are trained to target the collar-bone with their truncheons. Thomas Green had decided this was not a time for mere disarming or giving due consideration to his opponents and their welfare. He knew there was potential for death. He thought of the Pawley children upstairs – innocent, terrified, and in danger of their lives. He may well have also been incredibly angry at the violation of his peaceful surrounds. Tom Green was an old soldier. He believed in law and order. That was why he was a policeman. The situation he was presented with violated everything he stood for.

'We will have to charge them,' Sergeant Green finally said, solemnly and resolutely.

Pawley may have been the senior officer, but Tom Green, the dependable station sergeant, had taken control. Pawley ran through the options in his mind. There may have been a gun and ammunition in the station – under lock and key – for emergencies. If this wasn't an emergency, what was? Would firing a gun over the heads of the rioters escalate the situation? Unwelcome but familiar feelings resurfaced. Nearly eighteen years earlier, when he was a sergeant, Pawley had accidentally killed a colleague, Neil MacDougall, during police revolver practice at the Gravel Pits, Eltham, when he was based at Sidcup in Kent. There was no question it was a tragic accident and there was no recklessness involved. A gun that had been passed from MacDougall to Pawley simply discharged; nevertheless, MacDougall's death and guns were haunting presences in Charlie Pawley's life thereon.

Inspector Pawley paused for several seconds as he considered what his station sergeant was suggesting and then nodded. 'We will try it, but I don't think we will be strong enough.'
With Sergeant Green at the front the officers rushed out of the side door and steamed into the Canadians, taking them by surprise. As PC James Rose said later, with typical police understatement, they were 'using their weapons freely'. Although there were only eight policemen in the charge, the others being left to defend the windows and doors, they were successful in pushing the riotous contingent back into the yard in front of the house. Blood spurted from head wounds and the sickening sound of cracking heads and bones punctured the night air. Both PC Rose and Sergeant Fred Blaydon saw their colleague Thomas Green collapse as the teenage James Connors brought down a fence post on his head.

Blaydon had been in the force since 1891 and like Green and Pawley was soon to retire. He thought he'd seen it all, but never dreamed that he'd be engaged in a fight for his life at this stage in his career, and in Epsom of all places. Distracted by seeing Charlie Pawley also take a fearful blow to the head and staggering backwards, disorientated, he was relieved to turn around and notice Tom Green, one tough bugger, he thought, getting to his feet again. Fred had a house in Hook Road, which ran into Lower Court Road, and therefore the two men lived close and liked and respected one another. Inspector Pawley was heartened but concerned to see that his son, Harry, just back from the war and carrying wounds, was down in the yard in his shirtsleeves and braces standing shoulder to shoulder with his officers exchanging blows, but the numbers again were ultimately unassailable. The charge was over and almost every officer had now absorbed serious blows to the head and body, and they all instinctively retreated backwards into the police station.

Thomas Green was back on his feet but dazed from being struck so forcefully with the fence-post. He hadn't seen Inspector Pawley, PC Weeding and others reel backwards with blood pumping from head wounds and he moved forward again, believing he was leading a counter-charge and unaware he was alone. A big man stepped into his path as others pressed forward, eager to engage the other retreating policemen. This was MacMaster, who had successfully, and with terrifying strength, torn an iron bar from the police cell whilst trying to free McDonald and Veinot seconds earlier. The two men made eye contact. Green looked up, his head bare, having not retrieved his cap from the earlier fall, crimson-red blood seeping from a wound and streaking his face. MacMaster looked down, filled with rage and hate, his face twisted and eyes staring and burning. *'These fucking people ... silly bastard policemen with silly fucking rules ... scrawny, little Epsom bastards coming home and picking fights ... who is this fucking*

man getting involved? ... Bastard, fucking England that gave
me the galloping pox and now cannot get me home ...'

He lifted the bar high over his head with two hands, as he
often had in the forge at home with his father's sledgehammer,
and smashed it down on Thomas Green's skull with more
might than he had ever mustered before.

Two Red Ponds

Simultaneously, some Canadians had forced an entry into the
side window of the passage that ran alongside the police cells
and were able to break the lock of the door and free Private
McDonald. Inspector Pawley then stepped among them with a
key, past caring now for his own safety, opened the door to
Driver Veinot's cell and allowed him to walk out. Among
much cheering, the prisoners emerged through the window and
out into the yard.

'We got 'em!'

'They're out ... the boys are out!'

'Mac's free!'

Triumphalism pricked the violent hysteria like a balloon and
the men stopped fighting, roaring and throwing things.
Momentarily, they seemed unsure as to what to do next. Major
Ross exploited the interregnum by turning to Robert Todd and
instructing him to sound his bugle and the 'fall in', and again
the men did. Nursing gaping wounds, limps and bruises, they
staggered off into the darkness towards the park.

Following the distress call that had been put out to all the other
stations in Metropolitan Police 'V' Division, as the Canadian
soldiers made their way back to the camp, sweating policemen

on pushbikes began arriving, ringing their bells and huffing and puffing. The sight of them converging on Epsom from the country roads and lanes, on their wobbly bicycles, would have been reminiscent of a *Keystone Cops* comedy were it not for the tragic backdrop. A motor car also arrived from Wandsworth, containing Superintendent Boxhall, the young area commander, and other officers, but they too were just minutes too late.

As the prisoners were being freed some concerned Canadian soldiers had recognised that Sergeant Green was in a bad way: laying face down, he was not moving, and a pool of dark blood had formed, silhouetting his head. Six men picked him up by the arms and the legs, still face down, and ran him across the road, away from the melee, to prevent further damage. They knocked on the front door of the house called Park View, almost opposite, that belonged to Charles Polhill, the butcher. Mr Polhill, reluctant to answer the door and thinking that it was an injured Canadian they were carrying, shouted through the letterbox for them to take the body around the back.

'Please open this door now' commanded a soldier authoritatively and Mr Polhill, not wishing the same treatment meted out to the police station to be repeated on his property, did so. The men laid Sergeant Green down gently in the hall and for the first time on his back.

'He's a policeman,' explained one of the soldiers.

'Let me see him, I will do what I can for him,' said another, wearing a Glengarry cap. He knelt down besides the Station Sergeant. 'Bring some dry salt, quick.'

Mr Polhill fetched the salt and some water and the soldiers crouched around the sergeant, rubbed his hands with the salt and bathed his forehead and the wound over his left eye with the water. The irony could not have been lost on all present. A policeman that had been viciously attacked by rioting soldiers

54

was now being tenderly cared for by the same. Eventually the Canadians stood up and said they had to go. Charles Polhill looked at his clock and noted the time was 12.30am.

He then walked across to the police station, where by now at least three dozen officers, in uniform and plain clothes, surveyed the aftermath. Mrs Pawley and her elder daughters had come downstairs and were making welcome cups of tea as well as tending the best they could to the wounds, lacerations and bruises. Joe Weeding was looking ill and seemingly delirious; Albert Monk was bathing a nasty cut over his eye; Spencer Hook complained of being badly winded; PCs Barton and Bewick held injured arms with good arms; and Sergeants Shuttleworth and Durham examined badly bashed and bruised hands.

Monk was thirty-three years old and had worked as a machinist in Bedfordshire before signing up for the police in 1905. Constable Hook, known to all as George, like Tom Green had served with the army in India, and also in the Boer War, and as a reservist had fought in the Great War just ended. He had not banked on being involved in a battle situation again, and so close to home. George Frederick Barton was from Brentford, Middlesex and had worked as a compositor in the print industry before joining the Met in 1900. He had been promoted to sergeant in 1905, but for some reason, possibly at his own request, was reduced in rank back to Police Constable just before he arrived in Epsom in 1908. Thomas Bewick had listed his profession as a commercial traveller when he had joined the force in 1906 at the age of twenty-eight years. Peter Durham had previously been a porter in Tottenham Court Road before deciding to become a policeman in 1901.

'They dropped a bleeding log on my back,' complained Sergeant Bill Kersey, a cockney from Bromley-by-Bow, who had been in the force since 1893. 'Feels like the bastards may have broken it. To add bleedin' insult to bleedin' injury one of them grabbed my 'elmet, and you know what? When they marched off I see one of the buggers wearing it. Cocky swine.'

Charles Polhill entered the station looking very distressed and troubled. 'I've got one of yours in my hallway. I'm afraid he is in a very poor condition.'

It was only then that Inspector Pawley and most of his other colleagues registered the absence of Thomas Green.

Sergeant Herbert Shuttleworth, a constable for twenty-three years, having been a porter before joining the Met, was one of the first men through the butcher's doorway and was visibly upset to see his colleague and friend lying unconscious on the hall floor, his blood soaking into the cushion now supporting his head. He knelt down gently beside him and took his hand.

'Tom, can you hear me, Tom? Help is coming, Tom.'
There was no response and the constable looked up at the others in the hallway with a helpless look and a film misting his eyes. How had a skirmish in a beer house only a few hours earlier come to this?

Dr William Thornely, the police surgeon, had already been called and on his arrival at Epsom was ushered quickly into Charles Polhill's hallway. He was able to determine that Thomas Green was still alive and he instructed that he needed to be taken to the Epsom Infirmary urgently. Major Ross and Colonel Hugh McDermott from the camp arranged for a military ambulance to take the injured sergeant straight away. The time was now 1.00am. McDermott had driven from Woodcote camp earlier under the order to fetch the prisoners, but had been prevented from proceeding down Wilmerhatch Lane by the mob. Because of this he had taken a circuitous route into Epsom and parked by the Clock Tower before proceeding on foot to the police station. By this time, though, the prisoners were out. McDermott had stayed on with Major Ross and they had assisted the police and the injured in every way they could inside the station and were among the people in the hallway standing over Sergeant Green while Dr Thornely examined him. McDermott was the son of a church man and originally from Jamaica. He had recently been the Chief Medical Officer at Woodcote, but was now based at the Orpington camp. The reason for his presence at Epsom on this night is not clear.

It was a Corporal Sydney Arthur Bartlett who actually ferried the fading policeman to the Infirmary in the ambulance that had been intended to fetch the prisoners. Bartlett had not been involved in the riot. He had enthusiastically enlisted when war had broken out in 1914 and was among the first contingent to arrive in Britain and then to serve in France with the CAMC. By 1915 he was invalided back to England suffering from rheumatism and injuries to his left leg. There, his medical problems increased, as syphilis was diagnosed, followed by a paralysis of his leg and a loss of speech. He arrived at Woodcote camp in 1917, buckled down and was soon made a corporal.

Dr Thornely could never have imagined that he would be involved in such a high-profile case again in such a short space of time. Only six years earlier it was he who had been called to the bedside of the suffragette Emily Davison when she threw herself in front of the King's horse in the 1913 Derby. She had suffered terrible injuries and died soon after at the newly built Epsom Cottage Hospital. The events were recorded on film and the incident became the defining moment in the long campaign to grant women the right to vote. Prime Minister David Lloyd

George finally partly acceded to their demands in 1918. Thornely had diagnosed Davison as having a fractured skull and he believed that Sergeant Green had suffered the same fate. He asked the Epsom Infirmary (which stood on the site of the current Epsom General Hospital) to keep him informed of the patient's condition. This they did. At 7.20am on Wednesday 18 June 1919, Dr Thornely's telephone rang to inform him that Station Sergeant Thomas Green had never regained consciousness and had just died.

Thornely's later full statement was more revealing and illustrative of the fearful violence that Sergeant Green had been subjected to:

> There is a severe contusion over the left eye, causing great swelling of the eye-lid; another contusion high on the forehead of the right side; there are further contusions across the vault of the skull; there is also a slight abrasion on the upper lip. The only other sign of injury is a slight abrasion on the right elbow. On raising the scalp, there was found to be an extensive haemorrhage, chiefly on the left side of the head; there was a fracture of the skull on the left side. On opening the skull further extensive haemorrhage was found; there was a fracture of the skull extending from the left orbit, along the left temple and across the vault of the skull to the right side; there was no laceration of the brain or apparent haemorrhage into the substance of the brain. I consider that the death was caused by a blow from some blunt instrument over the left eye, causing the fracture of the skull, the result in haemorrhage and shock; there is evidence of other very severe blows.

This statement tells us much. Green's death was no unlucky blow or two. This unfortunate, courageous policeman had taken a vicious beating, which was glossed over, as we shall see.

In Epsom town dawn had broken to reveal the full extent of the damage to the police station and some surrounding buildings. The route from Woodcote Park down to the town was also clearly marked by a trail of vandalism. Two policemen and an armed British soldier stood guard defiantly outside the station building, but the twisted metal railings, general debris and broken windows told the sorry story. Townspeople had already gathered in Ashley Road as word of the nocturnal battle had spread. Children risked the ire of the policemen and the soldier to peer in to the station garden and point at the blood staining the remaining flagstones. The occasional Canadian soldier strolled past unaware, at this point, of the fate of the Station Sergeant.

For some, though, the abiding memory that morning was in Rosebery Park, where passers-by and sightseers were baffled and then horrified to see the two ponds streaked red. A few hours earlier the soldiers had knelt down on the way home to camp to bathe their wounds and clean themselves up. The fence that ran from the park gates along to the entrance to the police station had almost been stripped clean of slats. Outside the station building itself, among the broken glass, smashed masonry and assorted debris, lay a solitary dice used in the Crown and Anchor game.

CHAPTER 3

THE DAY AFTER

The Town

The curiosity shown by the townspeople of Epsom in the very early morning of Wednesday 18 June 1919 had developed into firstly resentment, then anger and finally, by mid afternoon, rage, as the news of Sergeant Green's demise had spread from shop to shop, street to street and house to house. Rumours that circulated for a while that PC Joe Weeding had also died added to the feverish atmosphere. In addition, the all-too-visible sight of their familiar and generally well-liked constables reporting to work and sharing guard duties outside the bedraggled station building, swathed in bandages and sporting cuts, bruises and black eyes, served to stir up a thirst for revenge among the Epsom public. Canadian soldiers were ordered not to go into town and those that had been away, in London at the Maple Leaf Club, for instance, were steered away from the police station when they disembarked from the train at Epsom. With the knowledge of the fatal outcome of last night's riot now in their possession no convalescents were now walking up or down Ashley Road at all.

Most of the Epsom policemen lived close to one another and within walking distance of the station. Tom Bewick and Percy Taylor were a few doors in either direction from Sergeant Green in Lower Court Road itself, Sergeants James Shirley and Bill Kersey and Constables Peter Durham and Alf Galloway all lived in Miles Road, a turning off Hook Road, and Harry Hinton, Arthur Orchard and Joe Weeding were all on the other side of the railway bridge in Middle Lane, whilst Page Janeway's house was in Station Road and Ernie Short lived in Pikes Hill, just off Station Road. Ernie was unusual among the Epsom police in being an Epsom man, having worked as a gardener before joining up in 1900. Their camaraderie would have been high and all are likely to have attended the station the next day regardless of their injuries and shift patterns. The crowd cheered them and the press took pictures, but any glory was tempered by the thought of their dead colleague and his bereft family.

There were plenty of comings and goings that morning for the crowd and press to observe, and when Lord Rosebery's black carriage arrived from his nearby Durdans residence, at noon, there was hush and removal of caps as the old man climbed out. He loved Epsom and its people loved him. Theirs was certainly not an old-fashioned squire-and-serf relationship, as Rosebery had been around for many years and given much to the town, financially and otherwise. He had famously been expelled from Oxford University for purchasing a racehorse and entering it into the Derby. It finished last, but Rosebery was to have much better luck later in life. His passion for horses and love of Epsom and the surrounding countryside persuaded him to buy The Durdans estate in 1878. The Durdans was Epsom's premier stately home, with a long history, and had been visited by King Charles II, King George V, William Gladstone and many others. Rosebery had started life as Archibald Primrose, but when his father died he became Lord Dalmeny and later the Earl of Rosebery. In 1894 he succeeded William Gladstone as Prime Minister. Along the way he had married a member of the moneyed Rothschild dynasty. Lord Rosebery once said he had three ambitions in life

61

– to become Prime Minister, to wed an heiress and to win the Derby. He achieved all three.

He was now seventy-two years old and in common with so many of the families of Epsom had lost a son in the war. That loss had cut him down mentally and a stroke had nearly killed him physically. He was much perturbed by the previous night's events and Sergeant Green's tragic fate. The Ladas public house getting smashed up would also have troubled him, as the pub had been renamed (from The Fox) after his beloved horse, Ladas, that gifted him his first Derby win in 1894 and was buried in the ground of The Durdans. The elder statesman, with the help of a stick, walked into the station and had a conversation with Inspector Pawley, no doubt asking for his sympathies to be relayed on to the Green family. Pawley, who could have had little or no sleep and had just had four stitches inserted into his forehead, must have been in a poor state by this time.

Henry Banks Longley, who lived in the affluent College Road and boasted a servant, was a Yorkshireman and the young leader, at forty-nine, of Epsom Urban Council. He was sufficiently concerned about the potential for more trouble in the town that he sent the following telegram to the War Office and the Canadian Military Headquarters, although he believed the threat resided with the Canadians rather than from the enraged locals:

STRONG ACTION SHOULD BE TAKEN AT ONCE, AS INHABITANTS HAVE NO SECURITY AT NIGHT. OWING TO ITS POSITION THE CAMP IS DIFFICULT TO CONTROL EFFECTIVELY EXCEPT WITH A LARGE GUARD. ALL LICENSED HOUSES AND CLUBS SHOULD BE MADE OUT OF BOUNDS, AND THE CAMP EVACUATED AS SOON AS POSSIBLE. THERE ARE NO MILITARY POLICE IN THE DISTRICT.

IMMEDIATE ACTION NECESSARY FOR SAFETY OF
INHABITANTS ... STOP

What Longley perhaps did not know was that the police had already requested military assistance during the night so they could go to the camp and make arrests whilst injuries and evidence were still fresh. They knew that going into the Woodcote camp without military back-up was hugely dangerous. It had been demonstrated that the men were capable of large-scale violence and that the military command was incapable of controlling them. Discipline had dissipated in the face of the war ending and the demobilisation delays. Permission was being sought from Major George Cornwallis-West, who was the military officer with this responsibility, but no response was received and when Superintendent Boxhall chased this up angrily in the morning he was told that Cornwallis-West was uncontactable because he had just left for racing at Ascot! This did not go down well with Boxhall and the matter was immediately passed upwards to Sir Nevil Macready, the Metropolitan Police Commissioner.

The church was also concerned about the incendiary situation in the town and the Bishop of Winchester arrived at the lecture hall in Station Road to deliver a speech. He did his utmost to puncture the anger felt by the townspeople towards the Canadians, although it is not recorded just how large his audience was. He said:

It is painful to us that an incident so tragic should have occurred as that which happened in Epsom last night, and which cost the life of a public servant belonging to the town, and a great deal of injury to others. We shall be far removed from attributing this to anything like the habitual conduct or the average character of our Canadian brothers. We know what splendid heroism they have shown, and we regret that a part of

63

their unit, in the greater trials of peace, should have been led, no doubt under trying circumstances, into an affair with such painful results. I should have felt disrespectful if I had said nothing about what has happened, but we pass to brighter thoughts of what Canada has done for us, and what we have done and what we are still trying to do for Canada.

The young men of Epsom, returned Tommy or not, would have not been listening to the Bishop of Winchester or anyone else, even in the unlikely event they were present. Not only had the Canadians been playing fast and wide with their women and acting up in the town when in numbers – they had now run riot and bludgeoned to death the local police sergeant. Their natural reaction would have been one of rage, anger and, possibly, fear. If the police could not protect them, who could? They too were seeking comfort in numbers and threatening terrible revenge attacks. Lone Canadian soldiers in the town, or thereabouts, were in serious danger over the coming days. Local paper *The Epsom Herald* recognised this and in its issue of 20 June appealed for calm and implored that local people should 'show no acts of hostility'.

However, the statement released by Canadian Headquarters in London that was carried in the following day's newspapers enraged Council leader Longley and the people of Epsom further. It read as follows:

The incident preceding the disturbance at Epsom, which is deeply deplored by the Canadian authorities, appears to have been due to the feeling of hostility which has been steadily growing between the Canadians and demobilised Imperial soldiers, which recently came to a head at Guildford. Since civilians were fined as the consequence of that affair a number of Canadians have complained at different times that when out alone, or in small parties of two or three, they have been attacked by a gang of civilians.

It has not been possible as yet to ascertain the reason for last night's occurrence, but according to some of the men a Canadian soldier who was walking with his wife was insulted by a gang of civilians. A disturbance ensued and several Canadians were placed in the police-station. Several Canadians returned to the Camp with the news, and a large number of men, resenting this treatment of their comrades, went down to Epsom with the idea of securing the release of the prisoners.

The officer of the day having failed to prevent the men from leaving the Camp went down to the town with them in the hope of averting a disturbance. This officer entered the police station to make enquiries, and as he did not appear for some time the Canadian soldiers, being under the impression that this officer had also been arrested, rushed the police station. Considerable damage was done to the premises. One policeman was so seriously hurt that he subsequently succumbed. Several other policemen were injured and five or six Canadian soldiers, one of the latter severely. After the affair at the police station the men returned in groups to Camp and went quietly to bed. Complete order prevails at the Camp, but the Canadian authorities have taken the most drastic measures to prevent any recurrence of the disturbance.

At the same time it was announced that the Canadian Red Cross had voted £200 for the family of Sergeant Green. This would equate to some £8,000 in today's money. Although the statement was predictably defensive of the Canadian men it was too much for Henry Banks Longley and he issued a reply on behalf of Epsom Council repudiating the contention that the riot was a result of the attitude of the civil population, and protesting against the explanation being issued *at all* before judicial inquiries had begun. At this point, before higher forces had become involved, it looked like a war of words and a blaze of publicity may have ensued.

The Canadian statement is interesting in its basic inaccuracies and its immediate downgrading of the riot, which was termed an 'affair at the police station'. Two soldiers were held at the police station, not *several* as the statement claimed; plus according to the statement it was a *disturbance*, not a riot, *small parties* of soldiers had been attacked by *gangs* of civilians, a Canadian soldier walking with his wife was insulted – there was no reference to a fight in a pub – and most importantly a policeman was not *killed*, but was seriously hurt and *subsequently succumbed*. And how good of the rioting soldiers that when they returned to camp they *went quietly to bed*. Also, one wonders who the soldier referred to as being very seriously injured was, as he was never mentioned again, and what exactly were the drastic measures introduced to prevent any recurrence? However, the most surprising thing about the statement was that the stance and choice of language would soon be adopted by the British authorities as well.

The Courts

Despite some minor damage to the Court House, which stood almost opposite the police station, it was business as usual on the Wednesday morning. Mr and Mrs Shield, the caretakers of the court buildings, had been only too aware of the previous night's events, but they had stayed inside, frightened that the Canadians would turn their attentions fully to their building. They had even heard some soldiers debating whether they should move into the High Street and smash the town up 'proper'. The magistrates sat and firstly ordered that all the public houses in Epsom be shut until the following Monday. With feelings running so high it could have been more inflammatory to have closed the pubs to the locals than run the risk of stray Canadians turning up in the odd bar. It was Inspector Goodenough, who was deputising for the recuperating Inspector Pawley, who applied under the Closing in Times of Riot Clause of the Intoxicating Liquors Act 1910. Goodenough explained that there was strong feeling in the town over Sergeant Green's death and more trouble was anticipated. The two magistrates, Messrs Jay and Dorset, were not at first unanimous.

'I think it is a very proper application,' said Dorset.

'It is a very serious to step to take. Have we any definite evidence that the civilians will riot?' asked Jay.

'You only have to go to the other side of the road to the police station to get evidence,' countered Dorset, impatiently.

Inspector Goodenough stressed there was only a rumour that the Epsom people were planning a riot and revenge attacks. It did not mean they actually were.

'If my friend on the bench could have been in my house last night he would know all about it,' rumbled on Mr Dorset, who had been called 'Dad' by the Canadian soldiers and who was missing the point as to who Inspector Goodenough was expecting trouble from – the locals.

Mr Jay assured Goodenough that they would do whatever he felt was necessary and asked if there was extra police and whether military help had been requested. Later that day the order to close the public houses and clubs was rescinded as news came of the Canadian curfew on all their men, which rendered it unnecessary.

Afterwards the magistrates dealt with the case of a Thomas Noble, a Canadian soldier who had absconded from the Seaford camp in Sussex, and who was for some reason in Epsom. He was remanded in custody whilst an escort was sent for to take him away. Detective Bell said that at 2.45pm the previous afternoon (Tuesday) he had been with other officers, but was in plain clothes himself, making enquiries, when he stopped the prisoner in the High Street and told him who he was and that he suspected he was an absentee.

The prisoner replied: 'Oh yes, I am a soldier. I was discharged from the Woodcote camp some time ago and I am up here from Seaford.'

When Noble was asked by the court if he had anything to say he claimed he was struck in the face and continually tripped by the police. If these allegations were true, and they may well not have been, it gives an indication of the state of relations between the police and the Canadian soldiers only hours before the situation in The Rifleman.

The inquest on Thomas Green was opened by Gilbert White, the Coroner of West Surrey, at the Epsom Infirmary where the dead sergeant still lay. White had presided over the inquest on Emily Davison, the suffragette, six years earlier, where Dr Thornely had been the police surgeon, and he too probably did not expect to be involved in another sensational case in the town again. In that 1913 case he had historically opined that Emily Davison did not intend suicide when she ran in front of the King's horse, Anmer, ridden by jockey Herbert Jones, during the running of the Derby, but that she merely intended to disrupt the race. The fact that Miss Davison purchased a return train ticket to Epsom that day led many to concur.

Mr White opened the inquest by stating that the evidence would show that Sergeant Green's death was due to injuries received at Epsom Police Station during a riot by men who apparently came from the Canadian convalescent camp. The matter was being investigated by police, he stated, and while their inquiry was proceeding he proposed only to take formal evidence that would enable him to give a certificate for burial,

68

and this was the reason that the inquest was taking place so quickly after the incident. Why normal procedure was not being followed and why it was so important to bury Sergeant Green so quickly was not explained.

Sergeant Bill Kersey was called to identify Thomas Green officially. Kersey had been commended in 1916 and was a long-serving Epsom officer who would have known Sergeant Green very well. His son William and daughter Alice were the same age as Thomas's Lily and Nellie and had gone to Pound Lane School too. He had been a widower since the children were little and his colleagues admired how he juggled his responsibilities. He could confirm that the body was indeed that of his colleague Station Sergeant Thomas Green. Gilbert White then adjourned the inquest until the following Wednesday (15 June), but before he closed the meeting he said he had been asked by Sir Rowland Blades, the Member of Parliament for Epsom, to read a letter from the War Office:

Dear Sir Rowland,

With reference to your call here today Mr Churchill asks me to thank you for the information you have submitted to him, as to the local conditions at Epsom. The whole matter will be the subject of a searching investigation. In the meantime he understands that prompt and adequate steps are being taken by the Canadian authorities to prevent any recurrence of the disorder. Mr Churchill desires to express the greatest sympathy with the relatives of Sergeant Green, who has died as a result of his injuries.

Yours faithfully,

A MacCallum Scott, Parliamentary Private Secretary.

Here is confirmation of Winston Churchill's personal involvement the day after the riot and already there is a reluctance to use words such as 'killed' or 'murdered'. It is almost as if Churchill has delivered an inquest verdict himself by saying he 'desires to express the greatest sympathy with the relatives of Sergeant Green, who *has died as a result of his injuries*'. After this letter was read out, the foreman of the jury asked if an assurance could be given that any witnesses they might require would not be repatriated or removed from the district before the close of their enquiry. The soldiers, he noted, were anxious to return to Canada, but if any of them were sent away considerable difficulty and delay might result. Gilbert White could not give that assurance, pointing out there was nobody present from the camp. Inspector Pawley intervened, saying he felt it could be taken for granted that any soldier implicated in the riot would remain at Epsom and that if the jury required any man to be called he was sure that the Commandant of the camp would see that he was available, including officers. Pawley's confidence in the full co-operation of the Canadian senior command would soon be shown to be misplaced.

The foreman of that jury was James Chuter Ede, a man with a great future ahead of him. Despite an apparent double-barrel name (Chuter was his mother's maiden name), which gave an impression of his being part of the gentry, Chuter Ede was in fact from more humble beginnings than, perhaps, even he realised and was most certainly a born-and-bred Epsomian. In 1841 his grandfather, James, is listed as living on Epsom Common in the poor Wells area. His occupation is shown as 'miller' and he lived in a basic cottage with his wife and three children, one of whom was James senior, Chuter Ede's father. Life would have been hard. There were no grand houses on the Common and although close to the town centre the community there was very much rural and poverty stricken. Ten years later,

Chuter Ede's grandfather was dead, and the family were living on the High Street in Epsom, operating as millers and bakers. The railway had now arrived in Epsom and the town was growing as new houses were being built to accommodate incoming residents whose work was in London. Epsom was becoming a desirable place to live and the prospects for shopkeepers were improving. Twenty years later still, in 1871, the business led by Chuter Ede's grandfather's widow, Elizabeth, was a thriving grocers and bakers and young James senior was helping his mother run the shop whilst one sister was doing the books and another was working as a shop assistant. When Elizabeth died in 1875 James assumed the proprietorship of the business and in 1881 he married Agnes Chuter, daughter of James Chuter, a successful builder and brickmaker, who had premises at one time next door but one to the Edes. Their son was born the following year and was democratically named James Chuter Ede. After attending the Epsom National School in Hook Road, where he showed great ability, he went on to Dorking on a Surrey Technical Instruction Committee Scholarship and then on to Battersea Pupil Teachers' Centre (by now he had decided he wanted a career in education) and finally on to Cambridge University. He became active in the National Union of Teachers and developed a thirst for politics. The year before the Canadian riot James had stood for parliament in Epsom as a Labour candidate, but then, as now, the town was staunchly Conservative and he failed to win the seat. Nevertheless, the journey from poor millers on Epsom Common to parliamentary candidate in a couple of generations was a remarkable one.

Chuter Ede was a Unitarian Christian, like his father, and held strong religious views. He was also a genuine champion of the people and it is clear from his questions at the inquest that he wanted to see justice for Sergeant Green and ensure that the murderer or murderers would not be able to evade the legal process. The budding politician would soon see how the high-level politics he aspired to actually worked. He was young and idealistic and what he did when the inquest of that day closed was typical of his innate decency. He took a rose he had picked earlier from a fellow juror, Lieutenant Commander Chamberlain's, garden and gently placed it on the cold, stiff body of Sergeant Green.

The Camp

Meanwhile, across the Atlantic, the *New York Times* was one of the first international newspapers to report the events in an article entitled 'New Riot by Canadians' in their 19 June issue. The paper clearly linked the incident to unrest over continued postponement of homeward sailings even though the Canadian government itself had not made this suggestion in its statement. The article said:

> There is much sympathy here for the Canadians, who repeat-edly have been assigned for homeward sailings or given dates, only to be told that further postponement was necessary, owing to strikes of dockworkers at Liverpool and other ports or to lack of transport. The unrest has not been confined to the Canadians. There have also been protests by Australians and New Zealanders. Some Scottish units, composed of veterans, recently held a demonstration against being sent back to France while men who had not seen active service remained in England or were demobilised.

Thomas Green or the circumstances around his death were not mentioned. The language in the British *Times* the following day was less sympathetic towards the Canadians and applauded the police for their bravery in fighting odds of twenty-five men to one and was peppered with proud talk of plucky truncheon charges. *The Daily Chronicle* was even more strident, calling the outrage 'intolerable'.

At the Woodcote camp the mood was sombre and pregnant with gloomy foreboding. The inflammatory cocktail of adrenaline, alcohol and anger from the previous night had dissipated and sore heads, throbbing bumps and bruises pumped away mercilessly. Colonel Frederick Guest had addressed the men early in the morning and told them that they would all have cause to regret their part in the death of Sergeant Green and that the police would be sure not to let the matter rest. He was ashamed and that made many of the soldiers ashamed, but uppermost in most minds was the growing realisation that last night's events could only prolong their wait to get home. It was a depressing thought and some men were more depressed than others.

Sergeant William Dowers had had no idea the previous night that things were as bad as this when James Connors had come in the early hours to his billet, gabbling away about having thrown a policeman over a hedge, and complaining of broken ribs. He had seen blood on Connors' tunic, but still did not imagine that anybody had died, let alone a policeman. Looking around now in the cold light of day there were several men, like Alphonse Masse, the Frenchman, wandering around with a bandaged head and looking disorientated, who could not pretend they did not take part in the riot. Dowers felt deeply apprehensive. He knew he may be questioned by the police and he wanted to do the right thing, but how could he incriminate his countrymen?

His superior officer, Sergeant Major Parsons, was having a similar thoughts, but he had a better idea than Dowers as to who played a leading part in the disturbance because the previous night he had accompanied Major Ross to the police station and had witnessed the riot unfold. He believed that James Connors and Robert McAllan were among the ringleaders and both men were clearly injured. Connors' involvement did not surprise him: he had been in the Orderly Room at the camp for various misdemeanours and could be particularly truculent.

When the police finally arrived at the camp in mid-morning it was not in large numbers. Major Lafone, the Chief Constable for 'V' Division, Inspector John Kenneth Ferrier of Scotland Yard, who had been assigned the case, a Sergeant Davey and PC James Rose, from Epsom station, came through the gates quietly and discreetly conversed with Colonel Guest and other senior officers. Guest and Majors Bird and Ross told the policemen they could not identify any of the men at the riot, which the officers must have found hard to believe, especially in the case of Ross.

Mindful of the potential of more disorder resulting from too strident an approach the senior policemen then asked if they could see any men who had been treated for injuries. It was harder for the Canadian top brass to thwart this request and they said that the policemen could see the medical officers the following day. This must have been the Canadians playing for time to enable them to seek guidance, from higher up the command chain, on how to play the whole affair. Guest then asked Ferrier whether he would consider delaying questioning any Canadians until an armed force of 400 men could be obtained from Ripon to ensure order. He said he feared that interrogation might provoke another outburst.

Ferrier agreed the low-key approach, but pressed for permission to allow one officer to view the soldiers only. The Canadian officers could not refuse this without appearing too obstructive and James Rose was led around the camp. Rose may have volunteered for the job as he had been in the thick of things during the truncheon charge at the side of the station and believed he could pick some people out. Also, contemporary court reports indicate that he may have been especially enthusiastic in his work. In the war years there were several instances of him arresting people for not having enlisted to fight while there are no other reported incidents of other officers making similar arrests. In January 1919 he single-handedly raided a gypsy camp on Bookham Common (about eight miles from Epsom) and made some arrests of 'absentees' under the Military Services Act. He had been born in 1891 in Iford, Wiltshire and had become a Metropolitan Police Officer in 1911. In 1916 he had married Isabel Stammers at the St Barnabas Church in Temple Road, Epsom. He bore a scar over his right eye from being stabbed on duty.

Rose quickly identified James Connors and a private named William Lloyd as being involved in the fracas, stopping just short of saying that Connors was the man who struck the fatal blow to Sergeant Green. (It would later emerge that Connors was not the man who struck the fatal blow to Thomas Green and that William Lloyd was not even present at the riot.) Ferrier took Connors and Lloyd away for questioning at Bow Street Police Station in London and requested that other soldiers who were showing injuries to be moved to another military hospital in Orpington, Kent, where they could be questioned at a later date. It had been decided that if and when charges were preferred that any hearings should take place at Bow Street Magistrates rather than Epsom because feelings were running so high in the town. By coincidence an Epsom resident, Mr EW Garrett, was one of the Bow Street magistrates.

Inspector John Ferrier was a top-level appointment indeed. Born in Dundee, he had joined the police force in 1896 and had worked closely with Sir Edward Henry, the highly regarded and only recently retired Metropolitan Police Commissioner, in pioneering the fingerprint system in Great Britain. As Inspector General of police in Bengal, Henry had seen how they used finger and palm prints to convict criminals and, when he was appointed Assistant Commissioner of the Met, he set up the first Fingerprint Bureau with young Ferrier as an eager disciple and champion. Ferrier is credited with introducing fingerprinting into France, the USA and Canada. He was assigned the job of protecting the Crown Jewels when they were toured around the globe in the World's Fair exhibition in the early 1900s and at the show other exhibitors were demonstrating the various fingerprinting techniques that were developing. The following extract from *Suspect Identities* by Simon A Cole gives us some clues to Ferrier's personality:

> The Prison Bureau's exhibition was upstaged, however, by Scotland Yard, which sent Detective John Kenneth Ferrier to the Exhibition as part of the detail to guard the Crown Jewels. Ferrier spent little time with the royal treasure. Instead he took up residence near New York's exhibit and also began demonstrating fingerprint identification. Reports have it that the young, handsome Ferrier cut a rather dashing figure ... [he] was a master showman, performing dramatic demonstrations ... in which he left the room and returned to identify which one of a group of spectators had left a fingerprint on a test surface. For those who wanted more serious instruction, Ferrier stayed in the United States and trained identification clerks in the Henry system.

In 1912 Sir Edward Henry was the victim of an assassination attempt at his home in London. The would-be murderer was entrusted to Ferrier on his visits to and from court. The failed assassin turned out to be an aspiring taxi driver who had been refused a licence because of a previous drunk and disorderly charge, but the potential gravity of the offence points to Ferrier being, if not the most senior, the most trusted on-the-ground officer at Scotland Yard's disposal. He was an ambitious young policeman who a few years earlier had applied for the post of Chief Constable of Lincoln, but had been unsuccessful.

Shortly before being tasked with the Epsom case he had been giving evidence at the trial of Sidney Hume, who was the defendant in a murder that was sensationally billed in the newspapers as the Ham Common murder. This case was also quite delicate as Hume had been an RAF pilot who had been shot down and served in various German prisoner-of-war camps and had subsequently suffered from severe mental illness, especially delusions. During one such attack he shot and killed a private in the Medical Corp who was caring for him at the Latchmere Military Hospital, Ham Common. Whilst the murder was a cold-blooded one, because of Hume's war ordeal there was not an appetite to see him hanged, and he wasn't. Private Aldridge, the victim, is recorded as a casualty of the First World War and perhaps Ferrier had been told of a desire for a similar outcome in the case of Sergeant Green.

He may have been told that by Major Edgar Mortimore Lafone, the Chief Constable of 'V' Division within the Metropolitan Police, who was present at Epsom Police Station during the Wednesday. Lafone, who later would be bestowed an OBE, was the son of a Conservative MP and was a bridge between the aristocracy and the police force. He was an old Harrovian who fought in the Boer War and was present at the siege of Ladysmith, an engagement where his brother William perished. On retiring from the army in 1906 he became Deputy Chief Constable of Kent and in 1909 was appointed a Chief Constable in the Metropolitan Police. Lafone does not figure very much in any documentation after the Wednesday so one imagines he was sent down by the Metropolitan Police Commissioner, Sir Nevil Macready, to settle John Ferrier in on the case and assess the situation.

Macready had by now heard about Major Cornwallis-West and his trip to Ascot and how the army did not support his police officers at a time of their greatest need, and was furious. He sent a steaming telegram to Winston Churchill complaining of 'the culpable inaction of the military authorities' and demanding answers. Macready may or may not have been aware that, although Cornwallis-West was only a year older than Winston Churchill, he had been married for a time to his mother, Jennie Churchill. At this point, though, in 1919, he was wed to the celebrated actress Mrs Patrick Campbell (Beatrice Stella Tanner).

In the files held in The National Archives at Kew there is a note filed by Sir Nevil Macready where he stands by his charge of 'culpable negligence' on the part of the military not responding to Epsom's request, but added it that it 'may not be necessary to pursue the matter'. Between his angry telegram and this hand-written note Sir Nevil had obviously received some answers, but not, it appears, the ones he was expecting.

'A most capable and genial officer'

Epsom residents who purchased their *Epsom Advertiser* (incorporating the *Epsom Observer*) on the morning of Friday 20 June 1919 would have read a detailed account of the riot in their town that had not been subject to any political or editorial interference or sensitivity testing. Their reporter on the ground clearly attributed the riot to a culmination of bad feeling between 'certain ex-servicemen of Epsom and Canadian soldiers'. The paper had no qualms about referring to the killing of Sergeant Green as a '*murderous* onslaught by Canadians' and labelling the rioters as 'ruthless law-breakers'. The paper was also keen to highlight the injuries that the town's brave constables must have inflicted on the soldiers and applauded their efforts under such crushing odds. Elsewhere in the paper was carried an appeal from the Epsom police that there should be no acts of hostility displayed towards Canadian soldiers and that residents should assist in making the duties of the police, civilian and military, as light as possible. The police also used the paper's columns to thank the residents for their many letters, gifts and good wishes that had arrived at the police station. A Mr Justins Van Maurik of Edenbridge, Kent had sent in 100 fine cigars to be shared among the officers, the distribution of which led to some bureaucratic difficulties.

A resident of Ashley House, one of the buildings adjacent to the police station, wrote into the *Epsom Advertiser* describing the damage done to the building, which, among other things, housed the registrar of births, deaths and marriages. He said the large stable gates were torn down, as were cast iron gutters that were then used as battering rams, and he wondered if this was how the Canadians repaid them for the free use of part of their premises as a canteen for the past three years. In a surprising echo of today's headlines, the resident wondered whether if he had taken the law into his own hands would he have been arrested and imprisoned by a 'do-gooder' judge? He also claimed that the roads leading to the police station were blockaded by soldiers to interfere with any reinforcements arriving, and saw this as evidence of pre-meditation. He concluded that Head of the Fire Brigade Captain Capon's brand-new motor fire engine should be utilised to quell any further disorder by firing jets of water at the miscreants.

Finally, the editorial in the newspaper struck a partially diplomatic chord:

The deplorable events on Tuesday night form by far the most unpleasant chapter in the history of Epsom during the war, a history which, on the whole, is one which can be viewed with feelings of pride. Regrets as to what took place in the wrecking of the Police Station are also, so far as the inhabitants of the town are concerned, not unaccompanied by feelings of pride, created by the thought of the really magnificent way our local police stood up to hundreds of Canadians. What these few police did against so many soldiers deserves to be publicly recognised in some way by the townspeople of Epsom. Probably nothing greater in the way of heroism has been performed by that little band of policemen struggling against what anyone would have considered to be overwhelming odds, struggling, and so far as preventing the administrative portion of the building from being wrecked is concerned, triumphing. It was really a victory for the cause of order against disorder, but it was a victory – and that is the saddening part of the matter – at the cost of the death of Station-Sergt. Green, a most capable and genial officer.

The conduct of the Canadian soldiers from the time they first arrived at Woodcote Park in 1915 has, on the whole, been wonderfully good. Let that not be forgotten in these days when feelings run high. It is within the last few months that some of those who wear the maple leaf badge have given the inhabitants and the police cause for complaint. The reasons may be various, as to what preceded the raid ...

But no good reasons can possibly be adduced by the Canadian soldiers who took part in Tuesday night's monstrous proceedings for what they did. They suggest that some of their number were the subject of an unprovoked assault by civilians during race week, and that this assault was the origin of the almost nightly fights since with the youths of Epsom. They seem to have grievances against the police for arresting any of them, presumably claiming the right to do whatever they like in the streets without hindrance, and grievances even because some of them were arrested at the races for gaming. As regards the bellicose relationships with the youth of Epsom, the fault may not be all on the side of the Canadians; very possibly not. In any case it needs two parties to quarrel, and the lads of Epsom should be sternly discouraged from doing anything likely to contribute to continued disturbances. But whatever reasons and excuses the Canadians may put forward, there are paltry reasons and excuses for such action as was committed on Tuesday night.

Meanwhile, following on from his letter to Winston Churchill on the Wednesday, the local MP Sir Rowland Blades had been granted an extraordinary audience with the man himself the next day. Things had moved on among the higher echelons in the last twenty-four hours. Sir Rowland had been the chairman of the family printing business and was now making his way in politics following his election victory. This day he found himself in front of Churchill, General Sir Charles Harrington,

Deputy Chief of the Imperial Forces, General Romer, Chief of Staff to Sir Douglas Haig, and Mr MacCallum Scott MP, Churchill's Parliamentary Secretary. Blades was able to impress upon them the seriousness of the situation, as he saw it, and they assured him that troops had actually started on their way to Epsom. (These must have been the men from Ripon that Colonel Guest from Woodcote camp had referred to in conversation with Inspector Ferrier earlier.) Later Blades relayed all this to Mr Chuter Ede, who seemed much concerned about the continuing threat from the Canadians in Epsom, and Blades even offered to arrange for his political rival to visit the War Office to see for himself that troops were being dispatched. This suggests that Chuter Ede may have showed some scepticism, and he would have been right to, because there is no record of any troops in significant numbers ever arriving in Epsom.

Up at Woodcote camp, as the police had requested, the soldiers showing visible injuries were moved to another military hospital in Orpington, Kent. On Thursday Inspector Ferrier and some Epsom constables went there to see if they could identify any further rioters or attackers. A further seven men were rounded up and sent to Bow Street for questioning with a view to being charged along with William Lloyd and James Connors. It is strange that the constables did this when almost without exception they had all made and signed statements saying they could not identify anyone in the rioting or fighting. There is no indication that any further enquiries were going to be made to identify any other ringleaders or rioters other than these nine men. This meant that unless the men now in custody spilt the beans on others, anybody else that was seriously involved, but did not sustain a visible injury, would avoid arrest. Conversely, it also meant that anyone that had sustained a visible injury but was not heavily involved in the riot could now be on quite a sticky wicket.

The procession of distinguished visitors to the Ashley Road police station had continued on the Thursday after the riot, the most prominent of which was Sir Richard Ernest Turner, VC who was the Chief of the Canadian General Staff. Turner was a Boer War hero, having won the Victoria Cross, and had also led his men in the First World War. He was given a brigade on the Western Front, but has since been accused of being out of his depth in the more mechanised method of warfare in France, with a particular failure of command in St Eloi in April 1916, where Canadian forces were decimated by their own artillery barrage and suffered over 1,300 casualties. After that Turner was effectively given a desk job and made General Officer of the Canadian troops in Britain, becoming a Lieutenant Commander in 1917. He may have asked Churchill *not* to send the troops in, assuring him everything was well under control at the Woodcote camp, and Churchill would have been relieved by this as it would be hard to keep a lid on things if Epsom was effectively under military rule.

After the visit Turner issued a Special Order that was distributed to all Canadian personnel in Britain and was carried in *The Times*:

With deep regret I feel compelled to refer to certain disturbances which have recently occurred.

All ranks are aware of the senseless acts of rioting which took place at Witley camp during the last weekend. Fortunately the better elements in the camp prevailed and the trouble is now at an end. Had these elements only recognised earlier the seriousness of the situation, or, had they at the commencement of the trouble realised the consequences of inaction, they would never have permitted the disturbance to reach the dimensions it did. I believe that they have learnt their lesson and that they will join with promptness and vigour in the suppression of any further outbreaks of this nature in the area.

A more serious and shameful disturbance has since occurred at Epsom, the details of which are known to all. For such a disturbance there can be no conceivable or possible excuse. It is a piece of criminal folly which every decent Canadian will condemn and regret.

These disturbances were, in certain respects, similar. In both instances the active participants formed a very small minority of the soldiers concerned. On both occasions the attitude of the majority was, for a time, at any rate, passive. While, finally, in both cases there arose a general feeling of resentment at the excesses which inevitably occurred. These points of similarity disclose, on the part of the men concerned, a profound misapprehension of their duty under such circumstances.

Apparently on both occasions the majority considered themselves innocent spectators. There can be no innocent spectators at a mutiny. Every soldier present is involved either as a supporter or opponent. There can be no neutrals at a mutiny. The man who, out of curiosity, hangs about the outskirts of the crowd is in the eyes of the law almost as seriously involved as the actual ringleader. In such a situation there are only two courses open to you. Either to remain in your huts, unless otherwise ordered, or to assist to your utmost in quelling the disturbance. It must be clearly understood that, in the presence of mutiny, inaction is almost as serious a crime as active participation.

From now on, therefore, every one of you must assist actively and promptly in suppressing the spirit of disorder wherever it manifests itself. Collective disorder must be stamped out – it must never be allowed to gain headway. The man who being present at a mutiny fails to assist in suppressing it will find himself in the same class as the ringleader, who is a criminal and disgrace to Canada. He will be subject to the same treatment during the disturbance; and will be liable to severe penalties upwards. There can be no possibility of further misunderstanding.

An impression seems to be abroad that there will be a general amnesty for military offenders upon the declaration of peace. So far as I know this is a totally false impression. The Canadian Military Authorities will show no leniency to men who have been found of guilty offences of a mutinous nature; indeed, a special record of such cases is being maintained.

It is now only a matter of weeks before the force of which we are all so proud will have ceased to exist. We who are left in this country form only the remnants, but in our hands its reputation lies. In the few weeks which yet remain that reputation may suffer irreparable harm.

I am not going to remind you of our record in France. That point has been emphasised before – apparently without avail. I am not going to remind you of the distress which these outbreaks cause our friends and families at home. Of that you yourselves must be fully aware. What I have to say to you now is that these disturbances must and shall cease and that whatever steps are necessary will be taken to ensure that they do cease.

Turner's missive is rambling, repetitive and muddled and is unlikely to have struck fear into the hearts of the Canadians troops. On the one hand, he is reassuring Winston Churchill that everything is under control, but what underpins this statement above are his real fears of a recurrence and even appeals to the men – 'from now on, therefore, must actively assist in quelling' – as if a further outbreak of disorder were a given. He says that there will be no amnesty for military offenders on declaration of peace (peace had already been declared, by the way), but then adds, 'as far as I know'. He also says that the men should stay in their huts if a riot developed, but also that to do nothing is equally mutinous as to riot. Confusing. The point of the statement was to warn and frighten the Canadians and he said that he considered the Epsom Riot to be mutiny. If so, why did he not go as far to say that any men found guilty in a court of rioting would then be subject to the military charge of mutiny? Even if he didn't carry it through later, if he had wanted to make the men sit up and take notice this would have been the way. Perhaps he was worried that even though he had raised the spectre of mutiny if he actually *did* signal his intention to level charges of mutiny it would trigger exactly that. This statement smacks of a military command that is wary of its own soldiers and has a fragile veneer of control.

Private Shelby Bowen was one Canadian soldier who was not listening to Turner, or anyone. He was convicted at Bow Street Police Court for being drunk and riotous and causing grievous bodily harm to a police officer just a couple of days after the Epsom Riot. He was among a large group of Canadian soldiers apparently pushing people off the footway in the Strand.

When the police intervened he embroiled himself in a fight with them and shouted, 'We'll show you what Canada can do!' When it looked like he was going to be carted off he appealed to the 200 or so colonial soldiers in the vicinity, 'Come on Canada; give them another Epsom!'

The magistrate sentenced him to four months' hard labour.

CHAPTER 5

THE ARRESTS

'We are not manslaughterers'

Fourteen miles north of Epsom, in central London on the Friday, eight Canadian soldiers were charged in the Bow Street Police Court with being concerned together in the manslaughter of Thomas Green. The ninth man, William Lloyd, had been able to prove beyond question that he was not present at the riot. A decision had clearly been made before the men were charged not to expend time trying to discover who had wielded the fatal blow to Green, and not to pursue a murder charge. Indeed, according to Ferrier's statement to the court, he had told the defendants that they were being held and charged in connection with the *manslaughter* of Sergeant Green and Allan MacMaster allegedly retorted, 'We want to get fair play. We are not ringleaders. We don't want to be manslaughterers.'

It seems therefore that police had decided, or someone had decided for them, they were pursuing a maximum of a manslaughter charge from the off, and not murder. Manslaughter is a charged levied by prosecutors when somebody has been killed unintentionally, but not accidentally. Unlike with murder there is an absence of malice aforethought and as such a manslaughter conviction carries lighter punishments and sentences than murder. This seems a strange decision to have been taken when Sergeant Green was clearly killed from a premeditated vicious blow to the head during a planned attack on his police station. It seems stranger still that the manslaughter

87

charge decision was taken before any substantial evidence and statements had been gathered. Strangest of all, in my eyes, is the alleged response from MacMaster – 'We don't want to be *manslaughterers*.' I have never heard of anyone use the term manslaughterer. On Google as I write there are only 5,000 references to the term and most of those relate to a heavy metal band, but there are 10,200,000 references to the word murderer. Even if Ferrier had couched his enquiries and charge to MacMaster, and the others, with the word manslaughter it is highly unlikely that MacMaster, who maybe would not have understood the important difference between manslaughter and murder under British law, would have replied with a word that he had never used or heard. He would have protested, surely: 'We are not murderers' or 'We are not killers.'

This indicates to me a policeman slavishly interpreting an instruction to keep the word 'murder' out of any statements or documentation that he was drawing up.

The defendants stood before the magistrate, Mr Garrett, the aforementioned Epsom resident. All were in hospital blues and six of them had their heads wrapped in bandages. Besides MacMaster they were: Private Frank Harold Wilkie, aged twenty-one, of the 102nd Battalion; Gunner Herbert Tait, twenty-nine years old, of the 11th Canadian Division; Private Gervais Poirier, twenty-four; Private Alphonse Masse, twenty-seven; and Private Robert Alexander McAllan, forty-five, all of the CAMC; Private James Connors, nineteen, of the 13th Canadian Highlanders; and Private David Yerex, thirty-one, of the Canadian Forestry Corps.

Inspector Ferrier testified that he had told James Connors that he was making enquiries into the rioting at 12.15pm on Wednesday at the Woodcote camp. He added that he had reason to believe [PC Rose's identification] that he was one of the men involved and should therefore arrest him. Connors made no reply and he was taken to Epsom Police Station, which must have tested his nerve considerably and been a strain on the officers present, as many of them believed he was the killer of their colleague Tom Green. He was later taken on to Bow Street. At 7.00pm on the same day Ferrier saw each of the other defendants at the Canadian Military Hospital in Orpington. After cautioning them he asked if they wished to give any explanation of their injuries. Statements were made by Tait, McAllan, Poirier, Wilkie and Yerex. Ferrier handed these to the magistrate, but they were not read out in court.

MacMaster apparently said to Ferrier at this time, 'I could not tell you how I came about my injuries. I don't know anything about it at all.' This he, of course, undermined when he also said: 'We are not ringleaders.'

Poirier added: 'It is only the fellows who got hit that got taken. There were others. It is not fair.' If true, this was an admission that he too took part in the riot.

Alphonse Masse merely stated in French that he knew nothing about it. The magistrate remanded all eight defendants for a week.

Allan James MacMaster was born on 25 November 1889 at Lower Hillsdale, Judique North, Nova Scotia to John MacMaster, a blacksmith, and his wife Mary and he had seven brothers and sisters. The above birth date comes from his army record, but on the Canadian census the date given is 5 October 1892 so, for some reason, it seems he pretended to be older than he was to the military authorities. It is not clear why, as he was easily old enough to serve by 1914.

Catholic, Gaelic-speaking Scottish highlanders settled in the Judique region towards the end of the eighteenth century and the beginning of the nineteenth and MacMaster was descended from these first pioneers. Of course, Nova Scotia itself means New Scotland. Judique was and remains a small community of fewer than a thousand people on the western side of Cape Breton Island. It was principally a settlement sustained by fishing and farming and John MacMaster would have worked hard shoeing the horses used in the agricultural industry to feed and clothe his large brood of children in harsh conditions. Allan MacMaster's childhood was not an easy one. At various times he was stricken with diphtheria, small pox and typhoid fever. He suffered from 'turns' and was occasionally difficult to control and his family attributed this to one or more of the diseases that had nearly killed him as a child. Later in England he would describe the fits he had had since infancy, which 'varied in frequency from once a year to twice monthly'. It was only then that epilepsy was diagnosed.

At the age of nineteen, and doubtless with an uncertain employment future ahead of him in Judique, MacMaster sailed for Michigan in the United States to seek work. He described himself as a labourer and was joining his friend John McDonald, an earlier émigré from Nova Scotia. He paid his own fare and in his pocket he had $48. Things could not have gone well for young Allan because by 1916 he was back in Judique working as a blacksmith like his father – most probably with him. On 4 March of that year he volunteered with the 106th Battalion of the CEF at nearby Antigonish and surprisingly, given his medical history and problems, he was welcomed with open arms. The battalion was known as the Nova Scotia Rifles and their motto was 'None So Reliable'. Whether MacMaster volunteered out of a sense of patriotic duty or because of the difficult economic conditions that prevailed we cannot tell, but on 15 July 1916 he boarded the *Empress of Britain* at Halifax and set sail for Liverpool. He would have had his Ross rifle, shoddy boots and a belt that would soon turn mouldy. He set foot for the first time in England at Liverpool on 26 July 1916 and was boarded on to a train to Shorncliffe camp at Sandgate in Kent, where the 106th Battalion was broken up and MacMaster was transferred to the 26th Battalion.

Some time after 27 September 1916 MacMaster arrived at the Front and saw action at the Somme, and one can only imagine what horrors he may have endured. By Christmas 1916 he was in hospital in Etaples, Le Havre and Boulogne, having originally gone down with appendicitis. In March 1917 he was able to return to his unit at the Front, but took ill once again and was returned to England where he was treated in various hospitals for a number of ailments, which now included gonorrhoea and syphilis. In February of 1919 Allan MacMaster walked through the gates of Woodcote convalescence camp riddled with venereal disease, angry, ashamed, frustrated and burning to get home.

'Let's go, boys!'

William Lloyd was the only man arrested who did not have any visible injuries. As we have seen, he had been identified by PC Rose as one of those at the front of the mob. Lloyd was able swiftly to prove this as erroneous, as he had stayed the night at a Mrs Beauchamp's lodging house in Epsom town and had civilian witnesses who were with him at the time the riot was taking place. Elizabeth Beauchamp, a widow, kept a sweet shop and lodging house on South Street, by the corner of Sweetbriar Lane, on the far side of Rosebery Park to the police station. It is not clear why Lloyd chose to pay money to stay in a lodging house when his camp was just up the road. Perhaps the attraction was Mrs Beauchamp's seventeen-year-old granddaughter Doris, who figures in his statement, or Mrs Maidment, Doris's mother. More important, though, was that Lloyd's statement was startling in many ways and could and should have led Inspector Ferrier to the killer. The crucial document read as follows:

> I wish to make a voluntary statement and this after having been cautioned by Inspector Ferrier, that anything I may say will be written down and may be used in evidence against me.
>
> On the Tuesday, 17th June, I was staying at Beauchamp's lodging house. I may say I lived there for four nights, from Saturday 14th. On Tuesday, about quarter to eleven, I saw the

girl Doris standing at the door of the shop and we entered the house by the side door of the shop. Mrs Maidment (Doris's mother), also her Grandmother Mrs Beauchamp was there and gave me supper. During this time a civilian came in and we all sat talking together till about 12.30 in the morning when a Red Cross ambulance drove down. We went outside to see if it was a Canadian ambulance and whilst standing at the door a Canadian sergeant came up to me and asked if I wanted to go to camp. I told him I was living at the house that night.

He went away and soon after two Canadian soldiers came up to us and asked for a drink. I asked what was the matter and one of them said: 'We've had a row down the street and have just killed a policeman.' I don't know who these men are and could not identify either of them, they were both short men. They then left, and the girl Doris asked me to go down with her to the Police Station to see if it were true. So Doris, her mother (Mrs Maidment) and [her grandmother] and I walked to the Police Station where we saw an ambulance and a crowd of civilians outside. We waited outside about five minutes and then went home, and I went to bed and did not arise until 9am next day. I may say I can't hold a fork in my hand as my left forefinger and thumb is dead, or practically so, and Mrs Maidment used to cut my food for me.

One of my chums, Eddie Lapointe, who sleeps in the same hut, No 83, 4th Division and next bed to me, told me that on Tuesday night on his getting to the camp gates at about 11pm he saw a lot of Canadian soldiers dressed in blue, very excited, and Major Ross talking to them trying to quieten them when a tall soldier said: 'Let's go, boys.' And the crowd went, and he (Lapointe) went with them. He told me that on the way down they tore fences down; that he was in the middle of the crowd and saw the big soldier, who had led them from the camp, strike Sergeant Green with an iron bar over the side of the head, and that the Sergeant fell down, and he heard somebody cry out: 'Kick him!' but he does not whether that was done or not. That's all he told me.

93

On the night of the 17th, Lapointe and I were passing the police station about 10.15pm or 10.30pm and we saw some Canadian soldiers arguing with five or six policemen and a little beyond the Police Station we passed on through the park, and I saw the policemen chase the soldiers away as we passed through the park. On our way through the park there was a group of about 15 Canadian soldiers, one of whose mouth was bleeding. They asked us to stay with them. We refused and passed through and they abused us and called us 'Conscripts' and that we had a yellow streak down our backs.[1] We walked up the Briar Walk at the top of which I left Lapointe and went to my lodgings, and met Doris outside the door as I formerly told you, and was with she and her mother till I went to bed at about 1.15am.

This statement has been read over to me and is true.

Bearing in mind this statement was taken on the Thursday at Bow Street, where Ferrier did not get very much from any of the other arrested men, it should have taken the Inspector to the heart of the events of the night before last. Although Lloyd was clearly not involved he had provided evidence of a comrade who had witnessed the killing. He even had a description of the murderer and his colleague (Lapointe) should have been able to point him out quite easily. Lapointe's version of events as told

---

[1] French Canadians had not rallied to the cause as enthusiastically as their other countrymen mainly because Britain was not their Mother Country and as predominantly Catholics they felt they would have a hard time among a chiefly Protestant army. As the demand for men became greater the government looked to the French-speaking population, principally in Quebec, to volunteer and when this did not work, despite the formation of French regiments, conscription was introduced. This became a dividing issue and a dangerous bone of contention between British and French Canadians, both at home and abroad.

to Lloyd also indicated malice aforethought on the part of the 'big man'. He also had knowledge that Sergeant Green had been struck with an iron bar when this was not generally known. The perceived wisdom at that point was that the sergeant had been viciously kicked in the head. Sir Nevil Macready had written to the Home Secretary, Edward Shortt, stating exactly this on the day after the riot.

Lapointe was a vital, compelling witness and from the point of view of getting justice for Sergeant Green and solving the case, a breakthrough. Yet instead of grabbing his cape and charging straight back down to Epsom to see Lapointe whilst nerves were still fraught and the events and scene of crime still steaming, Ferrier chose not to. In fact Inspector Ferrier did not get face to face with Eddie Lapointe until four days later on 23 June 1919, by which time he had clammed up and made an anodyne statement where he was not directly involved, could not identify anyone and did not see anything significant. Strangely, Lapointe does not appear to have been pressed on what Lloyd told the police. There was no attempt to put Lloyd and Lapointe together to iron out the anomalies in their statements. It must have been a fairly quick session with Lapointe as Ferrier combined the trip to Epsom with attending Thomas Green's funeral.

Men being men, they would have talked. Lapointe would not have been the only one to have seen MacMaster deliver the fatal blow with an iron bar to Sergeant Green. The soldiers that administered first aid to Green in Charles Polhill's house would also have been unlikely to have kept that whole intense experience to themselves. Lapointe knew the killer was MacMaster, now Ferrier knew the killer was MacMaster, and if he had cared to dig so did half of the Woodcote camp.

Other less obvious, but nonetheless striking, questions arise from William Lloyd's statement. He refers to the two short soldiers who volunteered at the guest house that they had just killed a policeman. These also were potentially the murderers of Thomas Green and although Lloyd was quick to say he could not identify the men (even though, unlike outside the police station, they would not have been in darkness), Mrs Maud Maidment, her daughter Doris and the other civilian present at the guest house (who was a travelling salesman for Crosse and Blackwell and only lived in nearby Battersea) all saw them too. Interestingly, among the arrested men, Robert McAllan was 5'4" and Herbert Tait 5'5". Could they have been the two men who asked for water? Did Ferrier not consider this?

Why were these witnesses not asked to make statements and why were they not taken to the camp to try and pick out the men? Unlike the Canadians, who were rapidly closing ranks and saying nothing, the Maidments were Epsom people and therefore presumably strongly motivated to help catch the killer or killers of their well-liked town police station sergeant.

Sergeant Shuttleworth, in his statement given to Ferrier in the immediate aftermath of the riot, talks about the Canadian soldiers surrounding the police station and says 'one of them I believe I could identify'. Why then did Ferrier not whisk him up to the camp and see if he could pick the man out? In normal circumstances omissions like this would point to an incompetent investigation, yet Ferrier would be commended for his handling of the case. Inspector Ferrier, as we have seen, was also a champion of and expert in fingerprinting technology, so why didn't he, when hearing of Lapointe's mention of an iron bar, get back down to Ashley Road and conduct a search for what was likely to be the murder weapon? Were the prints of one of the men he had in custody on the iron bar? If so, he had a result. If he were really committed to solving the crime he would have also ordered that the two ornamental concrete-bottomed ponds in Rosebery Park – the ones that were red with soldiers' blood in the morning, according to civilian reports – be drained, because his policeman's instinct would have told him that this was where the murderer would most likely have disposed of the weapon. Who knows if it does not still rest there, undisturbed in mud, at the bottom of the surviving pond to this day?

Of all the people Inspector Ferrier did *not* take statements from the most inexplicable candidates are Private McDonald and Driver Veinot. Here are two men that were not only the catalyst for the entire riot, but were centre stage during the most crucial stages of the evening. They were broken out. They must have seen MacMaster wrench the iron bar from their cell. They would have emerged into the epicentre of the fracas around the time, or just after, Sergeant Green suffered his fate. It is likely that neither man would have co-operated with the police, but for them not to be questioned at all flies in the face of police procedure, common sense and logic.

The detective's actions seem inexplicable if one, naturally, believes that he wanted to crack the case and bring the perpetrators of Sergeant Green's slaying to book. However, if one posits that he did not want a murderer on his hands and needed to move the case through the courts on the least contentious charges possible, and as quickly as possible, then his behaviour makes perfect sense. Indeed, his heart probably sank when he took William Lloyd's statement, as he did not want to hear this. A clear identification of a killer, if made public, would lead to pressure for a murder charge, which could lead to a death sentence, which could lead to David Lloyd George's nightmare scenario of a groundswell of anti-British feeling in Canada and other parts of the Commonwealth. Ferrier knew who the 'big man' was that Lapointe referred to. He had him in custody. He had looked into his eyes and seen his army and medical records. And now, ironically, he was keen to avoid his being identified as the killer of Sergeant Green.

If one looks at the statements in this case gathered together as a whole, it is extraordinary how almost all of the witnesses were quick to say they could not identify anyone they encountered on the fateful night. With the soldiers, perhaps, it is to be expected that they would close ranks and adopt a 'no names' stance, but equally, as was seen by Lloyd's statement, they were not an entirely harmonious group and most were desperate to go home and keen to avoid anything that would keep them in England any longer. I doubt if among the up to 1,500 men at the camp and the 400 who rioted there would not have been some who were prepared to point a finger, should they have been pressed, which they were not. The fact that all of the policemen (with the exception of James Rose and Sergeant Shuttleworth, initially) were all so definite they could *not* identify anyone I find strange. Granted, the gas lights around and outside the station were put out and it was dark outside. Even in the dark, though, if you are fighting toe to toe, as the police and the soldiers were, you see faces in close proximity. If you couldn't, how would you be able to land truncheon blows? And there were plenty landed, as we know. Moreover, the lights *inside* the police station were not smashed and soldier after soldier who tried to get access into the building via the door and windows would have been clearly seen and the light from inside the station would surely have given some visibility to events immediately outside. It stretches credibility that nearly all the police officers would state that they could not identify anyone involved in the riot when they most certainly wanted their colleague's death avenged. In the same way that there was a concerted effort to keep the words 'murder' and 'killing' out of the investigation there was also a will to avoid any individual being specifically identified with anything more than being a rioter.

CHAPTER 7

THE MEN

Volunteering

James Connors was the youngest of the accused, being born in 1899 in Montreal, Quebec, and only fourteen years old when the war broke out. He was one of seven children born to Irish parents, James M Connors and Essie Rooney, and at the time of his enlistment he put his occupation down as a farmer. He could not have been working long when he signed up at Barriefield, Ontario to the Queen's University Field Ambulance in August 1916, as he was still only a boy of sixteen. However, this boy was so keen to get in the army, for whatever reason, that he lied about his age, giving his birth year as 1897. By then he was 5'6" tall with fair complexion, grey eyes and light brown hair.

Young James Connors arrived in England on 5 November 1916 and joined the 13th Canadian Field Ambulance in April 1917 and in the September was hospitalised after being gassed. He was discharged to Base Details and his condition seemed not to improve. In May 1918 he contracted pneumonia and was returned to England and in December arrived at Woodcote camp suffering from pleurisy. After apparently recovering he was re-admitted for 'pleurisy' again in April 1919. Concerned about his health, the authorities did not discharge him from Epsom, and instead gave the boy duties at the camp as an assistant cook.

He was still a teenager and had seen things he never thought he would. He was ill and he knew it. The weight was falling off him and yet here he was, still in England. He wanted to go home to his mother and father and his brothers and sisters. He *needed* to go home, but the top brass kept promising they'd be sailing soon, and then there would be another excuse. Now the bastards were going on strike at the docks. He was angry and scared. More scared.

Robert Alexander McAllan was old enough to have been Connors' father and was the eldest of the men charged. He was also the only one to have been born in Britain. He came into the world in Glasgow in 1874 and in 1907, listed as a builder, he sailed for a new life in Canada. He had married, but by the time he volunteered as a soldier in August 1915, at the late age of forty-one, was a widower. He gave his profession as a stone-mason then and his next of kin as William McAllan, his brother, of Kipping, Sterling, Scotland. William's wife on one census return is listed as a prostitute, which demonstrates a startling honesty or a raw sense of humour. McAllan was a small man of just 5'4" and this, and his relative old age, may explain why he never got to see action in France. His army records also reveal he suffered from flat feet and varicose veins, which raises the question to why he was accepted in the first instance. He arrived in England on board the *Empress of Britain*, the same vessel as MacMaster, but slightly earlier in May 1916. He turned up on the staff at the Woodcote camp in August of 1917 and at some point after was appointed a military policeman.

The next defendant, Herbert Tait, was born in Plympton Township, Lambton County, Ontario in 1888. In 1911 he was in Gold City in Algoma, Ontario, presumably prospecting for the precious metal. He volunteered with the 149th Battalion of the CEF in February 1916 when he was living at Wanstead, Ontario with his parents. He'd obviously found no gold. His military record has him at 5'5" with a fair complexion, blue eyes and brown hair. Tait departed for England on the *Lapland* in April 1916, and was soon transferred to Canadian Machine Gun (CMG) Depot. In April 1918 he went to France to the CMG Reserve Pool before being taken on strength with the 4th CMG Company. In June 1918 he was charged with drunkenness and causing a disturbance at Divion, now the site of the Commonwealth War Graves Commission cemetery. In January 1919 Tait was still in France and was transferred to the 2nd CMG Company, but in March he was returned to England. In May 1919, only weeks before the riot, he arrived at Woodcote camp with lacerations to his head, presumably from some fight or other, and like MacMaster was suffering from venereal disease.

Orchitis was the ailment that the next defendant was recorded as suffering from. David Wellington Yerex was an unlikely looking aggressor, having suffered from myopia as a child, and normally wore thick-lensed spectacles. His orchitis manifested itself in an inflammation of the testicles and it is very likely that this too was a side-effect of a sexually transmitted disease. He was born in Galt, Ontario in 1887, the son of Andrew and Mary Yerex, who were of French extraction. At the time he enlisted in the Canadian Forestry Corps (CFC), in 1917, Yerex was working as a labourer and was a bachelor. He arrived in Liverpool in July 1917 and was taken on strength at the CFC Depot at Sunningdale, Berkshire. In September he was posted to 74 Company CFC in France and remained there until invalided to England, suffering from the orchitis, in April 1919.

On 8 May 1919, barely a month before the riot, he arrived in Epsom.

Exactly one week later Private Frank Howard Wilkie walked through the Woodcote camp gates. He had come from the Witley camp nearby to prepare for demobilisation, though he was not sure how the move to Epsom furthered this process. To add to his frustration and discomfort he was still suffering from a nasty case of gonorrhoea. Wilkie was born at Guelph, Ontario in 1897. He enlisted in the CEF at Hamilton, Ontario in September 1916, but did not proceed to England until April of the next year. On 4 September 1918, shortly before the war ended, he was wounded and gassed and evacuated to England. Back at Witley he was treated for his wounds, and for venereal disease, yet was still appointed Lance Corporal before his move to Epsom. This may give some indication as to how common-place sexual disease had become among the Canadians in England.

Gervase Lawrence Poirier was never too sure about his exact name. On his Attestation Paper he signs himself Jervus, and elsewhere Jervis, yet he was baptised in the church of St Hyacinth in D'Escousse, Nova Scotia as Gervase. He was born in 1893 to Albert Poirier and Agnes Cordeau. He enlisted with the 64th Battalion, CEF, at Halifax, Nova Scotia in February 1916 and was described at that time as being 5'7" with a fresh complexion, grey eyes and brown hair. He arrived in England in April 1916 with a bang, being almost immediately confined to barracks for ten days for 'misconduct'. In May he was transferred to the Canadian Engineers Training Depot (CETD) at Shorncliffe. He was sent to France in July as a sapper with the 43rd Tunnelling Company. In October 1916, close to Ypres, he came under heavy shell fire and was temporarily

103

buried alive.[2] Poirier suffered from severe nasal obstruction, a middle-ear infection and, no doubt, intense trauma from the terrifying experience and was returned to England.

Poirier entered Westcliffe Hospital for about a month and when discharged he was posted to the Garrison Duty Company at Crowborough in Sussex. He was made Acting Lance Corporal, but was later returned to the Canadian Engineers Reinforcement Depot (CERD) as a sapper. He never returned to the Front, being in and out of hospital with recurring nasal and hearing problems for the next year. In fact, his ear drums had been destroyed. In June 1918 he was transferred from the Engineers to CAMC Depot and on 13 June of that month he was assigned to the Woodcote Park Convalescence Hospital in Epsom.

The last of the men to stand trial was Alphonse Masse. He had been born in 1892 and was one of at least eleven children of Wilfrid and Eugenie Masse of Montreal, Quebec. The Masses lived in a region called Témiscouata, which was extremely remote, and given the late stage in the war and Alphonse's later appearance in Toronto it is likely he was a reluctant soldier and was conscripted rather than being a volunteer like his fellow defendants.

He attested at Toronto, Ontario in April 1918 and joined the 85th Draft, Canadian Engineers. He stood 5'5½'' in his socks

---

[2] No front-line role was much better than another in the quagmire of misery, butchery and torment of trench warfare, but the tunnellers faced unique dangers and death. Often looked down upon by other infantry and sometimes referred to as 'sewer rats', they worked underground, digging tunnels that could travel under enemy lines with a view to blowing them up. Often the Germans discovered them first and they found themselves captured, killed or blown up themselves. A constant threat was the collapse of any tunnel and being buried alive in the middle of nowhere.

and had brown eyes and dark brown hair. He gave his profession as a carpenter. On arrival in England in August he was assigned to the 2nd Canadian Engineers Reinforcement Brigade (CERB) and in January 1919 to the 1st CERB. For reasons that are not clear he was then transferred to the CAMC and from there to Woodcote Hospital on 15 May 1919. Clearly, he saw no action at all.

Of the eight young men that were to face trial four of them (at least) were suffering from venereal disease and two of those four had not even been to France. Contrary to later reports that hardly any of the soldiers had seen action, six of them had, and most of them had been injured. Five out of the eight had been in Epsom only a matter of weeks and four of that five had literally just arrived. They were a motley bunch, but not in a particularly humorous sense of the word. They were diseased, injured, shattered and being pushed around from pillar to post, but not to the one place they wanted to be pushed – home.

Doing their Bit

Canada is a relatively young nation. It is now the second biggest country by land area in the world (after Russia), but was not officially constituted as the Canada we know now until the middle of the nineteenth century. In 1867, with the union of three British North American colonies through Confederation, Canada was formed as a federal dominion of four provinces: Ontario, Nova Scotia, Quebec and New Brunswick.

Large-scale emigration from England, Scotland and Ireland to Canada had been accelerating from the early nineteenth century and the British operated Canada as a colony. The

Canadians themselves, though, fast developed their own unique personality and culture and developed strong relations with their biggest neighbour, the United States of America, after an earlier war between them, and progressively but diplomatically steered a course that would one day bring them independence from the British Empire.

Yet when Britain declared war on Germany, following that country's invasion of Belgium, Canada had no qualms over standing shoulder to shoulder with the Mother Country. In 1914 many Canadians were still fresh immigrants and half of the men that eventually became soldiers had been born in Britain. Loyalty to the Empire, family ties 'at home', romantic memories of their childhoods and perceptions of their ancestry simply erupted into a patriotic rush to enlist and 'do their bit' in France, where the front line of war was quickly established. There was no doubt, in Canada as in Britain, about where right and wrong lay and the sentiment articulated by Sir Arthur Conan Doyle that 'there are times when every one of us must make a stand for human right and justice or never feel clean again' was widely felt.

The man whose task it was to recruit, train and organise the Canadian volunteers into an army capable of aligning with the British in their resistance to the Kaiser was Colonel Sam Hughes. Indeed, it was a moment such as this that he had been waiting for all of his life. At sixty-one years of age he was the Minister of Militia in Sir Robert Borden's Conservative government and as a Victoria Cross recipient in the Boer War he felt qualified to lead a bolstering of Canada's military capability. It was he who led a campaign for Canada to fight alongside Britain in the southern African Boer war. He perceived the threat to Canada to be the United States initially (even though there had been no hostilities between the two countries for a century), but when war in Europe seemed inevitable his excitement was palpable, so much so that at one point he feared that Britain might not have the backbone to take on the might of Germany and was mightily relieved when war was declared.

Sam Hughes' lasting achievement was to set up a military training camp at Valcartier, Quebec and create the CEF within a remarkable few weeks. He promised Britain 22,000 men on the outbreak of war, but was soon ready to send 30,000, and by late September of 1914 ships packed with Canadian soldiers were sailing for Europe. Hughes joined them in England expecting to command his men in the theatre of war, but was promptly disabused. The Canadians were part of the British Army and as such were to be commanded by Major General Edwin Alderson, and Hughes had to accept this.

Alderson had secured his reputation in the Second Boer War when he had successfully commanded Canadian troops. From the off, though, the two men clashed: Hughes said his men were ready for battle, but Alderson disagreed. The Englishman took the Canadian troops to Salisbury Plain and spent several months transforming them into tough, capable and better-disciplined soldiers. A more fundamental and damaging disagreement between the two leaders was over the Ross army rifle that Sam Hughes had championed. Alderson thought it unsuitable and wanted the CEF to adopt the British-made Lee Enfield, but Hughes resisted and frustrated at every opportunity despite mounting evidence of his gun's unsuitability. Hughes' reputation would continue to falter as the soldiers struggled with other faulty equipment and through his propensity to make promotions based on patronage that undermined the effective-ness of the army. He was autocratic and prone to interfere at every level and would eventually be forced to resign in 1916.

Although some thoroughly unsuitable Canadians were sent home, Alderson's work on Salisbury Plain, and elsewhere, on Sam Hughes' recruits was beginning to pay dividends. By February of 1915 the first Canadians were sent to Europe. Trench warfare had already established itself, as had the relentless loss of life. By Christmas of 1914, 60,000 British soldiers had been killed.

It was in Belgium though, at Ypres, where the Canadians were involved in their first significant engagement. On the morning of 22 April 1915 the front line manned by French, Algerian and Canadian troops became the first to experience the horror of a German chlorine gas attack. The first they knew of it was a wall of green fog floating towards them from no man's land. Behind the cover of the toxic clouds were German soldiers advancing. The gas, if directly inhaled, burnt and choked the men, and they writhed in agony as they battled for breath whilst ripping at their tunics in their blind, dying panic. 'Piss on your handkerchiefs and tie them over your faces,' yelled one officer, and for some it worked, the gas setting up some sort of chemical combination with the urine and crystallising it. Survivors would later call the gas the 'devil's breath'. The Algerians broke the line and fled at this unexpected and unfathomable terror, suffering massive casualties as they did so, and the Canadians were forced to defend twice the length of front line in the face of this malevolent onslaught. Against the odds they managed to do so and gave no ground, but not before half of their number had been injured and 6,000 men had died.

The loss was felt keenly in Canada. The journey from the excited patriotism whipped up by Sam Hughes, and others, to a muddy grave on a European battlefield was all too rapid and real. The men of Canada had been urged to 'do their bit' in the recruiters' equivalent strapline to Lord Kitchener's 'Your

108

Country Needs You', but few at first really thought that doing their bit would entail swift and agonising loss of life. The country took solace and immense pride from the fact that their men had acquitted themselves so well and not fled, as many more battle-hardened and better-trained men had in the past and would do in the future. Compared to the British soldiers the Canadians may have been ill-disciplined and irregular, a criticism that had been often levelled, but their bravery was now proven.

A year after Ypres, in April 1916, the Battle of St Eloi ended in disaster for Canadian troops. British forces had previously blown a series of underground mines to destroy German defences, but the effort had left massive mud-filled craters to occupy. When the Canadians relieved British troops they found few actual trenches in which to take cover and most of those were waist-deep in water, in which faeces floated and rats swam. The entire Front was also under observation and constant fire from the Germans, who eventually managed to drive the Canadians out of the craters, and confusion through-out the division, and command, followed. The Generals did not know where their troops were much of the time and it is a sad fact that Canadians were often firing on Canadians. Over 1,000 men died here and the bungled operation cost Major General Richard Turner his job. General Sir Julian Byng assumed command of the Canadian Army shortly after.

Byng came from an aristocratic family with long traditions and attended Eton, where he picked up the nickname Bungo. Class and patronage may have played a large part in his rise through the military ranks, but his time in command of the Canadian men would prove him to be a clever, tactical and effective wartime leader and etch his name into military history.

The Canadians under Byng went on to the play their part in the Battle of the Somme during 1916. This was a disaster in terms of the cost of human life and the British lost some 400,000 men; the Canadians over 20,000. In April 1917 the Battle of Vimy Ridge would become the CEF's finest moment of the First World War, but not so fine for the many men who lost their lives and those who were seriously injured. Vimy Ridge was German-held high ground along an escarpment at the northernmost end of the Arras offensive. If the combined four divisions of the CEF, fighting together for the first time, could overcome the three divisions of the German Sixth Army it would be a massive victory and had the potential to change the course of the war.

The Canadian Corps, bolstered by their new-found cohesion, training and Byng's meticulous planning, captured most of the ridge on the first day of their assault. The town of Thelus fell on the second day, as did the crest of the ridge, and finally a fortified knoll located outside Givenchy-en-Gohelle was captured by the Canadians. The Germans then retreated. It was a spectacular victory and one in which the Canadians took, and still take, great pride. Historians have contended that it was this event that marked Canada's coming of age as a nation.

Later in 1917 the Canadians lost thousands more soldiers at Passchendaele as part of General Haig's ill-fated Flanders offensive. Between August and October of 1918 the Canadians were engaged in the taking of the ancient city of Cambrai, but cumulatively this episode claimed even more lives than the Somme. The following month, hostilities were officially halted.

The Canadians lost around 70,000 lives during the whole of the First World War campaign, which represented over ten per cent of the men who enlisted. Half of the Canadians who died were British-born. The British themselves suffered nearly a million deaths among a shocking total of almost ten million young men from all over the world. In addition to the 70,000 Canadians who perished were those that were injured, or became ill, and had to be sent back from the Front to be treated and then convalesce in England. There were a number of hospitals in the south of the country and one of these was Woodcote Park in Epsom.

The area covered 350 acres and on one side bordered Lord Rosebery's land and on the other ran into Epsom Downs itself. The construction of the camp began in November 1914 and was completed in remarkable time in February 1915 by the UPS Brigade. In those few months enough huts were built to house up to 5,000 men, a drainage system and power station installed, and, among many other things, a recreation room and ground, a post office, a hospital, a chapel, a hairdressers' and a rifle range were all erected. Like other Canadian sites in England it became a town within a town.

The huts themselves were where the Canadians spent most of their time, and these measured 120 feet by 20 feet with each housing 50 men. They were timber framed and built on wooden supports to prevent any part of the floor resting on the ground. The sides were constructed externally of corrugated iron and lined internally with matchboarding. They were fitted with hospital window frames and sashes and louvre ventilators in the gables. They were heated by three slow combustion stoves and lit by electric lamps.

The first convalescents arrived in June 1915 – forty Australians (including Troopers Maynard and Pinson who upset Inspector Pawley so), casualties of Gallipoli, the ultimately failed attempt by the Allies to take Istanbul in Turkey, which resulted in nearly 9,000 Australians being killed and another 20,000 being injured. Gallipoli has become to the Australians what Vimy Ridge is to the Canadians – a defining event in their respective identity and history. The sacrifices made are recognised, remembered and grieved over on ANZAC Day, 25 April, each year.

Later, Commonwealth troops damaged in the Battle of the Somme joined the Australians and soon the convalescent hospital hit its peak of 4,000 men. In July 1916, with the colonial men settling in, many of them cultivating and decorating small plots of garden outside their tin huts and relations calm and cordial, King George V and Queen Mary visited to open the new tea and recreation room. If the later Epsom Riot marked the low point of the camp, this Royal recognition signified the high.

The top brass were acutely aware that to keep such a large contingent of soldiers on Epsom Downs, twiddling their fingers and killing time, carried some risk and efforts were made to keep them constructively and healthily occupied and discourage them from spending too much of their wages and time in the little town's pubs and clubs, thereby putting undue pressure on the social infrastructure. Concerts and moving pictures were laid on and a baseball team was formed that played other Canadians and London Americans, but activities such as these, well intentioned as they were, were no substitute for the lack of female company and interaction with human beings other than themselves. To meet this need the soldiers would travel into London, by train, to visit the Maple Leaf Club, a social club and hotel opened by Rudyard Kipling in 1915 where Canadians passing through the capital could stay and indulge in everything the city had to offer. Those that were not inclined to travel up the line sought similar pleasures and pastimes nearer home.

When the war ended in November 1918 the Canadians expected they would be travelling home imminently, but the logistics of moving large bodies of men across the globe prevented any smooth demobilisation and when local labour disputes exacerbated the situation the soldiers became increasingly agitated. The men in the hospitals, many of them 'venereals', were at the back of the queue.

Not all the troops were waiting to go back to Canada, though. In all, around 22,000 soldiers elected to stay in Britain and return to the families, towns and villages they had left when they had emigrated for a better life some years earlier.

George Kimberley was one such man. He left Woodcote camp to return to the family he had bade farewell to, in Tipton in the Midlands in the 1900s, rather than return to Canada. His story, while not directly connected to the immediate events in hand, is a poignant one and illustrative of the Canadian war experience. George was born in 1887 and was a teenager when he immigrated to Canada. When war broke out he joined the 8th Canadian Infantry (Winnipeg) Battalion. He was one of the men sent to Salisbury Plain for training and perhaps the grim reality of soldiering was too much, because his military record shows a pattern of poor discipline. He lost three days' pay almost immediately for being AWOL. He most probably visited Tipton. Later he received one day's Field Punishment No 1 for insubordination and then five days of the above for being 'drunk falling in for parade'. Field Punishment No 1 consisted of the convicted soldier being placed in irons, handcuffs or some other restraint and being attached to a fixed object such as a fence post or gun-wheel for up to two hours a day. The rest of the time he would be made to do hard labour. The troops called this humiliating ritual 'crucifixion'.

George was in Belgium for the Second Battle of Ypres in 1915 when the first gas was unleashed and he suffered gunshot wounds to his head and left shoulder. More black marks punctuated his disciplinary record, including 'drunk on active service' and 'drunk in barracks', but in June 1916 he was involved in defending an attack by the Germans on the Canadians' positions around Mount Sorrel, south east of Ypres. He and his countrymen were literally blown from their positions and overwhelmed by the German infantry. George lost part of his skull to flying shrapnel and his speech was permanently affected, as was the sight in his right eye. Hospital records saw him classified as dangerously ill and unlikely to survive. He made some sort of recovery, though, and was well enough to be sent to Woodcote Park. His medical assessment on arrival said it all: 'Gun shot wound three inches by one and a half inches in rear half of skull, which pulsates. Slight pustulent discharge. Complains of pain at site of wound. Headache, dizziness. Total right-sighted blindness. Speech now better, except when greatly excited. He is no longer physically fit for war service.'

George left Epsom for Tipton to the comfort and caring of his parents' home rather than return to Canada. He became well known in the town in the years after the war because he was a walking, living reminder of the violence of the trenches with the visible silver plate in his head and his unseeing and frozen eye. Although he reached an accommodation with his physical injuries one can only imagine the mental pain he had to deal with. In 1926 a young boy witnessed George, now aged thirty-eight, jump into the canal and drown. The coroner returned a verdict of 'Death from misadventure, consequent from injuries he received in the Great War.' His gravestone bears the inscription 'He Fought a Good Fight'.

CHAPTER 8

THE FUNERAL

Dayspring in his Heart

From first light on the morning of Monday 23 June 1919 Epsom prepared itself for the funeral of Thomas Green, which would be, besides the annual Derby and Oaks horse races, the most public single event ever to have taken place in the borough. Early rising well-wishers delivered tributes and wreaths to the garden of 92 Lower Court Road, quietly placing them on the grass, not wishing to disturb the morning and mourning of Lily and Nellie Green, who readied the house in preparation for the many members of the extended Green and Card families who would be arriving shortly. Later in the morning the poor children from the borough, under no specific instruction, went into the surrounding fields and meadows and picked wild flowers, which they respectfully placed in their unkempt bundles outside Sergeant Green's house.

The Green family had spread far and wide since Thomas Green's childhood in Billingshurst. His parents were both now dead, but he had sisters in London, a brother who had emigrated for Canada and another, Edgar, who was a police officer in Egham, Surrey. When Thomas and Lilian had begun their married life, and he embarked on his career as a police constable, they first lived in the St Pancras area of London. Although army life would have conditioned him to the ways of the world, the contrast of life in the capital, and especially the kinds of people he would have been encountering daily, would have been in sharp contrast to the quiet existence the couple would have been accustomed to in deepest Sussex. St Pancras was an area that despite (or because of) the bustling railway terminuses was largely poverty stricken and awash with crime and prostitution.

Thomas Green must have adapted and acquitted his duties well because in July 1903, at the age of thirty-five, he was promoted to Sergeant and transferred to 'W' Division. In 1907 he was elevated again to Station Sergeant and given the berth of Putney Police Station at 129 Lower Richmond Road, Putney, London. Here he lived in a spacious three-bedroomed apartment above the station with his wife and his growing family. In 1911 he was offered the position of Station Sergeant at Epsom Police Station. Although fewer than ten miles south of Putney and just off the Portsmouth Road it was a country posting and one of the more rural stations falling within the Metropolitan Police boundaries. Horsham and its surrounds, where both Thomas and Lilian still had family and friends, was just a handful of stops further south down the railway line. Now aged forty-three and hoping there might be one last promotion to Inspector and an enhanced pension before his retirement, Thomas Green and his wife had decided Epsom would be a pleasant place for their young children to grow up and took the step. The red-bricked house they were offered in Lower Court Road seemed new and solid and the school just around the corner in Pound Lane felt homely and ideal for the girls. As for the job, Green was aware that on race days the town became lively, but on the whole it was a bit of a backwater. He looked forward to the quiet life.

At the so-called Brighton railway station on Station Road early on that funeral morning more people were arriving in the town than were commuting up to London, steadily increasing in

116

number as the afternoon drew near. Metropolitan Police officers from the entire force, and not on duty, had been given permission to pay their respects to their colleague and a special dispensation had been made for them to travel on the rail network at one quarter of the normal price. Officers had been asked to dress in their tunics and black gloves and Inspectors to wear caps. It was estimated that by the mid-afternoon seven or eight hundred uniformed officers were present in the town.

The shops in Pound Lane, just around the corner from Lower Court Road, had decided not to open as a mark of respect. Walter Clarke, the grocer; Florence Cooper, the draper; Harry McCoombe, the butcher; Charles Pellett, the bootmaker; and George Marlow, the greengrocer all knew Mr and Mrs Green and the girls very well and they and their staff would either line the route of the cortege that afternoon or attend the service and the burial. Most houses on the route and elsewhere in the town would be drawing their curtains later and almost every other shop in the town would shut between three and four o'clock.

During the morning more formal floral tributes arrived at the house, including one from the Canadian Record Office and another from Sir Rowland Blades. Blades, along with Lord Rosebery and Henry Banks Longley, Chairman of the Council, issued a letter calling for a fund to be set up for Sergeant Green's family and to benefit the other officers involved in the siege. It read as follows:

The wish has been generally expressed that the signal bravery of the Epsom police in circumstances fully reported in the papers last week should be publicly recognised by opening a fund in Epsom and neighbourhood. The proceeds would be devoted, first, to supplementing, if necessary, the provision for the wife and family of Station Sergeant Green, who lost his life in the gallant performance of his duty; and secondly, in pre-

117

senting a memento to each of the police who took part in the fight, not one of who escaped without more or less serious injury.

Probably there is nothing finer in the noble records of the police than this heroic defence of order against disorder, and it is thought that many beyond the immediate neighbourhood would like to join in this tribute of appreciation of fidelity in the face of great personal risk. In the absence of the Commissioner, the Assistant Commissioner (General Horwood) has seen and fully approved this letter. Subscriptions will be gladly received by the treasurer of the fund (Mr H.B. Longley).

Down at the Epsom Police Court, almost next door to the Wesleyan Church where the funeral service would be held a few hours later, Mr Tritton, the Chairman today of the magistrates, put on record the bench's appreciation of the gallant behaviour of the men of Epsom Police Station before morning business started as usual. He said that all the inhabitants of Epsom would desire to join in the expression of admiration of the conduct of the police in very difficult and trying circumstances and extended their deep regret over the loss of Sergeant Green. Inspector Pawley, who was present, thanked the Chairman: 'What we did was a very small effort in preserving order. We did our best as far as our abilities and the number of men permitted. It is a matter of gratification and pride for us all to know that we have the praise and appreciation of the British public.'

By 2.00pm the roads were lined two, three and four deep along the route from the Greens' house in Lower Court Road, left at Pound Lane and right on to Hook Road. At the junction of Hook Road and East Street, passing The Rifleman, the cortege would turn right again into the High Street, where the crowds were particularly thick, all the way to the police station and the

118

Wesleyan Church, left at Ashley Road. Until the cortege came into view the crowds chattered and basked in the sunshine with a nervous anticipation, but like a river running along the line, as the procession appeared in the distance, hats were removed, heads were bowed and a solemn, perfect silence prevailed with just the sound of mournful music hanging in the air. Those who were present would never forget the day.

The procession from the house was led by the band of 'V' Division of the Metropolitan Police and followed by the undertakers' carriage of Messrs G and J Furness transporting the coffin, and then the carriage containing Lily and Nellie. Furness, the undertakers, had given the services free of charge as some of the staff had served as special constables in the town and knew and had worked with Thomas Green. The coffin carriage was smothered in flowers and pulled by two elegant black horses, who somehow knew also how to bow their heads, and either side of the carriage marched four stiff-backed police sergeants. Behind was an impressive column of hundreds of constables. Lily and Nellie had been trying so hard to honour their father, and represent their mother, by keeping strong, but as they looked out of the windows and saw the girls that they went to school with now grown-up, the children from their street and nearby, and complete strangers, their faces etched with grief and openly weeping, they held each other tight and started to cry.

Outside The Rifleman the landlord, William Herbert, stood with his head bowed and hands clasped behind his back as the line passed, astounded and appalled that the incident in his beer house had led to all of this. Herbert was not in any way to blame, but he wondered if the brawl could have been handled differently, and if it had, would Thomas Green be alive today? He knew that the town had been boiling over; he had heard the whispered conversations of the returning Epsom men and

119

witnessed their rage towards the Canadians. Yet he had a living to make. Even though it was only a couple of miles away, he wished he still had The Plough in Ewell – a country pub that his father had run, and where he spent much of his childhood, and which he had taken over himself nearly twenty years earlier. It was quiet there, and took less money, but its tranquillity and rural rhythm now seemed terribly alluring.

As the horses steered left at The Spread Eagle, the imposing town centre pub, children stood on the high entrance steps to gain a better view whilst men stopped their bicycles, dismounted and stood still, rushing to remove their caps. In sight now was the Wesleyan Chapel on the left and the battered and bruised police station opposite. The Reverend George Alway stood outside the chapel to receive Sergeant Green as the carriage stopped and the eight police sergeants lifted the coffin of their colleague up on to their broad, defiant shoulders. The band played Chopin's funeral march and one or two women in the crowd swayed and fainted, their connection, if any, to Thomas Green unknown. The church officials ushered as many as could be accommodated into the chapel and the majority of the rest of the crowd waited outside, straining to hear George Alway's poignant address.

'The representative character of the people at the service here today shows how deeply we all deplore the unhappy circumstances which brought about Sergeant Green's death,' he began.

A noble life has been snatched from us by the intemperate passions of some misguided men, but we must not allow our sorrow and indignation to carry us to blind and unreasoning judgement.

Those who knew best were those who saw the true spirit of Canada in her sons who had worshipped in this very church,

120

and those who had been privileged to minister to them day and night in hospital and sometimes had been called upon to commit the dust of their dead to earth. These people know how sincerely the Canadians mourn with us today and how earnestly they lament the loss sustained.

The late police sergeant was a loveable and helpful man, the memory of whose genial personality will abide with us forever. His spirit was the spirit of service and no man found him anything but a brother. No woman was there that was not treated with Christian courtesy and noble chivalry, and no children ever found his protection unavailing. Of late the shadow of illness has fallen upon his home life, and a few days before he died there was the prospect of its lifting. But he faced his sorrow as he faced his duty, and there was always dayspring in his heart.

The service over, the procession continued up the hill to the cemetery, also in Ashley Road. The cemetery was relatively new, having opened in 1871, and the first internment was of a Mrs Elizabeth Dorling, who was the mother of Isabella Beeton of cookery book fame. Thomas Green's plot was positioned fairly close to the chapel, from where the various graves were spreading outward. As the entourage wound up to the cemetery the four local Justices of the Peace walked behind the last mourning carriage. They were Messrs Squarey, Pollen, Dorset and Jay, and behind them were Sir Rowland and Lady Blades flanked on each side by Henry Banks Longley and his Vice Chairman of the Urban Council, WG Langlands. Following them were the senior policemen Assistant Commissioner Horwood and the Majors Lafone, Tomblin and Olive. James Olive and William Horwood neatly encapsulated the culture conflict at the top of the Met, with Horwood having been recruited from the higher echelons of the army or the aristocracy, as often had been the case, and Olive working his way up from a humble bobby on the beat.

At the gates of the cemetery six boys from the Dr Barnardo's home in Epsom stood in line, three on each side of the gate, and removed their caps as the procession passed through. Soon the graveside was severely congested and more and more people pushed into the cemetery with little hope of seeing the actual internment. Around the graveside was Thomas's brother Edgar, two of his sisters, his brother-in-law William Bowers Card and an assortment of other in-laws, nephews and nieces. They slowly walked around, looking at the scores of wreaths and carefully reading the messages. A tribute from Lord Rosebery read 'Honour and Regret'. Lord Rosebery's wreath lay next to one from two young boys – Freddie and Wally Bennett – who often went fishing with Sergeant Green.

The coffin bore the inscription:

THOMAS GREEN.
DIED 18TH JUNE 1919.
AGED 51 YEARS.
A NOBLE HUSBAND.

At the head of the coffin was a beautiful wreath of roses, carnations and, fittingly, lilies, from Thomas Green's widow, Lilian. The message clipped to the flowers was jerkily written, as Mrs Green could only write it with her left hand due to the paralysis on the right side of her body. It read: 'With deepest love to my dear, noble husband, who was killed doing his duty. From his broken-hearted wife and daughters, Lily and Nellie.' Unsurprisingly Sergeant Green's widow and children were just about the only people in the whole affair who were not skirting around the fact that their loved one had been *killed*.

As the rites were being read the finality of it all over-whelmed Lily and Nellie. Whilst physically supporting one another earlier they now seemed to collapse, merging as one heaving, sobbing black smudge, barely able to stand. The adjacent mourners closed in, enveloping and supporting them as others retreated, leaving a huddle of stricken family members trembling and clutching and holding one another as the first shovel loads of soil landed noisily on the wood. This pathetic sight and the stirring, familiar tunes of the National Anthem and then 'The Last Post' ensured if there had been a dry eye in the entire cemetery there now was not.

CHAPTER 9

THE COMMITTAL

Marked Sixpences

Back in Epsom, at the Court House, on the Wednesday two days after the funeral the adjourned inquest re-opened. Frank Wilkie, dressed in hospital blues, and James Connors, in khaki uniform, had been brought down from the cells at Bow Street Police Station to be present. Wounds on Connors' head were still visible. Inspector Pawley gave evidence where some fresh specifics were revealed. Firstly he told how he had rung the camp after hearing the bugles and noise and was told, somewhat disingenuously, 'It's all quiet up here, although there is a noisy mob down the road.' He confirmed that the idea of charging the soldiers was Sergeant Green's and indicated that Green led the rush at the side of the police station. Nine constables out of a total twelve present at the station, at that point, took part in that charge. Presumably Pawley's civilian son Harry was a tenth man.

When Pawley's evidence was finished the Canadian Officer, Major James Ross, took the stand. He was 5'9" tall with a dark complexion, brown eyes and brown hair. He had been born in 1885 in southern Africa and had served with the South Africa Rifles before immigrating to Canada, where he had trained as an accountant. Ross volunteered with the CEF at New Westminster, British Columbia in March 1915. He was commissioned Lieutenant in the 47th Battalion and arrived in England in June 1915. In March of the following year he was transferred to France as Adjutant and, at some point, he was wounded and recommended for the Military Cross and mentioned in Despatches. The following year he was awarded the Distinguished Service Order for 'gallantry and devotion to duty in the field'. Suffering from arthritis and trench mouth, Ross was returned to England in August 1917 and then posted to the 1st Central Ontario Regimental Depot (CORD). In September he was admitted to the Moore Barracks Canadian Hospital at Shorncliffe because of 'debility'. He only remained a few days and was then posted back to 1st CORD until January 1918, when he went to the 3rd Reserve Battalion. In March 1918 James Ross, now a major, was seconded to Woodcote Park Convalescence Hospital at Epsom. In August 1918 he had married Beatrice Winifred and they set up home at Bedford Park, Chiswick, in West London. She was the daughter of a stage actor and Ross put his own father's occupation down as 'Capitalist' on his marriage certificate.

Under cross-examination he was asked whether some of the officers in the crowd were not seeking to control the men, but were actually agitating them. Ross, justly proud of his war record and professionalism, bristled at the suggestion. 'That is a distinct falsehood,' he replied.

He also revealed that after he had entered the station with Inspector Pawley and the mob had besieged the building, he had found his way out of the back yard and scaled a number of garden fences before finding himself in South Street. He had arrived back at the station via the High Street and passing the Clock Tower, then turning right into Ashley Road. By this time, Ross stated, the prisoners had been freed and some of the soldiers were turning toward the High Street, and he implied that an escalation of the riot was likely. Ross was able to persuade them that they had done more than enough damage for one night and reminded them that there would be terrified women and children in the town. The men turned and made their way back up to Woodcote camp. It was then that Major Ross re-entered the police station to help with the casualties and they were informed that Sergeant Green was lying gravely injured in the house opposite. On questioning, Ross said he saw a bugler at the camp, but did not know if the same man was outside the police station, a point that conflicted with the evidence of others. Major Ross was probably acutely aware that if he identified Robert Todd he could be putting the young private seriously in the frame as an accessory.

Major Bird, an adjutant at the camp, said that on the day of the riot there were 1,500 patients and 700 staff present in Woodcote Park. He added that on Saturday 14 June he had written to the Assistant Provost Marshall asking for more Military Police and that he had also requested permission to make all public houses out of bounds to the soldiers between 8.00 and 10.00pm. Clearly, the expectation of serious trouble was not only a police preoccupation.

At one particularly poignant moment Gilbert White produced the tweed cap that Sergeant Green had worn on the night of the attack, which had been picked up from the ground in the blood-stained aftermath. He commented that the question before them was whether the inquest should be adjourned until after the proceedings at Bow Street, or whether they should return an open verdict and leave the matter in the hands of the police. He pointed out that there had been no evidence by which they could identify the men who actually struck Sergeant Green. William Lloyd's statement, which was the key to that very question, was not mentioned, nor was Lapointe's. The coroner was clearly not in the loop on that score.

Connors and Wilkie elected to ask no questions or make any comment, not even to protest their innocence. The inquest was

126

then adjourned, again, pending the Bow Street proceedings against all the defendants.

These inquest details were reported in the *Epsom Advertiser* of Friday 27 June 1919 and by now the newspaper's leader columnist, Touchstone, had had more time to reflect on the whole affair. Although the words below were likely written in the immediate emotional aftermath of Sergeant Green's funeral, his conclusions about the Canadian people generally could not be more patronising. Reading these generalised and insulting comments about the Canadians, it is no wonder that there was a movement in that country and others to lose the 'colony' status. If the *Epsom Advertiser*'s view was representative, then one can sympathise with the Canadians' objections to being thought of as little more than uncivilised savages, living off the land and accustomed to 'running riot at home'. If Prime Minister David Lloyd George had seen this editorial, which he may well have, telephone lines out of Downing Street would have been red hot:

> The outstanding event in Epsom has been the tragic death and remarkable public funeral of Station Sergeant Green. His death was a lamentable event because it meant a useful life unnecessarily sacrificed. A comparatively few wild spirits, in an endeavour to overcome the salutary forces which restrain disorder, took the life of a man who was merely doing his duty, and in the act they have degraded their countrymen and stained the honour of their own land.
>
> It is possible to judge too harshly in matters of this kind and before judgement is passed on Canadians as a race it is only fair to look at all the factors which go to make up this tragedy. In the first place it is possible that we Britishers have erred in making too much of the Canadians. We were grateful to them for the manner in which they came to the aid of the Mother Country. We are indebted to them for many a gallant

127

stand, and more than once they helped the Empire out of a very critical and perilous position. In our gratitude we were apt to make the utmost of the work of our Colonials. Over and over again they were extolled while our own lads, whose exploits were just as glorious and who individually did just as much heroic deeds, were given little praise. That was a mistake because it gave to the Colonials an exaggerated idea of their part in the war, and it also left a grievance rankling in the minds of our own soldiers. That may be one of the predisposing causes for the unfriendliness which has been seen between the two sets of men in Epsom and elsewhere.

Again the Canadians and the Australians were made much of when they came into our midst to recuperate and rest. The laudation and the friendliness shown had the effect of making some of the men unduly sensitive of any slight and quick to resent a grievance, real or imaginary.

Perhaps the chief cause of the culminating disturbance was the fact that in the Colonies life is freer of restraint. Many of these men have come from thinly populated areas where a man is very largely his own policeman and where law and order are of a primitive nature. Discipline in their armies is slack and they have found the restraint of camp in Epsom irksome. Coming, as they have done, into contact with our ordered conditions, under which they have not been able to run riot as they would do at home without interference, their exaggerated ideas of the meaning of the word freedom led to a revolt.

When passions were aroused freedom turned to revolt, and the sturdy resistance of the police fed the flames and made the men do what they must now be heartily ashamed of. We do not seek to palliate their offence. They acted like savages and must have lost all sense of fair play. At the same time the Englishman's sense of justice prompts him to look at the facts squarely in the face, and there is a disposition already among the thinking population to temper the first hot indignation with which they viewed the riot and its consequences.

The event has shown us the difference between the silent discipline of our older civilisation and the newer, less apparent

128

The Green family circa 1902. Thomas's father, George, (born 1829) holds baby Nellie.
Thomas is seated next to him with his wife, Lilian, standing by his side.
Baby Lily is standing on a chair. © Gordon Kirkham

Black and White Cottage, Billingshurst, West Sussex,
home to the Green family in the mid nineteenth century. © Tony Collis

Thomas Green and Lilian Card on their wedding day, 1895.
© *Gordon Kirkham*

Epsom Police Station before the riot.
Courtesy of Bourne Hall Musuem

Epsom police force before the riot.
Thomas Green is third from left in the second to front row.
Courtesy of Bourne Hall Musuem

Thomas Green as a young policeman circa 1895
© Gordon Kirkham

Epsom Police Station after the riot.
Courtesy of Bourne Hall Musuem

Wrecked police cell from the outside.
Courtesy of Bourne Hall Musuem

Wrecked police cell from the inside.
Courtesy of Bourne Hall Musuem

Police and soldiers guard the approach to the station after the riot.
Courtesy of Bourne Hall Musuem

92 Lower Court Road, Epsom.
ome of Thomas Green and family in 1919.
© Tony Collis

The Rifleman, Epsom.
The fight that led to the arrests of two
Canadian soldiers started here.
© Tony Collis

Canadian convalescents on parade at Woodcote Park.
Courtesy of Bourne Hall Musuem

James Chuter Ede,
Epsom politician
and foreman of the inquest jury.

Inspector John Kenneth Ferrier,
the Scotland Yard detective
in charge of the murder inquiry.

NUMBER EIGHT PLATOON

1 715833, Private W. Mansfield, Antigonish, N.S.

2 716138, Private Alex. McDonald, Antigonish, N.S.

3 716173, Private Angus McDonald, Antigonish, N.S.

4 716128, Private D. V. McDonald, Antigonish, N.S.

5 715838, Private J. C. McDonald, Antigonish, N.S.

6 716143, Private James McDonald, Antigonish, N.S.

7 716122, Private W. J. McDonald, Antigonish, N.S.

8 716205, Private W. M. McDonald, Antigonish, N.S.

9 716142, Private Jno. McIsaac, Antigonish, N.S.

10 716144, Private A. J. McMaster, Antigonish, N.S.

11 715834, Private A. E. McPhee, Antigonish, N.S.

12 716146, Private N. Moros, Sydney, N.S.

13 715153, Private W. G. Nicolle, Antigonish, N.S.

14 715156, Private W. M. Petipas, Antigonish, N.S.

15 716140, Private

16 716129, Private

17 715159, Private

18 716142, Private

19 716119, Private

20 715154, Private

21 715953, Private

22 716151, Private

*Allan J. MacMaster,
the soldier who later confessed
to killing Sgt Green is number 10.*

*Allan MacMaster (front)
with family members
at Timmins, Ontario around 1930.
© Buddy MacMaster*

FUNERAL OF CANADIAN RIOTERS' VICTIM.

Station-Sergeant Green, who died as a result of injuries received while defending Epsom Police Station against the Canadian military rioters, was buried yesterday at Epsom with full police honours. Above is general view of the cortege. Inset, Sergt. Green.

FUNERAL OF STN SERG GREEN 23.6.19.

PHOTO J & R CNS

Metropolitan Police Band leads the cortege at Sergeant Green's funeral.
Both Courtesy of Bourne Hall Musuem

FUNERAL OF LATE STATION SERGEANT GREEN. 23.6.19.

PHOTO J&R. SUTTON

Sergeant Green's funeral. The cortege enters Epsom town.
Courtesy of Bourne Hall Musuem

FUNERAL OF LATE STATION SERGEANT GREEN. 23.6.19.

PHOTO J&R. SUTTON

Police sergeants carry Sergeant Green's coffin to his grave.
Courtesy of Bourne Hall Musuem

A little girl makes an offering to PC Rose outside the police station.
Courtesy of Bourne Hall Museum

PC Rose and Inspector Pawley attend the Bow Street hearing.
Courtesy of Bourne Hall Musuem

Caricature of Justice Darling, judge at the trial of the Canadian soldiers.

Edward, Prince of Wales, pictured on his tour of Canada, 1919.

Lord Rosebery, seated centre, at the medal-giving ceremony to surviving Epsom policemen.
Courtesy of Bourne Hall Museum

Prime Minister David Lloyd George.

SOUTH WEST ENTRANCE.

Sentry box at the south-west entrance to Woodcote Park.
Courtesy of Bourne Hall Museum

Sergeant Green's daughters.
Lily is sitting, Nellie is standing.

1021 GUARDSMAN J. BRITTON
GUARDS MACHINE GUN REGT.
24. 7. 1917   547
22919 PRIVATE J. W. BROWN
NORFOLK   REGIMENT
23. 7. 1922   AGE 27   732
2009126 PRIVATE F. B. BRUNS
CAN. ARMY MEDICAL CORPS
25. 6. 1919   AGE 29   234
657062 PTE. O. L. BUCHANAN
1ST BN. CANADIAN INF
29. 11. 1917   241
715369 PRIVATE H. A. CAMERON
87 TH BN. CANADIAN INF.
8. 6. 1917   AGE 27   244
S/13185 PRIVATE M. CARRIGAN
GORDON   HIGHLANDERS
6. 12. 1916   AGE 25   646
3/6611 PRIVATE J. CHAPMAN
GORDON   HIGHLANDERS
23. 3. 1916   AGE 30   648
23099 PRIVATE P. CLARKE
LANCASHIRE   FUSILIERS
1. 2. 1918   644
5261 DRIVER T. CLEVENDON
ROYAL FIELD ARTILLERY
23. 10. 1918   651
220504 PIONEER A. COLLINGS
ROYAL   ENGINEERS
22. 11. 1914   652
455 SERJEANT W. A. COOPER
THE   QUEEN'S
3. 8. 1919   654

Memorial in Ashley Road cemetery
where Frederick Bruns is listed.
© Tony Collis

James Connors' grave at Brookwood Military Cemetery.
© Tony Collis

A plaque to Thomas Green in Epsom, unveiled by Chris Grayling,
Shadow Home Secretary and Epsom MP, ninety years after the event.
© Tony Collis

IN MEMORY OF
STATION SERGEANT THOMAS GREEN
WHO FOUND DEATH IN THE PATH OF DUTY
HE WAS KILLED IN DEFENDING THE
EPSOM POLICE STATION
AGAINST A RIOTOUS MOB.
JUNE 17TH 1919.

THIS MEMORIAL WAS ERECTED BY
THE OFFICERS AND MEN OF THE
METROPOLITAN POLICE FORCE.

Sergeant Green's headstone at Epsom Cemetery.
© Tony Collis

moral restraint imposed upon the people in our great Colonies. It has shown that our policemen are as ready as ever to protect the public from assault and to do their duty whatever the risks may be. It has also shown the perils of 'mob law', a very salutary lesson in these critical times.

Over in Canada a balancing view was struck by the *Calgary Daily Herald* of the same day, which dismissed the claims by Canadian Headquarters that the bad feeling in Epsom (and other bases) was due to 'rough civilians' attacking and goading the soldiers. Their understanding was that relations between the Canadians and the local populations they were living with were mainly cordial. *The Herald* had heard stories from repatriated soldiers about local shopkeepers profiteering at their expense, but firmly saw the root cause of the disturbances as being the delays in repatriating the Canadian troops.

'How can it be explained that 425,000 American troops were repatriated in June alone, making the total number of Americans repatriated about one half million, while all this difficulty remains about Canadian repatriation? If labor troubles are no obstacle to American repatriation, why are they allowed to impede the Canadian return?' the paper asked.

The *Manchester Guardian* in an editorial concluded: 'The only way of evading family quarrels and keeping our policemen alive is to repatriate the Canadian troops as quickly as possible.'

It is assumed here that the 'family quarrels' referred to by the *Guardian* are instances of British Tommies returning to find their partners engaged in, or having been engaged in, relationships with Canadian soldiers. For certain, some came home to find a child looking up at them that they knew could not be their own offspring.

On Friday 27 June 1919 the eight Canadian soldiers found themselves at Bow Street Police Court being charged on remand with being concerned in the manslaughter of Station Sergeant Thomas Green of the Epsom Police. They stood before Sir John Dickinson, a magistrate and judge, who was already a key figure in British criminal and legal history. Dickinson had presided over the preliminary hearing that culminated in Sir Roger Casement being hung for treason; he described DH Lawrence's book *The Rainbow* as 'filth' during an obscenity hearing; he sentenced Bertrand Russell to six months' imprisonment for anti-war activities; and committed the Brides in the Bath murderer, George Smith, to trial at the Old Bailey, where he was eventually sentenced to hang. Dickinson had recently lost a son at the Front.

Sir Richard Muir and William Lewis conducted the case on behalf of the Director of Public Prosecutions and Edward Abinger defended. Muir had only recently been knighted and this honour was bestowed in recognition of his reputation as the greatest public prosecutor of his time. He was born in 1857 in Scotland and came to London with the intention of becoming a stage actor, but after a stint as a parliamentary reporter for *The Times* he had entered the legal profession. From 1901 he represented the Crown on nearly every notable trial there was. He was a stern man who prepared for his cases with exacting meticulousness and he expected the same from everyone on his team, including the Scotland Yard detectives who gathered evidence for him. In the light of this it is surprising that he had not demanded his usual thoroughness from the police in the case made against the eight Canadian soldiers.

Such was his reputation that when Dr Crippen heard that his prosecutor was to be Muir he is said to of remarked, 'I wish it had been anybody else ... I fear the worst.' Muir's subsequent cross-examination of Crippen, who was on trial for the murder of his wife, Cora, is believed to be a classic of the art. Crippen was hung following this sensational trial. The doctor had been apprehended after sailing to Canada, of all places, with his lover dressed as a boy, but recent DNA evidence has thrown new doubt on his guilt and some are now calling for a posthumous pardon.

Sir Richard quickly laid out his stall. The prosecution was not able to prove that Poirier was in camp on the night in question, he began. He was found the next day to have been injured, and said that he had been struck in Rosebery Park at Epsom. He had complained that the only fellows who were arrested were those who got hit.

'It must be admitted', continued Sir Richard, 'that it is only those who were hit who have been arrested. That is a grievance which the prosecution is not in a position to remove. The evidence of recent injuries to the head immediately after the riot is in my submission evidence that they took part in the riot. There they are like so many marked sixpences, with the evidence clearly impressed upon them.'

CHAPTER 10

THE INQUEST

The Weight of Evidence

The following day was a Saturday, and still only ten days after Sergeant Green had been killed, yet the magisterial hearing at Bow Street continued and was concluded.

Gervase Poirier gave his evidence and said that on the night of 17 June he had heard a bugle being blown and later followed a crowd of soldiers going 'down town', thinking there was a fire. He said he took no part in the attack on the police station and that the injury to his head was caused by a brick thrown by a soldier in Rosebery Park, which was over a 100 yards away from the station.

Herbert Tait stated that he had been to Olympia in West London and returned on a late train. When he walked down from the station he came across a big crowd of soldiers and when in the thickest part of that throng he was struck down and became dazed. Both men were believed and subsequently discharged and the remaining defendants – MacMaster, Connors, Wilkie, Masse, McAllan and Verex – were committed for trial on charges of manslaughter, malicious damage and riot.

Robert McAllan had admitted to being in the crowd at Epsom, but said he was hit on the back of the head and could remember no more. Masse had an almost identical story to Poirier, yet he was not acquitted.

'I know nothing about it,' he claimed. 'I was coming from the train. There was a crowd. I was there about two minutes. I said to myself, "It is dangerous here. I had better go." Just then I received a blow on the head and fell.'

Wilkie was still displaying a nasty cut over his eye. He admitted to being in front of the police station and thought he had been struck with a sharp stone. 'As soon as I was hit I went back to camp. That is all I done,' he pleaded.

The curious thing about this committal was that Poirier's and Tait's alibis seemed to go unchallenged. Why did the other men not put forward similar stories? MacMaster and Connors may have had problems being believed, as the latter particularly had been singled out by PC Rose as being present in the front line of the riot. Masse did volunteer *his* alibi, but Wilkie and Yerex, at least, could have come up with something similar and tried their luck.

Poirier thinking that he was marching into town to put out a fire does not stand up to much scrutiny. It was pretty clear up at the camp why the soldiers were going down to the town. Some, especially MacMaster, had spoken angrily about their comrades being incarcerated unjustly and Major Ross and other officers had appealed loudly for calm. Even if Poirier had missed all this and just tagged along at the back he surely would have heard the conversations and shouting of soldiers, speaking in both French and English. Do soldiers going to put out a fire normally rip up fence posts and smash up pubs en route? Most of all, how does what Poirier is claiming here square with what Ferrier recorded him saying when he was first questioned? 'It is only the fellows who got hit that got taken. There were others. It is not fair.' There is no record of these questions, or others, being put to the Frenchman in court.

Herbert Tait may have been to Olympia – perhaps he had a ticket stub to prove it. But he would have first seen a crowd of soldiers as he turned into Ashley Road from whatever station he came in at. The soldiers had not overrun the town so it is difficult to see how he could have become embroiled in the mob by accident. He would have had to have joined them. Where exactly was he when he was struck and dazed? And what happened next? These were alibis that may or may not have been true, but why were they so easily accepted and not challenged at all?

The previous day PC James Rose had given evidence to the effect that he saw Sergeant Green struck down with a piece of fence-rail about six or seven feet long. He identified James Connors as one of the men who attempted to strike Green with a piece of railing, but now he did not think he actually struck him. Rose's stance had shifted radically from being convinced that Connors *had* struck Green when he picked him out up at the camp a week earlier. It was bizarre he was now saying that he saw Connors *trying* to strike him, but thinking that he didn't. What happened, then? Did Connors miss? Did Green jump out the way? Why was Sergeant Blaydon not called? He had made a statement saying that he saw Sergeant Green get up again after being hit by the fence-rail. He and Rose had seen more or less the same thing, yet Blaydon was not asked to corroborate and expand on that evidence. Why did Connors not have his say on Rose's evidence?

If Rose had stuck by his original statement that Connors had bludgeoned Green with the fence-rail then the Crown would be obliged to focus on an individual defendant and this, in my belief, is not what they wanted. Also, had things started to come on top for Connors alone he may well have decided to point the finger at the real killer, MacMaster, and again this was an outcome not desired by the Crown. (On a general note it is also odd that Rose had enough light to think he could identify Connors and, mistakenly, William Lloyd, and the

134

nature of the weapon that Connors was yielding, as did Blaydon, yet everybody else insisted it was too dark to make anything out.)

Sergeant Dowers, who was in charge of the hut that Connors slept in, testified that the defendant was not in camp at roll call, but he was back in his billet, boasting about chucking a policeman over a hedge, at 1.30am.

There is reason to suspect that by this time the defendants, other than Tait and Poirier, had been spoken to in a very English nod-and-a-wink manner and told that no murder charge would be brought against them. Even manslaughter charges would be downgraded and only riot charges would stick. If they played the game they would all be home in Canada for Christmas.

Mr Abinger stated that all the defendants pleaded not guilty and would reserve their defence. Sir John Dickinson went on then to discharge Poirier and Tait and commit the others for trial.

Everyone drew breath on Sunday and then on Monday 30 June 1919 the inquest was reconvened and concluded at Epsom Court. Major Percy James Sandy Bird, adjutant at Woodcote camp, was the first to give evidence. He had been born in Dublin some forty-two years earlier and was the son of a reverend. A married man, he lived at Willow Bunch, Saskatchewan when he volunteered with the CAMC in 1916. After some moving around and presumably service in France he had ended up back in England, suffering from trench fever and rheumatism. He had arrived in Epsom in 1917 and was appointed Adjutant Registrar in March 1918. He could confirm that none of the accused had any injuries prior to 17 June.

135

Jury foreman Chuter Ede pushed Major Bird on something that was troubling him.

'Are these six men the only men who the authorities know were in the riot? And how many people do the authorities compute were outside the station that evening?'

'Roughly speaking between 300 and 400 left camp although some of those returned without having gone as far as the police station,' replied Bird.

'There was considerably more than six, then.'

'Yes.'

One can picture the expression on Chuter Ede's face following this exchange. He found it fanciful that only six people out of three hundred or more could be identified, especially by those who knew each and every one of the soldiers. He was not about to let it rest. He said that the jury required reliable evidence from a medical officer at the camp that no man was medically treated after the riot other than those in custody. Chuter Ede was vexed and had smelled a rat. He pressed Bird about the bugler. In Chuter Ede's mind this man, whoever he was, bore some culpability for the riot, at least. He had called the men in and bugled them away again, and that had been testified. Here was one ringleader, as far as the foreman was concerned, who was not in the dock.

'The bugler's identity must be known,' insisted Chuter Ede.

Major Bird was literally lost for words and the atmosphere in the little court room could have been cut with a knife. The silence was deafening. Inspector Ferrier did not like the way this was heading and intervened.

'I have gone fully into the matter,' he told the court firmly, 'having been working night and day, and as far as I can ascertain these men are the only persons who were injured in the riot. I could find no persons other than PC Rose and

136

Regimental Sergeant Major Parsons who could identify a single man present at the riot.'

Really? What about Mrs Beauchamp, her daughter and her granddaughter, who had men in her house saying they had just killed a policeman? What about Charles Polhill, who was with the men who carried Sergeant Green into his house for half an hour with the lights on? None of these people were even asked to try and identify anybody. What about McDonald and Veinot, the prisoners? What about Sergeant Shuttleworth, who thought, in his statement, that he could identify at least one rioter? And, of course, as we have seen, there were plenty of others who said they could not identify people but who were not pressed or presented with contradictory statements.

Regimental Sergeant Major Parsons gave evidence next and must have realised that the game was up as far as the bugler was concerned. He admitted that the name of the man was Robert Todd and he was among those he saw marching to the police station, and that he saw him again after the raid, outside the station building. This was too much for the jury and they sent for Todd to be fetched from the camp immediately. James Chuter Ede believed that this man should be brought to account for rallying the men for such a dangerous and illegal mission. Within an hour the terrified and tiny ex-Barnardo boy was produced before them and sensibly, and probably acting on hurried advice en route to the court, said he had no evidence to give. One wonders if Chuter Ede was shocked by the youthful and slight-looking boy standing before them, clearly over-whelmed by the turn of events.

Having given evidence at the Bow Street committal on the Friday PC Rose was now giving it again at the Epsom inquest. Being in his home town and among people he knew and felt comfortable with, he gave some astonishing evidence. He talked about the run-up to the riot and how he had left his house in The Parade, a minute around the corner from the police station, following a call to help. He arrived almost at the same time as the mob. He described how he saw Sergeant Green struck across the forehead with a large piece of wood resembling a post. He saw him go down, but was himself surrounded and forced back inside the police station. He had not seen Thomas Green get up again. He then went on to say how he had attended a parade at Woodcote Park camp and identified James Connors as being in the front of the crowd, near the spot where Sergeant Green was struck down, armed with a long railing.

Again Chuter Ede was disturbed. 'Can you identify the man who struck the blow which knocked Sergeant Green down?' Rose replied: 'I did identify the man who to the best of my belief was the man, but owing to the weight of evidence there was no charge against him.'

What on earth does PC Rose mean? To what weight of evidence was he referring? Rose had not been subjected to any 'evidence' and even if he had it was not his place to judge what other evidence there may or may not be. Juries evaluate evidence, not witnesses. What he is telling us here, loud and clear, is that somebody had told him that he should not identify Connors (or anybody else) as wielding a blow on his colleague. That somebody may have said to him that other evidence suggested it wasn't him. Rose's language clearly suggests that things were taken out of his hands. You can imagine how the small-town bobby would have been in awe of the Scotland Yard supremo Inspector John Kenneth Ferrier: Dixon of Dock Green meets Sherlock Holmes.

Connors struck Sergeant Green and Rose saw it. As it happened, it was not the blow that killed him, but it could have been. Rose was not to know, because he had not seen the MacMaster attack. Only on Friday he had told the Bow Street court that although he saw Connors wielding a fence rail he thought he *didn't* hit Green with it, and now, forty-eight hours later, he was saying that he *did* see him, but 'evidence' had persuaded him otherwise. He was embarrassed by his about-turn and in the little police court in Epsom he more or less told them why. Surprisingly, Chuter Ede did not delve further. Arguably, it was at this juncture where he, the ambitious but principled young politician, saw the bigger picture.

If one accepts there was a conspiracy, for want of a better word, to engineer a quick trial and benign woolly charges to prevent Anglo-Canadian embarrassment, or worse, it is clear why Rose's identification would have been more than awkward. He was clearly pointing the finger at someone who had viciously struck Sergeant Green with a blow that may or may not have killed him. The burden would be to investigate further, bring different charges, and if the judicial system was allowed to take its course Connors could have ended up being hung. It was a long shot and it would have been a miscarriage of justice, but the risk was evident.

Gilbert White, the coroner, summed up and firstly made the comment that he believed that Epsom's new fire engine would have been an excellent thing to have been used to disperse the crowd. He'd been reading the local papers. He said that if the person who had struck the blow that had killed Sergeant Green could have been identified then he would have advised the jury to return a verdict of wilful murder. However, this was not the case. The men were working together to one end, that of releasing the prisoners, so if one of them had committed manslaughter all those who participated in the affair were guilty of manslaughter as well as the man who struck the fatal blow. The bugle was sounded, but while there was no evidence that Todd was guilty of rioting, it was for the jury to consider how far he anticipated the riot. There were no marks on him, he reminded the jury.

Under White's logic, then, up to three or four hundred men were guilty of manslaughter, but just six, who happened to carry visible head injuries, were being tried.

The jury returned a verdict after fifty minutes. 'The death of Sergeant Green was caused by a blow or blows on the head received while on duty.'

They found that the six soldiers committed for trial on Saturday at Bow Street and the bugler Robert Todd were guilty of manslaughter. They also added a rider that the police under Inspector Pawley acted with discretion and great valour during the whole proceedings, and the management of the inquiries by Inspector Ferrier was worthy of commendation. They also donated their jury fees to Sergeant Green's wife and daughters.

One can understand the plaudits they offered Inspector Pawley, but it is difficult to see why the jury would decide that Inspector Ferrier's 'management of the inquiry' deserved a commendation. The inquiry had been extraordinarily quick and limited in scope and as it stood nobody was going to stand trial for the murder of a much-liked, decent and brave local policeman. Some time later Superintendent Boxhall would send a letter to the Home Office urging that Inspector Ferrier be commended for his handling of a case 'that bristled with difficulties'. Is this code for 'Ferrier met the unusual, delicate and confidential demands of his masters'?

Meanwhile the young and diminutive Robert Todd, who had never caused any trouble and had merely done what he had been told, was one minute lying in his hut at the camp with hands locked behind his head thinking about nothing in particular and an hour later was in custody in Brixton prison among murderers and thieves, waiting to face the full might of the British judicial system.

Murder in their Hearts

A month after Sergeant Green's death, back in Epsom, and the town was busy trying to erase the trauma of recent weeks, move attention away from the upcoming trial of the Canadian soldiers and restore some normality. On Saturday 19 July Epsom's dignitaries staged their official Peace Celebrations and local publisher and stationer Pullingers produced the programme to commemorate the occasion. Henry Banks Longley chaired the Peace Celebrations Committee and was assisted by, among others, Inspector Wootten, Head of the Special Constabulary during the war years, and Mr Capon, Head of the Fire Brigade, who understandably was made secretary of the bonfire sub-committee. Epsom inhabitants assembled at the Clock Tower at 11.30am to sing 'God Save The King' and then they marched to the Alexandra Road Recreation Ground where there were sports such as sack and egg-and-spoon races and, later, dancing.

Mr Chuter Ede had arranged for a marquee where free tea was dispensed to men from local war hospitals, including Woodcote Park. There were now only a few Canadians left at the camp, but there *were* some, and Chuter Ede would have known that diplomacy was needed in order to show warmth to the soldiers (which he believed was important), but not to risk inflaming the locals, whose feelings were still running high. In the programme he extended 'a cordial invite' to the men and asked local hero, racing groom Sydney Martin, now the proud recipient of the *Médaille Militaire*, to meet and greet and generally keep an eye on things. Elsewhere Dr Thornely and Pound Lane School headmistress Mrs Chittenden acted as judges for the children's running heats and ex-servicemen were encouraged to take part in pillow fighting and the blindfold tandem race.

The finale was a torchlight procession from Waterloo Road up to the Downs, passing Sergeant Green's fresh grave on the way. At 11.00pm Mr Longley lit the huge bonfire and then, half an hour later, the crowd returned to the town, where they thronged once more around the Clock Tower and rendered a more raucous 'God Save the King'. This time around there was a notable absence of alcohol and no Canadian soldiers leap-frogging counters and plundering spirits from the local public houses.

At the Surrey Assizes at Guildford on 22 July 1919, three days after the Peace Celebrations, the full criminal trial of Connors, McAllan, MacMaster, Masse, Wilkie, Yerex and Todd began in earnest. They were indicted for the manslaughter of Station Sergeant Thomas Green and for riotous assembly. Justice Darling presided. He was a judge of long standing with an esteemed reputation. He had tried the Cortesi mob following a brawl when gang leader Darby Sabini had been shot at in one of the earliest London gangland armed power struggles. In 1903 he had sentenced the 'Finchley Baby Farmers' to death and Annie Walters and Amelia Sach became the first women to be hanged in the brand-spanking-new women's prison at Holloway. Albert Pierrepoint, legendary hangman, tied the knot. The two women ran a 'nursing home' for unmarried mothers to have their babies in and which, for a fee, claimed it would care for the babies afterwards. Instead they murdered them to keep running costs to a minimum.

Arguably his most famous trial was that of Stinie Morrison, who was found guilty of the murder of Leon Beron on Clapham Common in 1911. Darling had severe doubts about Morrison's guilt and was relieved when the death sentence he was obliged to pass was commuted to one of life imprisonment. It was a short life term, because ten years later Morrison went on hunger strike and died.

Not everyone thought highly of Darling, though. In 1900, when he was trying a case of obscene libel, he warned the press against reporting the indecent evidence. The editor of the *Birmingham Daily Argus* took exception and wrote a leader stating that Darling was 'an impudent little man in horsehair; a microcosm of conceit and empty-headedness'.

Only three years before the Epsom Riot trial Justice Darling was the judge in the appeal of the aforementioned Sir Roger Casement, the Irish patriot, poet and revolutionary who had been found guilty of treason. Darling heard the appeal and refused it and despite protests from the likes of Sir Arthur Conan Doyle and George Bernard Shaw, Casement was hung at Pentonville Prison in August 1916. Another of the coincidences that pepper the Epsom Riot saga was that one of the jurors on Casement's trial was William Bowers Card – Thomas Green's brother-in-law.

Sir Ernest Wild KC was prosecuting. Wild was an MP at this time and had been spearheading an effort to get a law through parliament outlawing lesbianism in the same way that male homosexuality was then illegal. He was also a leading freemason and would soon become the presiding judge at the Old Bailey. He was assisted by Cecil Whiteley KC who was also destined to become a judge and would go down in the legal history books as the man who cross-examined Frederick Bywaters in the famous Bywaters and Thompson murder trial a few years later. Edith Thompson, an attractive married woman, and Bywaters, her lover, bludgeoned to death Thompson's husband, Percy, allegedly at her behest. Frederick and Edith were both found guilty and hung on the same day.

Mr Harold Benjamin defended Connors and McAllan and Mr Edward Abinger the other prisoners. Edward Abinger had represented the aforementioned Stinie Morrison and years later would publish his autobiography, *Forty Years at the Bar*, the title being, hopefully, a play on his professional life rather than his private one.

After Sir Ernest opened the case he referred to some evidence from Major James Ross. He mentioned coming across a party of fifty men when he first realised there was trouble and when he asked what the matter was they said, 'Two of our pals have been detained by the civil police.'

Justice Darling intervened. 'Were any of the prisoners present when the statement was made?'

Wild replied in the negative, but thought he was entitled to use it to show how the riot commenced.

Justice Darling disagreed. 'Riot cases are like conspiracy cases – easy enough to go on with, but difficult to commence.'

Wild concluded his opening address by saying that the prosecution believed the legal position was this: there was a riot and all the men charged took part in it. They had to prove five things:

1 That there were no fewer than three men present, and there were in fact about three hundred.
2 That there was a common purpose – the liberation of the two soldiers.
3 That the common purpose was attempted or executed.

4   That men helped each other, by force if necessary, against anyone who opposed them in their common purpose.
5   That such force was used as to cause alarm to at least one person.

Inspector Pawley had made a new statement to the Crown that matched the above points. He apparently said in his statement that 'the riot was no doubt pre-arranged and the five points under the Riot and Damage Act were covered'. Also, revised statements from Sergeant Kersey and others had added postscripts referring to them hearing the Canadians say; 'Come on, boys! Burn the fuckers out! Set fire to the show!' Presumably these new references to the rioters wanting to burn the place and subsequently throwing paper in to the building were to re-iterate that points 3, 4 and 5 above were covered too.

Even if all these pre-requisites were satisfied it is difficult to see how this proves manslaughter, however. Judging by Wild's detailing of what he was setting out to prove it does appear that the effort was being made to convict for rioting, not manslaughter.

Next, plans of the police station and the surrounding area were produced. The distance between the station and the camp gates was measured at a mile and 544 yards. Various photographs of the damaged police station were shown to the jury. Inspector Pawley then took the court through his now familiar evidence. When he referred to someone in the mob shouting 'We are going to get those soldiers out,' Mr Abinger objected, unless the prosecution proved first that all his clients were actually present. Justice Darling ruled that statements made by the mob were evidence of the riot, though they didn't necessarily implicate any particular individual. Mr Abinger replied by saying that he raised the point as his defence was that his

146

clients were not present at the riot and Mr Benjamin added that would be his defence too.

For the first time Pawley's evidence made much of the mob's threat to burn the station down and he said a quantity of wood and paper was thrown into the building to make the threat seem very real. This had barely been mentioned by anyone in earlier statements. Wild was keen to nail down the fact that no police entered the road at all and that all the fighting took place in the police yard and therefore on police premises.

Mr Abinger cross-examined Pawley: 'Why didn't you succeed in getting hold of one or two of the soldiers in the garden? It would have been easy to have opened the door and pulled one or two of them inside.'

Nobody was sure where Abinger was going with this, but Pawley's back arched and the sympathy of the court room was with him.

'What, with a murderous attack on and three hundred men against twelve? It would have been very foolish.'

'I suppose they had run amok?'

'They had murder in their hearts.'

The court was silent as Inspector Pawley fixed his eyes on Mr Abinger and delivered this dramatic statement. The defence counsel was quick then not to risk alienating the jury further. He assured the policeman he did not mean to cast any reflection on the courage shown by him and his colleagues. He had the greatest admiration for their conduct throughout.

Major Bird's evidence followed and in response to a probe from Abinger as to why the gates at Woodcote camp were not closed so as to keep the men in, Justice Darling rebuked him and said that the court was not holding an inquiry into the culpability of those in charge of the camp or as to how the camp was conducted.

After Major Bird referred to hearing the bugle the first time Abinger intervened again.

'If the men heard the bugle sound the general assembly would they fall in?'

'It would be their duty to do so as quickly as possible,' replied Major Bird with no hesitation.

This was an important point, especially in the light of the prosecution's own stated burden of proof that 'a common purpose must be proved'.

Major James Ross was next to take the stand. He quickly said that after hearing the bugle he gave orders it was not to be blown again. Those orders were given to Robert Todd, who Ross said he knew. In the dock Todd must have been despairing at the vital role he was now unwillingly playing in proceedings. The remainder of Ross's evidence was much the same as given at the committal and inquest. Before Ross stood down Justice Darling reassured him that there was not the slightest suggestion that he did not behave extremely well and did none other than his very best to stop the riot. The fact that the judge felt impelled to say this leads one to deduce that there *was* that slightest suggestion.

James Ross did not agitate the riot, but his actions during the disturbance and afterwards must call into question his authority and ability to react effectively in this situation, at least. It was never really explained (or asked) why he left the police station through the back door and hopped through a number of gardens at the beginning of the riot before returning at the front, via the High Street, by which time the prisoners were free and Thomas Green was laying somewhere dying. Did he panic and flee?

Ross was followed by RSM Parsons who, again, was more candid than his fellow officer. He had accompanied Major Ross to the police station and he saw McAllan and Connors among the crowd outside. He heard remarks such as 'Let's get them out!' and he noticed that Connors was not wearing a cap.

Mr Benjamin in cross examination asked if Parsons saw the men in the dock actually *do* anything. He said that Connors was looking on as if interested in the proceedings and he did not see McAllan do anything at all. He conceded that missiles were flying in all directions and it was possible for anyone to get hit. The prosecution ended the exchange by establishing that, in Parson's eyes, neither Connors nor McAllan were doing anything to *stop* the rioting.

Mr Abinger then asked the witness whether he gave the order for Todd to sound the bugle. Parsons said he did not and that any non-commissioned officer could give orders for it to be blown. He did not know who gave Todd the order on that night.

PC James Rose then gave his evidence and Mr Benjamin hinted that the constable's evidence that he saw Connors armed with a weapon outside the station could not be relied on as he had also identified William Lloyd as being there and he had subsequently proved himself to having not been present.

Charles Polhill, the butcher, and Dr Thornely followed, the latter explaining that Sergeant Green died from an extensive fracture of the skull and confirmed that the injury could have been caused by one of the pieces of wood produced in the court room.

Next Sergeant William Kersey of the Coroner's Office gave formal identification of the body of Sergeant Green.

The man in charge of Hut 83 up at Woodcote camp, Sergeant Dowers, was the next witness. He could swear that Connors was not in his hut before 11.00pm and said he was awoken at 1.30am by him entering the hut in an excitable state, saying he had lost his cap in the struggle down the town and

149

that he threw a policeman over a hedge. He also complained that some of his ribs were broken and pointed to blood on his tunic, which he said was a result of the struggle. Dowers said he did not take too much notice and thought Connors was talking rot.

Justice Darling was moved to interrupt at this point. 'Are you sure that Connors did not say something about having hit a policeman over the head?'

'I took it said he said "over the hedge",' replied Dowers.

His colleague Corporal Edwards opened up by saying that Robert McAllan was in the Military Police and had no right to leave the camp. He said he had no bandage on his head at 11.30pm, but when he saw him again in the guard room at 12.30am he did, and he said he was not up to doing his duty,

Again the judge asked a question directly: 'Why did you not ask McAllan to account for the bandage around his head?'

'It was not my business.'

A Private Rowe was questioned about his colleague Wilkie and confirmed that he did not have a head wound on the day of 17 June, but he did when he awoke the following morning. Mr Abinger was curious as to why this private did not join in the march on the police station when the bugle was sounded.

'Convalescents are not supposed to fall in at that time of night,' he said.

Justice Darling at this point interjected with humour that prompted laughter around the court: 'Maybe you were confusing the "fall in" sound with "turn in"?'

Private Cowley followed and also said that he did not make any enquiries about Wilkie's wounds and bandages. He said Wilkie was a good soldier and a well-behaved man.

'Why didn't you ask him how it happened?' insisted his Lordship.

'Well – I was only in charge of the hut.'

'But didn't you ask him how he became injured?' Justice Darling was becoming frustrated at the reticence of the witnesses.

'No, I thought perhaps he had hurt himself in a game.'

'What, in the middle of the night?' barked the Judge.

'I thought he might have hurt himself playing leap-frog or something ...'

'Or marbles ...' huffed Darling contemptuously.

Mr Abinger then commented that it would have been useful if a roll call at the camp had been called that night, but Justice Darling did not think this would have served any purpose. This led to some more playful jousting between the Judge and the defence counsel.

'I would have thought that if the men had been placed on honour and asked if they were in the unlawful assembly the guilty ones would have said "yes". That happens at Court Martials,' Abinger expanded.

'I have known people not only on their honour, but on oath, who have not told the truth,' Justice Darling pointed out.

'Yes, no doubt you would sitting as a judge,' parried Abinger.

'And you have been in court at the time,' Darling finished.

This whimsical exchange concluded the case for the prosecution. Harold Benjamin then submitted there was no case against Robert McAllan to go the jury as it was proved that he had been in camp after the other men had left and that he had reported to his corporal at 11.30pm.

'If he had joined in the assembly or mob, that is sufficient,' the Judge clarified. 'It is not necessary to prove that he joined it at commencement. There are those, you know, who labour in the vineyard during the last hour and receive the same reward as those who have toiled all day.'

'There is no evidence he took part in the riot and there is only one witness who saw him near the police station,' Benjamin insisted.

Mr Abinger submitted there was no case against *his* clients to go before the jury. Not a single witness had sworn that any of them had struck Sergeant Green, and the only evidence before the court was that the men received injuries. The Magistrate at Bow Street had already discharged two men who received injuries without going anywhere near the police station.

His Lordship could not see any justification for withdrawing any of the accused from going before the jury and he adjourned the court for the day.

'A little jollification?'

On the Wednesday morning Mr Benjamin put James Connors in the witness box. For a nineteen-year-old boy he looked like he had lived a lifetime. His uniform hung forlornly on him, his features were gaunt and his spirit crushed. However, he put up a good effort under pressure. He had been gassed in France and suffered one complaint after another ever since and the last thing he wanted was to hang in England or waste away in Dartmoor prison. He did not want to take the rap for what happened that night. He knew he did not kill the policeman and almost certainly knew who did.

'On Tuesday, June 17th 1919, I had leave,' he told the court. 'I left the camp at 7.30pm, went to Epsom and commenced the return journey between 10.15pm and 10.30pm. I sat on a bench by the Ladas Hotel to smoke a cigarette when I heard cheering and then about 150 to 200 soldiers passed me. I followed the crowd for curiosity's sake and stopped outside the police station for about ten minutes, and during that time nothing in particular happened, only a good deal of shouting. After that I went home. At no time during the evening did I handle a wooden post, or use one, and I had no knowledge of the fact that two Canadian soldiers had been taken into custody.'

This statement neatly ticked all the boxes of avoiding intent and a common purpose and allowed for the fact that Connors had been identified at the scene. Bearing in mind his young age and poor health it seems likely that Connors received some coaching from counsel in formulating this.

During a forty-five-minute cross-examination Connors added that he had been with a girl who he only knew as 'Lil' who lived near Horton Asylum. He said that when he was outside the police station he was about eight to ten feet from the gate. At no point did he ask what the row was about.

This was too much for Justice Darling to swallow. 'What did you think it was all about?'

'I could not say.'

'Did you think it was a prayer meeting?' The court laughed as the Judge insisted: 'What did you think all those men were there for?'

'A little jollification, I suppose,' replied Connors, unwisely.

Further questioning from Sir Ernest Wild failed to get the defendant to admit to losing his cap or that he was at any time holding a fence post.

Robert McAllan was the next in the witness box. He said he was attached to the Military Police and reported for duty at 11.30pm. He was not supposed to leave camp, but thought he would go down to the town to 'see what was the matter'.

He asked someone outside the police station was told, 'There are two men in there and they are going to get them out.' McAllan thought this was no place for him and went back to the camp. On the way back he was struck on the back of the head by a stone.

Under cross-examination he helpfully, for him, added that he went down to the station in the execution of his duty as a military policeman. Why had he not stressed this in earlier statements? It would have saved him a great deal of discomfort and worry. He saw no sticks being used and said the crowd was quite orderly. He was hit by a stone as he turned from the station. He was not at the scene for more than two minutes.

Allan MacMaster, the only man present who knew beyond any doubt who had struck the blow that killed Sergeant Green, was next in the box. He did not give an inch. He claimed he went to bed at 9.30pm and got up again on hearing what he took to be the first part of the fire call. He then went down to the town with about fifteen other men, but at no time was he near the police station where the officer was killed. He never armed himself, and never saw or struck a policeman. On the way home he received a blow on the side of the head, which rendered him insensible. It was an unprovoked assault. Cross-examination elicited nothing further.

Masse's story was similar. He had been to Dorking and returned to camp, reporting to the guard room at 11.00pm. Just then a crowd of men were leaving the camp and he followed them to the police station. After a few minutes a considerable quantity of sticks and stones were flying through the air and he decided that it was too dangerous and turned round to go home. Before he had got far he too was struck by a brick.

154

Wilkie followed the party line too and under questioning was asked what he thought the sticks and stones carried by the soldiers were for. He was not forthcoming.

'You've been in France and seen some fighting?' pressed Justice Darling.

'Yes.'

'When you were in France and saw guns and swords being brandished about what did you think they were for?'

'For fighting purposes.'

'And when you saw sticks, posts and iron bars being brandished, what did you think those were for?'

'For breaking things up.'

'For breaking the police station up?' suggested Ernest Wild.

'I do not know about that.'

Yerex claimed he too was awoken by the disturbance in the camp and the sounding of the 'fall in' and got up and dressed. He said he could not find out what it was all about and followed the men into town. Because of his poor eyesight he had no idea where he was and when he turned round and headed for home he received three blows to the back of his head.

Under cross-examination Yerex also stated he did not know where the police station was. Ernest Wild thought it was odd that he had lived in Epsom but did not know where the police station was (even though he had been at Woodcote camp barely a month). This was an opportunity for His Lordship to deliver another quip – that a great many respectable people did not know where the police station was – and it was met with the expected laughter around the chamber.

The final defendant to face scrutiny was the young bugler, Robert Todd. The court reports at the time described him as

155

diminutive and he was likely still in shock at the turn of events. He had only done what he was told and now he was looking across at a stern English judge and a jury that could well decide he was *responsible* for the riot by blowing his bugle. Terrified, he had decided to tell the truth as he knew it, just like he had been taught at the Dr Barnardo's home.

He said that a threatening mob had shouted to him to blow the bugle up at the camp and he thought he ought to obey. He did not blow it of his own free will. The men went round to the huts calling out to the other soldiers, saying they were going to the police station to rescue two comrades. Major Ross, said Todd, tried to quieten the men, but failed, and then consented to go at the head of them to see if he could get the two prisoners handed over. One expects that Major Ross winced at this piece of evidence. On hearing that the Major was going to Epsom, Todd decided to go along and take his bugle in case he was needed. He described what happened at the police station and Veinot and McDonald being released and said that the men were then talking of raiding the town,

Major Ross had turned to him, he recalled: 'For God's sake blow something on the bugle to head the men towards camp.' He blew the 'fall in' twice and headed back to camp with a large mob behind him.

These exchanges described by Todd proved that Major Ross was being less than honest earlier with the court when he said he did not know who the bugler was and could not identify him. It indicated strongly that Ross's loyalty was to his men and not the British judicial system.

When Todd had finished giving his evidence Sir Ernest Wild for the prosecution remarked that there was no doubt that Todd was bullied into blowing the bugle and that the boy had told more truth in the witness box than the other six men put together. He then proceeded to conclude the prosecution's case:

> Everyone must regret that men who had come over to help us in the cause of order and right, for which we had been fighting for the past five years, should now find themselves in the dock. There is a very grave danger if people take the law into their own hands at a time when lawlessness is rampant and direct action is being preached. These men have taken the law into their own hands with the result that the death has occurred of a police officer. If I have proved the facts to your satisfaction, then you, the jury, it is your duty to return a verdict accordingly.

Mr Benjamin then addressed the jury on behalf of Connors and McAllan, saying there was no evidence that they took part in any rioting and therefore the charge of manslaughter could not be sustained.

Mr Abinger concluded for the other prisoners, but he firstly, unusually, praised his counterpart on the prosecution. 'Sir Ernest Wild represents that rare and refreshing fruit in counsel for prosecutions, in that he has been perfectly fair in the way he has put his case.'

He went on to say it was monstrous that the men must be convicted just because they had wounds. That their wounds were caused because they were in the forefront of the riot should not be a foregone conclusion, he pleaded. Windows were broken at The Ladas, half a mile away, he reminded the jury, and therefore people could have been hit by stones without going to the police station at all. The prosecution case broke down immediately Todd went into the witness box, claimed Abinger.

He was bullied into sounding the call – by whom? Not by the men in the dock, as they were in bed when the bugle was sounded, but by those who were the real perpetrators of the riot. Jury, you cannot convict the prisoners unless you find they were committed to a common purpose.

Major Ross was outside the police station at the time of the assault, but he was never asked by the prosecution if he could identify any of the men now charged. Why? This case has been presented in a chaotic condition *and the proper steps have never been taken to discover the real miscreants* [italics mine].

Justice Darling then began summing up and turned to the jury.

It has to be proved that the defendants, either of them or all of them, are guilty of manslaughter. There is not the slightest evidence that either of them struck the blow which killed Sergeant Green, but if it is proved to your satisfaction that the prisoners or either of them were actively engaged in unlawful riot in the course of which Green was killed then it is manslaughter against all those engaged in that unlawful riot in the direct execution of which Green came by his death.

It might be a shock to you to know that it is legally possible for four hundred men to be guilty of manslaughter. The men in the dock might not have seen Green and yet might be legally guilty as participators in the riotous assembly, but you might shrink from giving your verdict against them unless you are satisfied that the prosecution has thoroughly proved its case.

The Canadian authorities are as anxious as anybody in the country that the guilty parties should be brought to justice, and the complaint from defence counsel that the officer in charge of the camp had not been called to say there were no more wounded men in the camp must not be taken seriously. If, as Mr Abinger had suggested, a roll call had been taken was it not too much to expect of human nature that a man who broke away from the camp and took part in a riot would, when placed on his honour, come forward and say, 'I killed Sergeant Green,

and, in fact, I am such an honourable man that if you had not
been in such a hurry I was just coming up to tell you all about
it'?

At this juncture there was another ripple of laughter across the
courtroom.

'The jury must consider carefully the charge of manslaughter,' Darling resumed:

> whether any of the defendants are guilty of riotous conduct,
> and of riotously assembling together and injuring by force the
> police house at Epsom and attempting to secure the release of
> two persons in lawful custody. You must consider the case
> carefully against each prisoner and discriminate between them
> in any manner suggested by the evidence and the facts placed
> before the court.

The judge, having firmly steered the jury away from delivering
a manslaughter verdict, then dismissed them to deliberate.

Only thirty minutes later they returned. Robert Todd and
Robert McAllan were found not guilty on both charges; the
other five were found not guilty on the charge of manslaughter,
but guilty on the charges relating to rioting.

The murder of a policeman had been solved and tried in
record time (it was barely a month since the Epsom Riot) and
five men were about to be sentenced on the relatively minor
charge of rioting. From a pure justice point of view, most
would consider this to be an abject failure.

The foreman also said he had been asked on the behalf of
the jury to make the point that the soldiers were not used to our
laws, and coming from abroad were probably not aware of the
offences they were committing. This is a strange request, at the
least. Where did the jury think these men came from? Did they

159

think that in Canada it was within the law to riot, to smash up public buildings and bash people over the head with iron bars? Justice Darling addressed Todd and McAllan, telling them they had been acquitted and were therefore discharged and not into military custody. The oldest and the youngest defendant left the court free men, mightily relieved that the spectre of prison, or worse, had been lifted.

'As to you others,' continued Darling:

> the jury have found you not guilty of the very serious offence of manslaughter, and for that I am very glad, because had they found you guilty it would have been my duty to sentence you to long terms of imprisonment, but they have taken a merciful view and acquitted you of the grave offence. They have, however, found you guilty on evidence which permitted of no possible doubt of having taken part in a riot for the purpose of releasing from legal custody two comrades who had been arrested for resisting the police in the execution of their duty. You formed part of a huge and dangerous mob of soldiers assaulting a small body of men, at the first only twelve and never, even at the last, more than twenty-four, and you assailed a small body of men like that with such violence, some more than others, and actually killed one policeman, who was merely doing his duty as a servant of the State.
>
> I shall treat you exactly as I should men who have been bred and born in this country in so far as the sentence I am about to impose on you is concerned. There is no distinction between the way in which you behaved and the way many people are behaving at this moment. Their conduct may in some respects be worse than yours and they may have been soldiers. The law must be observed, and if necessary, it must be enforced by punishment.
>
> I regret more than I can tell you the position in which you now stand. You are men who have come over here, not as volunteers, but in obedience of the law passed in your own country, to fight for the same cause which was fought for by

the whole of the British Empire. You had no real grievance, but you banded yourselves together with others to release two men who were very soon to be handed over by the civil police, had you not interfered, to be punished, if they had deserved to be punished, by the officers commanding your own troops. I regret extremely that men who are not criminals in the ordinary sense, men who have never committed any criminal offence, should stand where you do convicted of a grave offence against society.

I cannot help noticing that the result of your riot was that a considerable amount of damage to property was done, injury was inflicted on a number of men loyally serving the State, and one was killed whom nothing could have been alleged except that he did not give way to the violence of the mob. The attack on the police station was such that women and children were placed in grave danger, and there was an attempt to burn the place. You were accomplices in all this.

The jury has recommended me to take a lenient view of your offence, because you may not have realised how serious it was. I shall take into consideration the fact that you have been wounded or invalided for a time, and excuse you the hard labour which would otherwise accompany the sentence.

The sentence of this court is that you be imprisoned for twelve calendar months.

Take them down.

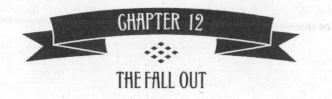

CHAPTER 12

THE FALL OUT

Jolly Good Fellows

The jury's verdict and the judge's sentence acknowledged the belief that they did not really have the murderer(s) of Sergeant Green before them (although they did) and therefore a British policeman's brutal killing in the grounds of his police station was going to go unpunished. A bunch of soldiers had received a token one-year prison sentence and that was that. Justice Darling had said he was going to treat them in exactly the same way as British men in his sentencing. There are no directly comparable cases involving British men, but it is stretching credulity that perpetrators of a riot that culminated in the death of a policeman and the wrecking of buildings would have got away with a year in prison in those times. Even now. Justice Darling's sentencing speech was also erroneous when he described the men as conscripts and not volunteers and this indicates poor briefing. His comments about the convicted men's injuries leads one to believe he was not brought up to speed, even privately, about the venereal disease backdrop to most of the men's presence in Epsom in the first place.

It is also surprising that the outspoken Justice Darling would not have commented about the failure to bring the real perpetrators to justice and the lack of a thorough investigation. Had he known about William Lloyd's statement and Eddie Lapointe or heard about Mrs Beauchamp, who had soldiers in her house saying they had just killed a policeman, then maybe he would have done. But His Lordship didn't know about any of that, and neither did the jury.

Normally such a vapid outcome in terms of justice for a murdered policeman would have prompted outrage, or vocal disappointment at a minimum, but no such reaction was reported in the national or local media. The sentencing was barely reported and it is hard not to conclude that Prime Minister David Lloyd George called in some favours from newspaper barons Lords Northcliffe and Beaverbrook to achieve this. There is also no record of policemen themselves protesting over the lack of justice for their colleague or any fingers pointed at the unseemly speed and superficiality of the investigation. Indeed what future publicity there was centered around praise and rewards for the detectives who investigated the riot and those officers who survived it. The quest for justice for Thomas Green, if ever there was one, had ended.

The commending of the police officers had started in earnest at the inquest in Epsom, but after the men had been taken down at Guildford Assizes Sir Ernest Wild mentioned to the Judge that the coroner's jury recommended that Inspector Ferrier ...

Justice Darling interrupted: 'The man whose conduct and bravery I should specially commend is Inspector Pawley.'

'He was mentioned as well, my Lord,' replied Sir Ernest. 'He was placed in a position of great difficulty, with very little assistance and an army of enemies.'

The judge's swift interjection at the mention of a commendation for Inspector Ferrier speaks volumes about what he may really have been thinking about the police investigation.

Back in Epsom Lord Rosebery had announced a fund for Sergeant Green's widow and the Metropolitan Police Fund had also awarded her a pension of £67 per annum, equating to some

163

£4,000 in today's money. The following month, in August, Mrs Pawley and her son Harry were awarded a gold and silver watch respectively in recognition of their efforts and bravery on the night of 18 June. The watches were presented in the police station garden by Inspector Pratt of 'V' Division. Inspector Pawley, Mrs Pawley and Harry all made grateful and self-deprecating speeches in front of other Epsom officers, local dignitaries and their families. Pawley joked that his son must have thought 'he was going over the top' again when he engaged with the marauding Canadians. At the end of the ceremony the invited guests burst into a rendition of 'For He's A Jolly Good Fellow'.

In the same month, quietly, an appeal was heard where Mr Abinger argued that the soldiers should be acquitted because it had been wrong to try the defendants *en-bloc*. The appeal was refused. At the same time, Edward, Prince of Wales set off on Lloyd George's Royal Tour of Canada, Australia and New Zealand with the aim of thanking these colonies for their support, effort and great sacrifice in the war. Robert Todd and Robert McAllan were now safely back in Canada, but it is unlikely they would be viewing the royal visit with any particular enthusiasm.

Meanwhile, back at Epsom Police Station, Sergeant Fred Blaydon was deeply troubled. Suffolk born, he had been a copper since 1891, nearly thirty years, and was close to retirement. He lived at 60 Hook Road in Epsom, a stroll away from Thomas Green's house, with his wife Elizabeth and grown-up daughter Elsie. Like Green he had policed closer into London, having spent some years at Streatham Police Station, and had a commendation under his belt before arriving in Epsom. He had been in the thick of the riot and had made the

164

statement that he had seen Sergeant Green go down and had seen him get up again. He had avoided serious injury himself, but was recorded as being 'lamed' in the aftermath. Something was bothering him so much that he felt compelled to write to the Metropolitan Police Commissioner, Sir Nevil Macready, directly. He must have considered his grievance incredibly sensitive to go straight to Macready and not his superior at Epsom, or Inspector Pratt of 'V' Division. He wrote from his home address asking for an audience with the Commissioner, saying mysteriously 'there were some men whose conduct should be explained'. He also wondered if those policeman who attended the station later (and were therefore not in the main riot) would get the same award as those who had risked life and limb.

We may never know what was exercising Fred Blaydon so. There had been much excitement over bravery gifts and potential cash awards that were to be presented to all the police officers who had been present at the riot and clearly Fred felt some of those were undeserving, but his comment about men whose conduct needed explaining is curious. He may have had an issue about cowardice shown by some of his colleagues in the heat of the battle; he may have had a problem with Inspector Pawley himself, and that would explain why he felt the need to go above his head. It is possible, but unlikely, that he felt that some of his colleagues had shown excessive violence towards the Canadians. Whatever it was, Sir Nevil wrote back to Fred Blaydon refusing him an audience and saying that the Epsom Riot case was closed. It is assumed that Fred Blaydon let his grievance drop at this point. This exchange of letters, though, has been preserved in The National Archives in Kew and an attached note, handwritten by Macready himself, is an instruction: 'The Epsom Riot case is closed, but any further correspondence should be drawn to my own personal attention.'

Strange that this exchange with lowly (in the scheme of things) Fred Blaydon should prompt such a dictate from the Commissioner. One would imagine that then, as now, the Commissioner's role would be strategic and political rather than operational. Why would Sir Nevil want to be so directly involved in the minutiae of this case? He must have considered it to be sensitive or potentially political to want to see any correspondence, from whoever, about the killing of Sergeant Green.

On 14 November 1919 Allan MacMaster, David Yerex, Alphonse Masse and James Connors were released from Wandsworth Prison to the charge of the 2nd Canadian Discharge Depot in London from where they would be shipped back to Canada in time for Christmas and receive dishonourable discharges. They had served only sixteen weeks of their one-year sentence. For some reason David Wilkie was kept in a bit longer, not being released until December and not setting down in Canada until the new year. He had already been deprived of his Lance Corporal status. A total of twenty months had therefore been served between all the men combined for the murder of a policeman.

Strangely, the following news item appeared in *The Epsom Advertiser* of 5 December 1919:

In response to the petition presented by Mr Bernard Abinger, solicitor, for the release of the Canadians imprisoned through the Epsom Riot, the Home Secretary, Edward Shortt, has replied that after consultation with the Canadian Authorities he has seen his way to decide that the men shall be released on December 15th and handed over to Canadian military escort, to be returned to Canada.

What is going on here? All the men with the exception of Wilkie had already been released by this time and handed over to the Canadian authorities. The inference was that the men were still in civil prison, and this was definitely not the case. One can only imagine that the government did not want the public at large to be aware that most of the men who were charged for the riot that killed Sergeant Green were already on their way home without any pressure from their defence counsel. It fits in with the pattern of unseemly haste and misleading statements that marks the whole affair. In five short months a policeman had been murdered, an investigation mounted, charges laid, a committal and trial heard and sentences imposed. Prison time had now been served and the guilty men returned to their home country of Canada. Extraordinary.

PC Harry Hinton had not been the same since the riot and was unfit to work. He was born in 1879 in the village of Wheatley in Oxfordshire and was a labourer when he signed up with the Met in 1904. His joining records reveal that he sported a tattoo on his right forearm. He had been unable to resume work fully since the night of the riot and was diagnosed with 'neurasthenia'. Harry resigned on 10 December 1919. He could not face policing any longer.

Neurasthenia was a controversial complaint because it was hard to quantify. Nowadays it would more likely be called post-traumatic stress disorder or a nervous breakdown. It was a matter of debate, then as now, as to whether it was a 'real' illness or not. Sigmund Freud believed (and one hopes that Harry Hinton did not know about this) that neurasthenia was a

167

result of excessive masturbation. Nevertheless, the Metropolitan Police were sympathetic to Hinton's plight and in February 1920 awarded him a gratuity of £273 19s 10d. This would have not been far off a year's wages and presumably his pension rights were intact. Harry had also volunteered to fight in the war in 1914 and had only been serving as a police officer again for a few months before the riot. It may have been that his war experiences contributed to his fragile condition too. Nearly eighty years later Hinton's daughters said that their father carried some guilt about his colleague's death. They said that he always felt, having been present at The Rifleman when the fracas began, he could and should have done more to nip the trouble in the bud. He could not be persuaded otherwise.

On the Wednesday afternoon, 14 January 1920, Lord Rosebery was driven in his black Hansom cab to the Epsom Police Court where he was to make presentations to the officers of Epsom Police Station in recognition of the gallantry shown in repelling the attack on the night of 17 June 1919. The old man was even frailer than when he had visited Inspector Pawley the day after the riot only six months earlier. He was helped to a bench in the court and remained seated throughout. It was announced that the fund launched by Rosebery and the Epsom MP Sir Rowland Blades had reached £575 15s 7d (approximately £30,000 in today's money), of which £310 (£18,000) would be given over to Thomas Green's widow. Lord Rosebery and Sir Rowland had decided that the remaining money was best used by awarding each of the twenty-four police officers commended with a permanent memento in recognition of their bravery. Lord Rosebery then proceeded to present each of the officers with a gold watch or medallion, inscribed with the words: 'In token of public appreciation of the gallant fight by Epsom police, 17th June 1919.'

He also handed to Harry Pawley a silver cigarette case, the gift of Sir Rowland and Lady Blades, in recognition of the assistance he gave to the police on the night of the attack. Finally, he passed to Inspector Pawley the cheque for £310, which he asked to be passed on to Mrs Green, who still being very ill was unable to attend.

Sir Nevil Macready was present and he stood and thanked Lord Rosebery on behalf of the whole Metropolitan Police Force and the old man replied with regret and sincerity: 'I wish with all my heart that I could express all that I feel on this occasion – but I cannot.' When he climbed into his carriage to leave the policemen and the other people present gathered in the courtyard and loudly cheered him.

The following month one of the officers present at the station the previous June died and became the second suggested fatality of the Epsom Riot. He was Page Mayes Janeway and he lived in Station Road in Epsom with his wife Emily, twelve-year-old son Leonard and eight-year-old daughter Olive. His role in the riot is unclear and he was not listed among the officers who suffered injuries immediately afterwards, yet he is listed on the Metropolitan Police Roll of Honour as having 'died from cancer believed triggered by injuries sustained in the Epsom Riot'. His death certificate is less specific, listing cancer in the glands of the neck and cardiac failure as the cause of death. He was commended, with the others, for his part in the defence of the Epsom Police Station.

Page had a rough deal in life, it seems. He was born in 1875 in Royston, Hertfordshire, but by 1881 he was in the Royston Union Workhouse with his grandmother and brothers and sisters. He joined the Metropolitan Police Force in 1897 and received a commendation in 1904 and would have been another looking towards his retirement. Perhaps he and his family believed that his cancer was a direct result of the trauma and injuries he received in June 1919, but this would a difficult one to prove definitively. The Met obviously some had sympathy with this view as he is clearly listed by them as a casualty of the Epsom Riot, and his body is buried in the plot directly next to his old colleague, Thomas Green, in Epsom Cemetery. Yet, rather bafflingly, they did not grant him a memorial stone at all, let alone one of the dignified splendour of Sergeant Green's.

Only three months later, in May 1920, a third man present at the riot died. It was generally assumed that all the Canadian soldiers that stood trial were well and truly home by this date, resuming their lives with their families. Although James Connors had been released into the custody of the Canadian authorities in November 1919, with the others, he had not been put on a boat home, but instead was admitted to hospital. During his time in Wandsworth Prison he had lost a further twenty-one pounds in weight and finally somebody diagnosed tuberculosis. A note on his file at this time records that he had suffered from 'a general weakness, defective hearing in his left ear, poor nourishment and a debilitated look'.

He was admitted to the Bermondsey Military Hospital in Ladywell, Lewisham where he spent his final weeks coughing, spluttering and miserably fevered as his life ebbed away, with no family or friends to comfort or sustain him. He died on 19 May 1920 at the age of just twenty and was buried in the Canadian section of the Brookwood Military Cemetery in Surrey.

In his statement to the police about his whereabouts on the evening of the Epsom Riot, Connors stated he had been seeing a girl called 'Lil' who lived close to the gates of Horton Hospital. On surveying the 1911 census I have been unable to find a 'Lil' who would be of a similar age to Connors and who lived in one of the roads close to the Horton Hospital entrance. However, just after that census was taken, a girl called Lil or Lily did move into a road near to the Horton gates, and she was almost exactly the same age as the young soldier. The road was Lower Court Road and her father was named Thomas Green.

CHAPTER 13

FINDING DEATH

Soldiers of Christ Arise

A year after the riot Epsom was almost back to normal. The Canadians had all gone home, the soldiers who had returned from the war were resettling, many struggling to find work, but nevertheless adjusting the best they could to civilian life. They had seen and done things they never dreamed they would, but most of them did not like to talk about it. The relationships that had been impacted on by the Canadian presence either completely broke down or gradually repaired. Most repaired. The local policemen put the riot behind them and most of them did not like to talk about it either. Many had retired or moved on. For those that remained their days were now more likely to be filled with ticking off children raiding birds' nests or men riding bicycles down footpaths than facing up to murderous mobs. Another Derby had been run and this time was won by a horse called Spion Kop with an American jockey Frank O'Neill piloting it to a comfortable victory.

On 11 June, almost a year on from Sergeant Green's funeral, a crowd gathered again in the Epsom Cemetery for another service – this time to mark the unveiling of his impressive memorial. The stone was a fine, tall, carved Celtic cross bearing the inscription that had been worded carefully by Lord Rosebery:

IN MEMORY OF
STATION SERGEANT THOMAS GREEN

WHO FOUND DEATH IN THE PATH OF DUTY.
HE WAS KILLED IN DEFENDING
EPSOM POLICE STATION
AGAINST A RIOTOUS MOB
JUNE 17th 1919.
THIS MEMORIAL WAS ERECTED BY
THE OFFICERS AND MEN OF THE
METROPOLITAN POLICE FORCE

Thomas Green would have been interested to know that he found death in the path of duty rather than being bludgeoned mercilessly by a crazed, syphilitic and epileptic Canadian soldier. Rosebery's words raise more questions than answers for the uninitiated: at best he was being tactful and at worst he was part of an orchestrated effort to bury the Epsom Riot from public view then and in the future. This inscription does not tell you that Green was murdered by a Canadian soldier – one could assume that he had, for example, been killed under the weight of fallen masonry from the under-attack police station. There is no mention of the policeman's signal bravery and no reference to him being a hero. Towns normally want to celebrate their heroes, but here an opportunity to do this is curiously missed. If the Metropolitan Police paid for the memorial, why did they not choose the wording? One can only imagine that Sergeant Green's family and Epsom colleagues could have only been disappointed with the woolly and almost weasley words that would mark their loved one's existence for evermore.

As at the funeral, the Reverend George Alway spoke about Thomas Green the man and Sergeant Green the policeman. Charlie Pawley was there, now retired, as was his replacement at Epsom, Inspector Goodenough. Further up the police tree was Divisional Superintendent Boxhall and finally Major Lafone. Sir Nevil Macready was not present, having been sent

173

by the Prime Minister, Lloyd George, to command the troops in Ireland and having now been succeeded as Commissioner of the Metropolitan Police by William Horwood. Macready would probably have been relieved not to have been there and risk being confronted by Sergeant Fred Blaydon. As before, family and friends encircled the grave. The numbers were not as great as at the funeral, but no less intense for that. When the Metropolitan Police Band struck up the hymn 'Soldiers of Christ Arise', written by the brothers and founders of the Methodist movement, John and Charles Wesley, and sung by the Green family's fellow worshippers from the Wesleyan Church, a car drove slowly through the iron gates and up to the graveside.

> Stand then against your foes, in close and firm array;
> Legions of wily fiends oppose throughout the evil day.
> But meet the sons of night, and mock their vain design,
> Armed in the arms of heavenly light, of righteousness divine.

Still singing, the crowd stepped on to the grass to allow the car to stop alongside the stone. In the back seat were young Lily and Nellie Green. In the front passenger seat, looking ruefully for the first time at her husband's resting place, was Lilian Green, having made a life-draining effort to come from her hospital bed to mark this occasion.

The ailing widow only survived one more winter herself. Leaving the hospital, she did return home to 92 Lower Court Road, dying there on 30 November 1921 at just fifty-two years of age. She was buried in the grave with her husband and her name added to the flank of the memorial. Fewer than twenty weeks later the only surviving members of the Epsom Green family – Lily and Nellie – were gone too. In April 1922 they boarded the passenger ship *Corsican* and sailed for a new life. Their destination was Canada.

174

CHAPTER 14

THE CONFESSION

'Do you want him?'

Allan James MacMaster was discharged from the Canadian military on 3 January 1920 at Saint John, New Brunswick. On discharge papers seen by the author the words 'dishonourably discharged' have been inked out and replaced by 'demobilised'. Who made that alteration and why? MacMaster firstly headed back to Judique, Cape Breton, to his father's home, no doubt hoping that the events in Epsom were a closed book. Having seen action in France and Epsom and experienced life and death at the extremes, he could not sustain resettling in such a rural and remote environment and after six weeks left again. This time he headed for the town of Cobalt near Ontario where he caught the latter days of the 'silver rush' that had begun twenty years earlier and had given birth to the town when the precious metal had been discovered by railway construction companies. He found regular employment in mining and hope for the future in prospecting.

On 30 April 1922 he married Cassie McCaskill, a fellow Nova Scotian from Whycoomagh who had been born to Neil McCaskill and Annie McKinnon in 1893. They set up home at 56 Laurier Avenue, Timmins, Ontario and it seemed that MacMaster's life had entered a phase of relatively quiet domesticity. He was now thirty-one. Their first two children were a boy and a girl named after each parent, but when Cassie fell pregnant again she became ill and on 17 January 1925 she died from cardiac failure and eclampsia.

The effect that this had on MacMaster must have been traumatic, but in the light of what had happened four years later one could assume that a blend of conscience and the residual influences of his Roman Catholic religion caused him to examine his past and torture himself over whether his misdemeanors and sins were the cause of the tragedy that had befallen his wife and family. Inevitably his thoughts would have regularly returned to the night of 17 June 1919 in Epsom and the policeman he killed. He *had* murdered Sergeant Green, even if a court did not find that he had. He had killed a man who had a wife and children. A man he did not know at the time of striking the blow was an English police officer; a man who had done him no harm whatsoever. And he had got away with it. He had not been punished in law and that was why he was being punished now. The need to confess to a priest and to the law grew inside him. Epileptic and tortured, he could not hold down a job and began to drink heavily and drift.

The enormity of confessing should not be underestimated. MacMaster could not have grasped that he was not charged with murder because there was not a will to do so – he believed that the police had simply not solved the case. By confessing, MacMaster would fully have expected to be sent back to England for trial and knew that the punishment for the cold-blooded, brutal murder of a policeman would be the gallows, despite his coming forward and the decade time lapse.

On the evening of 31 July 1929 MacMaster walked into the Police Headquarters at Winnipeg, Manitoba, Canada and announced he wished to confess to a murder. He was ushered inside. MacMaster was clearly drunk and, first things first, was charged under the Liquor Control Act. Some time later, when

176

he had sobered up, his statement was taken, rather sceptically at first. It was ten years and six weeks since he had committed this murder.

When the duty detectives heard his story, which featured Edward, the Prince of Wales, the Old Bailey, pardons and the murder of a station sergeant, they realised they were either on to something big or they had a lunatic in front of them, and Chief Constable Chris Newton was summonsed. Newton knew all about riots – in June 1919 he had broken a police strike in Winnipeg by bringing in an army of 'mercenary' police officers. Newton proceeded to take down MacMaster's statement in front of detectives Jack Bishop and Charles McIver. McIver would later become Chief Constable of Winnipeg too, serving in that post as late as 1953.

MacMaster's statement read as follows:

I, Allan J. MacMaster, of no fixed address, at present in custody at the Central Police Station, Winnipeg, Man., on a charge of the Breach of the Liquor Control Act, voluntarily state that I was a Private, Reg. No. 716144, originally in the 106th Battalion CEF transferred to the 26th Battalion CEF at Dibgate. Enlisted in Antigonish, Nova Scotia about the month of January, 1916. In July, 1916 proceeded to England, was encamped at Dibgate near Shorncliffe in Kent. After serving in France and convalescing at Uxbridge in Essex, I was transferred to Epsom at Farm Camp awaiting return to Canada for demobilisation.

On the night of 17th June, 1919, I remember that it was the night of the first Derby after the War; I was in company with a number of comrades who went to the Police Station at Epsom to effect the release of some comrades who had been arrested by the Civil Authority. Major Burd, 2nd in Command of the Hospital at Farm Camp tried to persuade us not to go, but he did not succeed.

177

I don't know who was the leader of the bunch that went down to the Police Station, but there was about 800 of us and we smashed in the Police Station and effected the release of the men. Sgt Green was in charge of the Police at this Station and he and the other Police charged us with their batons. I struck the Sergeant on the head with an iron bar. It was wrenched from one of the cell windows. I saw him falling backward, he was bareheaded at the time and I think he was bald. I was struck on the head by a police baton and my head was cut open. I walked to the road and over to the camp and had my head dressed by one of the Doctors.

The next day, I, with five other men who were marked in the affray, were removed to a Hospital near London for one night and then removed to Brixton Gaol. About the 5th July, 1919, we six men were charged before a Magistrate who released two men and sent the other three and myself to trial at the Fall Assizes. In October we came before Mr. Justice Darling at the Old Bailey on five or six charges including Murder, Manslaughter, Rioting and Assembling to Riot and Wilful Damage. We were acquitted on the Murder and Manslaughter charges and convicted of Rioting and sentenced to one year's imprisonment at Wandsworth Prison. Twelve days later this conviction was appealed and as a result the date of the commencement of the year's imprisonment was set back to the date from the time of the arrest.

I forget the name of one of the others convicted with me, but the other two were Private O'Connor and Private Wilkie. In December 1919, we were pardoned and released. I came to Canada on the Scotian and landed at St John's, N.B., and was discharged from the Army on 3rd January 1920. I went home to my Father's home at Judique, Inverness Co., Cape Breton, was there for about six weeks and went to Cobalt and have been engaged in mining and prospecting ever since.

The reason I make this statement is because I feel a burden on my conscience and know I would have to confess it sometime.

MacMaster's statement is littered with spelling mistakes [here corrected] and wrongly named people and places. The passage of a decade, the effects of drink and, perhaps, the legacy of syphilis had damaged his power of recollect. The riot did not take place on the night of the Derby, that was a fortnight earlier; it was Major Ross not Major Burd [sic] who tried to prevent the men from marching into town; there was no fellow defendant called O'Connor, though there was a Connors; and the trial was not held at the Old Bailey. This is the first time mention is made in public of Edward, Prince of Wales granting a Royal pardon to the convicted men. If correct, on what grounds was it granted? Was it normal for the Prince rather than the King to grant a pardon? The timing, if correct, suggests that Edward may have offered or agreed to this during his Canadian and American tour. He docked back in Britain on 1 December 1919.

Excited and intrigued, Chris Newton sent the following telegram to New Scotland Yard:

HANDCUFFS, LONDON

Am detaining Allan MacMaster, who admits being murderer of Police Sergeant Green at Epsom on June 17th, 1919.
Do you want him? Wire instructions.

Newton,
Winnipeg Police
City Police, Chg Attorney General's Dept.

He backed it up by the following letter:

Dear Sir,

Re Allan MacMaster
Murder of Police Sgt Green at Epsom

179

I have the honour to advise for your information that a man named Allan MacMaster, 39 years, came to Police Headquarters in the city on the evening of July 31st, 1929, and stated that he desired to confess to being the murderer of Police Sergt. Green of Epsom, England on June 17th 1919. MacMaster stated he was with the 26th Battalion of the Canadian Expeditionary Force and that his Regimental number is 716144. The story he tells in short is as follows:- 'Two of our men got arrested and locked up. As soon as we heard about it we all went down to town to take them out of the lockup. We made a rush at the building. Sergt. Green tried to stop me. So I picked up an iron bar and hit him over the head with it. He died the following day. Two other men and I were arrested for it and tried before Mr Justice Darling and sentenced to one year's imprisonment for rioting. We served five months and were pardoned by the Prince of Wales. The Police never found out who was the murderer of Green. This matter has worried me for a long time and I have made up my mind to confess so as to clear my conscience.'

I am enclosing herewith a voluntary statement in triplicate made by the subject of this communication in the presence of my two officers for your information and guidance. Please advise me as soon as possible what your wishes are in this connection.

Yours truly,

Chris H Newton

Commissioner Newton was probably pleased and surprised to have MacMaster walk into his offices and he was 'honoured' to relay the news to Scotland Yard, the most celebrated police HQ in the world. The telegraphic response from the Yard would have undoubtedly puzzled and deflated him. He and his officers perhaps harboured hopes of a nice sailing to England to deliver their cop killer to belated justice and Newton may have been already constructing a self-congratulatory press release in his head. Instead, he received this:

MACMASTER SENTENCED IN CONNECTION WITH THIS AFFAIR AND HE IS NOT WANTED. LETTER FOLLOWING.

The message was short and to the point and we do not know what further explanation, if any, was forthcoming in the following letter. Yet by any measure the information provided was misleading. MacMaster had confessed to a murder. He had not been tried for murder and therefore double jeopardy laws would not apply. Here was a written confession to an allegedly unsolved murder of a police officer, yet Scotland Yard dismissed it in fourteen words. They did not want further details, did not want to interview MacMaster and did not pass on this information to people that had a moral right to know, such as Thomas Green's family, those who fought alongside Sergeant Green on that June night in 1919 and the general public. Like many facets of this case, the confession was hurriedly and quietly buried.

CHAPTER 15

THE OTHER MAN

Circumstances of Death

It was Edward Shortland, a former detective, who stumbled upon the first information about 'the other man'. Like when he was a policeman working on solving a case, it was one of those nuggets of information that occasionally fell into his lap. Shortland was up at the cemetery in Epsom seeking out Thomas Green's monument, and although the Council offices at Epsom had given him directions, he could not find it immediately. Seeing an aged man pottering around and thinking he may be an odd-job worker or grave digger he asked him if he knew of the stone. The man promptly led him to the grave.

'I'm not sure where the other one is, though.'

Shortland jolted.

'The other one?'

'Yes, the Canadian soldier who got killed as well.'

Edward was flabbergasted by this aside. This elderly chap in front of him was nonchalantly stating something that, if true, put a whole different complexion on the affair and, certainly, it was not a claim he had ever heard before. Shortland knew dynamite when he heard it, but he was also trained to smell a rat.

'A Canadian soldier was killed in the riot?'

'He got killed and he was something to do with it, but I'm no expert ... and he's buried up here ... somewhere ... they'll know down at the office. They'll tell you. They know all about it.'

'So it's public knowledge?'

'Well, I wouldn't say that. It's knowledge. Probably hushed up. Wouldn't have been good, would it? Canadian soldier … Epsom policeman … policeman gets killed by soldiers … soldier gets killed by someone. It's not the sort of thing you shout about. Not then. But people in Epsom knew about it. Some of them did, anyway.'

'What was his name, do you know?'

'No idea.'

'What is your name?'

The old man laughed. 'My name? What are you – a policeman? No, I'll say no more. Ask at the cemetery office, I told you. You won't be the first.'

Shortland assumed that the man was intimating that a Canadian soldier had also perished in the riot and from the blows delivered by the policemen. He could barely contain his excitement.

A subsequent call by Shortland to the cemetery office based in the Council's building in The Parade – a stone's throw from the old police station – confirmed that there were indeed a number of Canadian soldiers buried in the cemetery and these were men who had died at either Woodcote camp, the Grandstand Hospital or Horton Hospital between 1914 and 1918.

'Is there one who was killed in the Epsom Riot of 1919?' Shortland asked directly.

'There is one soldier who we have been asked about in the past,' came the reply. 'His name is Frederick Bruns. He is buried in the Canadian plot and his name is on the War Memorial. He died in 1919.'

'He died in 1919? Do you have his date of death there in front of you?'

'I do. Bear with me ... Frederick Bruns died on ... 26 June 1919.'

Shortland's brain whirred and his heartbeat accelerated. This was just over a week after Thomas Green's demise. On checking, he would see that it was the day after Sergeant Green's inquest at the Court House and the day before the Canadian soldiers' hearing at Bow Street, where the defendants were sent to trial. He worked out that Bruns had met his death fewer than sixty hours after Sergeant Green's funeral. He knew there was a lot more digging to do, but another death at around the time as Green's in the midst of everything that was going on and with no mention anywhere was interesting to say the least. His policeman's gut instinct told him that he was on to something extremely significant.

A subsequent search of official records by this author threw up some explosive facts. Frederick Bruns' body had been discovered on 26 June 1919 at the chalk pit on Headley Road, Epsom, which was just outside of the Woodcote camp and almost on Epsom Downs, not too far from the race track. The cause of death on his death certificate was listed as a fractured skull. His body was discovered on the Thursday and an inquest was held just forty-eight hours later, on the Saturday, which must have been by special arrangement and highly unusual, and an open verdict was returned. A death certificate was issued and the case was closed with burial arrangements being made by the end of the Saturday. This was an astonishing rush job by any stretch of the imagination. As a former policeman himself, Shortland knew that no meaningful police investigation could have taken place.

Another piece of information emerged that Shortland felt straight away would have been akin to having a hand grenade thrown into the delicate structure of the well-made plans of the establishment at the time – although Bruns was a soldier in the Canadian Army, he was an American citizen. If the establishment had fretted about the impact on Anglo-Canadian relations over the killing of Thomas Green then the subsequent murder of an American soldier by English civilians would have sent them into an apoplexy.

Frederick Bruns had been born in Moose Jaw, Saskatchewan on 20 February 1888 to parents John and Helena Bruns. They must have been one of the early settlers in this small town, as the first homestead was established by James Hamilton Ross, who had become the initial permanent resident of the city only six years before. He and others were on a scouting tour, in search of the most likely spot for the Canadian Pacific Rail (CPR) lines divisional point. The CPR chose the tow site adjacent to the Moose Jaw River to ensure water supply for their steam engines. Both industry and commercial trade expanded with an agricultural settlement, and Moose Jaw, because it was a CPR divisional point, was the chosen location for major processing. By 1913 the population had burgeoned from Ross and a handful of others to 14,000 people. Frederick's parents had both been born in Germany and were first-generation immigrants to Canada, so fighting against the Kaiser may have presented the young Bruns with mixed emotions.

At some point John and Helena and the children crossed the border from Canada to America, because when Frederick joined the army in May 1918 his parents were listed as living in Agar, South Dakota. Frederick Barton Bruns, though, enlisted in the CEF at Toronto, Ontario and arrived in England on 15 July 1918. He was described as being 5'8½'' in height with medium complexion, blue eyes and fair hair. He was initially posted to the CERB at Seaford and promptly contracted venereal disease, for which he was treated at Etchinghill, the military hospital near Folkestone in Kent, between September 9 and Christmas Day 1918. Shortly after, in the New Year, he caught influenza and was sent to Woodcote Park Convalescence Hospital in Epsom. Frederick was present at Woodcote Park at the time of the Epsom Riot, but there is no evidence to say he took part. He was destined never to see France or enemy action, but nevertheless to meet an extremely violent end.

This author attempted to locate the inquest report for Bruns, but was told by both the Surrey Archive Centre and the Coroner's Office that all records had been lost, even though other inquest reports from the same period are intact. Similarly, my researcher in Canada attempted to glean more information from military archives and discovered there was a Circumstances of Death report on Frederick Barton Bruns, but on receiving it found only the brief death certificate details.

However, during further searching of local newspapers the following press report from the *Epsom Advertiser* of 4 July 1919 was located:

SOLDIER'S TERRIBLE FALL

60 feet down a pit

MYSTERIOUS WOUNDS, DOCTORS DIFFER

Mystery surrounds the tragedy near Woodcote Park Convalescent Camp, Epsom, last week when, as reported in the *Advertiser*, the terribly injured body of a Canadian soldier was found at the bottom of a chalk pit, between 60 ft and 70 ft deep.

At the inquest, conducted by Mr Gilbert White, at Leatherhead on Saturday, doctors differed regarding a wound on the deceased's nose and the jury returned an open verdict.

Corporal Joseph Arthur Lallander, CAMC, stationed at Woodcote Park Convalescent Camp, identified the body as that of Private Frederick Barton Bruns, who was about 25 years old and who had been in the Camp for about two months. On Wednesday last (June 25) they left the Camp together and at Ashtead station [the next down the line from Epsom] they parted, deceased going to Wimbledon and witness to Sutton.

Mabel May of 125 Gladstone Road, Wimbledon stated that she met the deceased for the first time at 9.10pm on Wednesday, and stayed with him for about an hour. Outside her house they parted, deceased telling her that he was going back by the 10.35pm train. He was quite sober.

Private Frank Durrance, Canadian University Corps., Woodcote Park Camp, said that on Wednesday last week he was on duty at No.2 gate at the Camp. Between 12.35am and 1am after a civil policeman, with whom he had been talking, left him, he heard three distinct shouts from the direction of the quarry. The first shout was loud, but the others grew fainter. As it rained shortly after he went into the sentry box. It was there he saw a soldier coming through the hedge from the path which led to the quarry. Witness challenged him and he replied that he was 'a friend from the hospital'.

Coming across to the witness he said: 'My friend has jumped the fence and I think has fallen into the quarry, I think he may be killed.'

Witness told him to go to the guard room if he wanted any aid, but he said, 'If I report to the guard room I am out of hospital without permission and I shall be punished for it.'

Witness therefore let him into the Camp and called out the guard who found the body in the quarry.

SHORT CUT TO CAMP

By the foreman of the jury, Mr A. Allen – He distinctly heard three shouts and not moans?

Superintendent Coleman, representing Surrey County Constabulary – There were nothing in the shouts to suggest to him there was a man in distress.

187

Lieutenant F. Cawthorne, officer in charge of the guard at Woodcote camp on Wednesday evening, stated that he was notified by the corporal in charge of No.2 guard that cries had been heard as if someone needed help. He sent two men with a lantern to search, and with another man he went towards the quarry, and afterwards went to the bottom where they found the body. It was outstretched with legs crossed, and the heart had ceased to beat. The depth of the pit was about 60 feet. There were no signs of a struggle on the top.

Captain Manford Robert Carr, CAMC, who was called to the quarry immediately the discovery was made, said there were severe injuries to the head, and death must have been instantaneous.

Sgt Kersey with Colonel Guest, Commandant of the Camp, and Major Bird, Adjutant, went to the bottom of the pit where there was a pool of blood, a piece of scalp and a quantity of brain. Half-way down the cliff in line with the spot where the body was found there were two heel marks. Several palings of the fence were broken away, but anybody who wanted to get to the edge of the cliff would have had to get under the middle strut. Witness opinion was that deceased knocked his head half-way down the side of the cliff as he fell. Near the pit was a short cut to the Camp from Ashtead, but he would not like to use it in the dark, although he knew it well. Had the deceased gone through the fence a little higher up he would have skirted the pit and it might be fairly said that he missed his way.

P.C. Rose deposed to find £5 in Treasury notes, silver and bronze coins, a permanent pass and a letter from the deceased's brother in the United States on the body.

Dr L. Potts, Leatherhead, who in company with Lieutenant Colonel McDermott, Medical Officer at the Camp, made the post mortem, said the skull was smashed to pulp. The jaw bone, chest bone and collar bone was fractured, as also was the fourth rib on the right side while the liver was ruptured. The heart and the lungs were perfectly normal and there was no disease about the man. There was also an incised wound from the tip of the nose running upwards to the nearside of the left

188

eyebrow. It was a very clean cut between two and a half and three and a half inches in length. Potts thought that all the injuries with the exception of this wound could be accounted for by the fall. In his opinion this wound could not have been caused by the fall, but must have been caused by a sharp instrument such as a knife, dagger or bayonet.

Lt. Colonel Hugh McDermott, CAMC, did not agree that the wound was caused by an instrument, his view being that the crushing in on the side of the skull tore away the side of the nose and the bone above.

Superintendent Coleman – He did not think any instrument had been used at the bottom of the pit, and if one had been used at the top one would have expected a good deal of blood about.

The jury retired, and after a time the foreman returned and asked if the inquest was adjourned whether the authorities could produce the corporal of the guard and the soldier who came through the hedge. Lt. Colonel McDermott replied in the affirmative with regard to the corporal, but said they did not know the other.

An initial reaction to reading these details could be that the case has no relation to the riot and the death of Sergeant Green. Edward Shortland, on only hearing the cryptic comments of the man in the cemetery and seeing a death certificate that referred to a fractured skull and an open verdict, developed a thesis that Bruns was hit in the riot with a heavy instrument (a poker?), suffered a fractured skull and didn't know it and did not seek medical attention at the camp knowing that to do so was inviting arrest. He walked around in a dazed state for a few days carrying a haematoma inside his head, which finally exploded when he was walking around on the outskirts of the camp and collapsed and died. His thesis continued that the powers that be were appalled by the news that another body had been found only a couple of days after Sergeant Green was

189

buried, and this time it was a Canadian soldier. Only it wasn't – it was an American, and this made things even worse.

Shortland thought that the powers were busy trying to limit the damage that could have been caused by the Sergeant Green affair and navigating the Canadian soldiers through the legal system, and this new development completely spooked them. Orders were given literally to bury the case as quickly as possible. An inquest was heard within two days and, unusually, on a Saturday. No investigation into the death was made, when a murder inquiry would have been normal, and an open verdict recorded. Private Frederick Barton Bruns was found dead in the early hours of Thursday 26 June, his inquest was heard on Saturday 28 June and by the close of that day he was forgotten. Not mentioned. Case closed.

On reading the additional information on the inquest covered in the above press report the initial reaction is to consider Shortland's theory flawed – or the first part of it at least. However, when one takes a step back and then reconsiders, there is no doubt that the investigation of Bruns' death was even more hurried and under-investigated than Sergeant Green's. One must conclude that even if there was no connection between the two incidents the government/establishment believed and worried that there *was*. A full investigation was not desirable at this sensitive time, whether there was any connection or not, and therefore Bruns, or at least justice for him, became another victim of the Epsom Riot. And here, at least, is the first connection between the deaths of Sergeant Green and Private Bruns.

Looking at the case we have the same ingredients: a Canadian/American soldier, a violent death, a broken skull, venereal disease, almost within a week of each other, almost within a mile of each other, no assailant identified and various Epsom

190

policemen involved in both cases. Crossovers in cast include PC Rose and Sergeant Kersey, Gilbert White, the coroner, Colonel Guest, Major Bird and Lieutenant Colonel McDermott, who was there in Sergeant Green's final hours.

The information revealed at the inquest also begs a number of questions. Why was the inquest held at Leatherhead and not Epsom? And why on a Saturday? Why was case handled by Surrey Constabulary when it was Metropolitan Police officers (Kersey and Rose) who attended the scene? Who was Mabel May, how did the inquest know she existed and how did they find her? If Bruns had met her for the first time, then he could not have told his colleague Lallander he was going to see her. There is a Mabel May in Wimbledon in the 1911 census (though not at Gladstone Road), but she would have only been fourteen in 1919.

If Bruns did catch the 10.35pm train he would have been back in Ashtead by 11.00pm, at the latest, so why did it take him over an hour and a half to get back to the camp? Where was he in that meantime? Why were ticket collectors at Ashtead (they did still exist in those days) not consulted to ask whether he did alight from that train and whether he was accompanied or not? If he didn't get off at Ashtead, did he get off at Epsom, the station before?

Who was the policeman that Private Frank Durrance was talking to when on guard duty? Why was he not traced and called to the inquest? Surely he was a key witness, as he was there, or thereabouts, when Bruns met his death. It has been suggested that he may have been off his beat and did not wish to get into trouble, but once he realised the seriousness of the incident, surely this would not have prevented him coming forward?

Who was the soldier that Durrance saw coming through the hedge? Why did he say he 'was a friend from the hospital' rather than give military name and number? Was he in uniform? Why was there no attempt to identify him and bring him to the inquest? Durrance saw and conversed with him – he must have been able to identify him. If he was not a soldier from the camp, who was he? What made him think his friend had been killed? If Bruns was his friend and he really thought that, surely he would have joined in the effort to help Bruns rather than worry about a minor charge for being out of the camp when he should not have been.

The evidence was that getting to the edge of the cliff would have entailed crouching and squeezing under a middle strut of a fence – would anybody really have done this intentionally or willingly? What was the incised wound running from the tip of Bruns' nose up to his forehead that concerned Dr Potts so? He was convinced this could not have been caused by the fall and that it was perpetrated with a knife or something similar. Lieutenant Colonel McDermott's alternative theory about the nose ripping so cleanly during his fall, causing such a precise incision, seems unlikely, to a layman.

When the jury enquired about an adjournment so the corporal of the guard and the mysterious soldier could be brought before the court why was not it granted, even if only for the former?

What were Bruns' parents told?

Where did the details of this inquest go? Why are records missing from the Surrey Coroner's Office and Surrey Archives?

This was certainly a mysterious incident and an even more mysterious response and investigation. Touchstone, the respected commentator for the *Epsom Advertiser*, certainly thought so. In his column the week after the inquest he wrote as follows:

Lately Epsom has become a town of sensation. For a week the inhabitants were stirred by the tragic riot at the police station, and following this there is a mystery which, although perhaps not so sensational, is being probed to the very depths in the hope of solution.

I refer to the tragedy in the vicinity of Woodcote Park camp when the body of a soldier was discovered at the bottom of a chalk pit, 60 feet deep, and in connection with the jury was not able to decide on the cause of death.

There were terrible injuries consistent with the fall, but an incised wound on the dead man's nose was the subject of a dispute between two doctors. One held the opinion that it was caused by a knife or some other sharp instrument, but the other, the camp Medical Officer, disagreed.

Hence the jury's open verdict. It remains a mystery as to whether the tragedy was the outcome of foul play or whether the victim lost his way in the dark back to camp and accidentally fell off the cliff.

The soldier who the sentry told the Coroner gave him information 'that his friend had fallen off the quarry' could probably have satisfied the jury one way or another if he could have been found afterwards. His absence, indeed, adds to the mystery of the affair.

Quite.

What exactly happened to Fred Bruns is impossible to prove. Bearing in mind that there were two people, at least – the 'soldier' and the policeman – in his close vicinity at the time of his death, who were *both* apparently untraceable afterwards, one is prone to lean towards some sort of foul play taking place. Whether it was directly related to the riot and/or Sergeant Green's death is a harder decision to make.

If it is accepted that foul play took place then one has to look towards a motive. Robbery does not seem plausible, bearing in mind the money found on Bruns. A drunken fight is unlikely as the victim had not been drinking, at least up until the time he parted from the girl. The most likely scenario is that another soldier had reason to want to hurt Bruns and that other soldier was the man who came through the hedge, but then why alert the guard to the incident? He did not have to.

If one thinks about exactly what was going on at that time of the tragedy another possible motive emerges. Sergeant Green died on Wednesday 18 June and local anger built from that morning to such an extent that the newspapers on Friday 20 June called on local men not to seek revenge on Canadian soldiers. The police did the same through the columns of the newspapers. The Borough Council was warned about the spectre of the inhabitants rioting. For a short time there was an order to shut the pubs and this was only rescinded when it was pointed out that this move could stoke up the locals further and that the town had been made out of bounds to the convalescents at Woodcote Park.

Even if the weekend and the absence of a noticeable Canadian presence in the town had served to dampen down the confrontational ardour of the Epsom men, those with revenge in their hearts would have seen their tempers reach boiling point again on Monday 23 June, as the whole town was given over to Sergeant Green's dramatic and poignant funeral. Forty-eight hours later something happened to Frederick Bruns: a Canadian soldier out late and alone in Epsom.

Bruns and the soldier he left camp with went to Ashtead railway station and not to either of the Epsom stations most commonly used by the Canadians, and the ones closest to the camp. I would surmise this was because they were forbidden from entering Epsom town and at heightened risk of being attacked if they did venture down. The locals, though, would have soon cottoned on to what the Canadians were doing and they would have been well aware of the route from Ashtead station back to the camp. It involved footpaths and woods and sparse lighting. They may have waited for a lone, unsuspecting Canadian alighting from the late trains.

Perhaps he was grabbed near the fence where soldiers customarily sneaked back into camp and set upon. Someone felled him with a vicious slug to the jaw and then others kicked him about a bit before dragging him to his feet and making sure he knew why he was being roughed up. One of their number, a man with a specific grievance on top of what had happened to Sergeant Green, produced a knife and flashed it upwards across the terrified soldier's face, with cruel results. This shocked the others and when Bruns cried for help they panicked and dragged him through the fence, muffling his cries with their arms and hands, and pushed him off the edge of the cliff face into the quarry. Thinking he may be dead (and they were right), they took to their heels and ran down Langley Vale and back into town, avoiding the main roads. One of them, though, was a civilian working and living in the hospital, as plenty Epsom people did, and it was he that had earlier alerted the others to the short cut and the soldiers going to and from London via Ashtead station. He thought it best to get back into camp unnoticed, but was seen by the guard. When challenged it was his first reaction to say he was 'a friend from the hospital' rather than his name and number, which if he was a soldier he surely would have given, and his conscience led him to mention the victim in the hope they could do something for him.

This is a theory and sadly, ninety years on, very hard to prove or disprove. However, an observer with no vested interest would surely conclude that a chain of events (or something similar) as speculated on above are more likely than a sober man falling down a cliff on a night-time walk he had obviously done several times before and sustaining an injury that one doctor was convinced came from a sharp blade.

To speculate a little further, which group of Epsom men had cause to wish to avenge Sergeant Green's murder more than most? The Epsom police. Who knows how upset and angry some of their number were, firstly about the cold-blooded murder of their comrade and also about the battering they themselves took. Did they also feel betrayed as they sensed which way the wind was blowing as far as punishing the murderer or murderers went? Was the mystery policeman who was talking to the guard a diversion? What was he doing up there in the first place? This is a longer shot and policemen in this country have not traditionally acted in this way – taking the law into their own hands so dramatically – but when they saw the law being manipulated as it was, who knows? Could this have been 'the conduct that needed explaining' that prompted Sergeant Fred Blaydon to seek a private and confidential audience with Sir Nevil Macready? Did he know something that was troubling him in the same way that Green's murder had drilled away at MacMaster's conscience?

Dr Potts from Leatherhead was convinced that Bruns had been attacked before falling or being thrown down the quarry, but Lieutenant Colonel McDermott was not. Or was he? Did he feel that supporting this thesis was just too dangerous to contemplate? It was bad enough trying to keep a lid on things over his soldiers murdering Sergeant Green, but to indicate that now, a few days later, one of his men had been murdered by locals would be provoking a mutiny, lighting a touch-paper that could ignite every other camp, and he did not want this and neither would his superiors nor government. The objective now was to get his countrymen home as quickly and as safely as possible. His country and his guest country were united on this, and nothing could be allowed to hinder that goal.

In the late summer of 2009 I visited the site of Bruns' death. The wide footpath that dissects across Headley Road to Langley Vale is still there. This is Chalk Pit Road. There was another pit, at what was is now known as Pleasure Pit Road, and this is nearer to Ashtead Station. It was known as Pleasure Pit then, but Bruns' death certificate gives place of death as The Chalk Pit, Headley Road (rather than Pleasure Pit, Headley Road), and I therefore believe that the incident took place at Chalk Pit Road.

At the entrance to Chalk Pit Road is a house called The Junipers, and as you walk up there is the RAC on the left-hand side and what was the quarry on the right. The chalk pit has been filled and an equine stables is in its place, although it still dips down considerably. The boundaries to the RAC are the boundaries of the old Woodcote Park Hospital. My first thought was that you would have to be seriously inebriated or disorientated to mistake the chalk pit for the way into the camp especially as – as the inquest established – you would have to bend down and climb between fence slats to reach the edge of the cliff top.

I took a closer look at The Junipers and wondered if the house stood in 1919. The present owner came out and confirmed that it had and that his garden was indeed perched on the old chalk pit. He showed me where his garage was slipping into the refill. I told him my business and he introduced himself as Robert Carr. I didn't say so, but I was mildly taken aback, because according to the inquest it was a Captain Robert Carr who was the first officer to view Bruns' dead body. Although he knew nothing of the events that had taken place ninety years before Mr Carr was able to tell me something about the house that may have some relevance. He was told by elderly residents when he moved to the area some twenty years earlier that The

Junipers was once an off-licence, but also a private, possibly illegal, drinking den frequented by jockeys who did not wish to be seen imbibing in the town's main pubs. He was told that Steve Donoghue, celebrated Derby-winning jockey, was said to be one of its patrons. Donoghue was at his peak in 1919. Further research showed that The Junipers was a pub as well as an off-licence and was owned for many years by Mellersh & Neale, trading as The Reigate Brewery.

Perhaps this is where Fred Bruns spent the missing time after alighting from the train at 11.00pm and when the cries were heard at circa 12.45pm? The walk from Ashtead Station should have taken him about thirty to forty minutes. Did he nip into The Junipers and have a drink before re-entering camp? Was this a habit of Canadian soldiers coming in this way? Were there some locals in there plotting violence and vengeance? Did they following him to the chalk pit footpath and knock him about? Would those signs of a struggle that were absent from the cliff-edge been visible closer to The Junipers? Seeing how seriously they had hurt him, did they drag him under the fence and push him down into the quarry?

What happened on that cliff top and who the mystery people were would have been known to only a few, and they are now certainly dead. It is beyond question that there was at least one man who knew what happened to poor Fred Bruns – the man who alerted the sentry – but my belief is that there were other men who lived out blameless lives in Epsom, perhaps delivering milk or letters, or toiling in the asylums, who knew exactly what happened to Fred Bruns and felt a shiver every time the Canadians in Epsom were mentioned.

If you stand today in front of Thomas Green's imposing headstone in the Epsom Cemetery and look beyond it, to the left and slightly downhill, your eyes will alight on the War

Memorial. Frederick Barton Bruns is on the Roll of Honour, his body lies in the plot beside it, and there is only one thing to distinguish him from the list of other Canadian soldiers who died here, in Epsom hospitals, and are commemorated. He is the only one whose year of death is 1919, the year after the war officially ended. Besides that tiny pointer nobody could have guessed at the unusual tragedy and drama that lay behind that meagre detail.

CHAPTER 16

THE COVER-UP

'It had to be like that'

David Lloyd George was born in 1863 and was the last (and first) Prime Minister to have been Welsh, the last Liberal Prime Minister and the last Prime Minister to be *proven* to have sold honours, including OBEs. Although born in Manchester, due to his father's teaching work being temporarily there, he was the son of very Welsh parents and lived most of his young life in Wales and spoke English as a second language.

His father died when Lloyd George was a toddler and the family moved in with his mother's brother, Richard George, in Llanystumdwy, North Wales. Young David's uncle was an influential figure in the town: a shoemaker by trade, he had a lively interest in politics and was an avid Liberal. He had a burning admiration for Abraham Lincoln, which he passed down to his nephew, who became a solicitor and soon had his own practice operating out of his uncle's house. He gained a reputation as being sympathetic to the underdog. At the same time Lloyd George's political views were developing and hardening and like his uncle he became a Liberal Party activist and campaigned for the party in the 1885 General Election. He was also a Welsh nationalist, resented English power and influence over Wales and supported the banishment of the Church of England from 'his country'.

In 1890 Lloyd George fought a bi-election for the Caernarvon Borough seat and won by a narrow margin. This made him, at twenty-seven years old, the youngest MP in the House of Commons. He soon became a noted figure for his strident and eloquent speeches and attracted much attention (and flak) when he opposed the Second Boer War. In 1906 the Liberals, led by Sir Henry Campbell-Bannerman, won the General Election and the new Prime Minister installed Lloyd George as his Minister for Trade. Then in 1908 new PM Henry Asquith, who had replaced Campbell-Bannerman, promoted him to Chancellor of the Exchequer at the young age for high office of forty-five.

With this new-found power Lloyd George quickly moved to implement some policies that impacted on the issues that had spurred him into public life in the first place. He introduced the old-age pension, pushing the demeaning spectre of the work-house away from the elderly working class, and he increased taxes on the more wealthy to pay for it. Not satisfied, he introduced the first National Insurance scheme and successfully reduced the powers of the House of Lords.

In 1912 he was accused of corruption, having bought Mar-coni shares in the knowledge that the company was to benefit from a large government contract. However, he was able to avoid any prosecutions on a technicality, but his reputation for having high moral standards was tarnished. He also lost some of his following when he failed to support women in their quest for equality and specifically the right to vote, despite having been on side with the suffragettes when in opposition. Women's leaders were deeply unhappy with Lloyd George over this and Emmeline Pankhurst was convicted of organising a bomb attack on his new Walton Heath home in 1913. In another link to Epsom, she appeared in the police court there, which is close to Walton Heath, in the same dock that would conduct some of the Sergeant Green proceedings. One of the other militants who carried out the attack on Lloyd George's

201

home, in which nobody was killed or injured, was Emily Davison, who would soon die under the hooves of the King's horse in the 1913 Epsom Derby and would be processed by the same police doctor and coroner as Sergeant Green.

When it became clear in July 1914 that Britain was likely to go to war with Germany, Lloyd George and three other members of the cabinet informed Asquith that they opposed this and said they would resign. When war was actually declared on 4 August, the other three duly resigned, but Lloyd George was persuaded by the Premier to stay on. He embraced the challenge solidly and was prepared to escalate the war in order to bring a faster victory. In 1915 he became Minister of Munitions and his credentials as an effective wartime politician were established. The following year the coalition government began to question Asquith's leadership abilities in this time of crisis and Lloyd George agreed to work with the Conservatives to remove him. Asquith was toppled and Lloyd George was now in charge of the country and the war effort. His resolve and quick thinking under pressure served him well and these years were his finest. The country generally gave him much credit for Britain's eventual victory over the Triple Alliance and in 1918 they rewarded him by re-electing him, in a landslide, as Prime Minister. He had been a masterful leader in a time of conflict, but how would he fare in peace time? He laid out his stall by famously pronouncing: 'What is our task? To make Britain a fit country for heroes to live.' It rapidly became apparent that this was a pledge on which he was unable to deliver.

The returning war heroes often found that the Britain they came home to was fit for very little. Prices had increased manifold and although wages had jumped in line that was all very well if you had a job that provided pay. Unemployment was rife and disillusionment soon set in. It was not uncommon to see young ex-servicemen selling matches or begging outside railway stations and other public places. Other men, many of whom knew nothing but soldiering, became unemployed or under-employed civilians dodging passing pushbikes on the road rather than flying shrapnel. Life-threatening adversity was exchanged for comparative life-numbing inactivity. These were men who had not made the 'supreme sacrifice' by pure luck, but had lived cheek by jowl with death, terror and horror for many, many months. They had seen things that their worst nightmares could never have conjured up and lost friends and comrades on a gargantuan and sickening scale. They had lived among rats that rolled around the trenches, plump on the blood and gristle of the dead. They endured each day in the knowledge that it could be their last, their fates likely to be sealed by a sniper's bullet, a German bayonet, by being blown to bits, buried alive, diseased, or even by firing squad if they demonstrated 'cowardice'. They came home to see their fallen comrades deservedly celebrated, revered and remembered, but themselves largely ignored and forgotten. They shared a trauma like no other and these men clammed up and rarely spoke of their experiences again.

In the early months of 1919 industrial unrest spread across Britain at the same time and with the same velocity as the deadly influenza. There were strikes by cotton workers in Lancashire, miners nationally, tube workers in London and many others all over. In Glasgow a general strike led to rioting on the streets and clashes between police and demonstrators. However, the potential dispute and militancy that struck most fear into David Lloyd George's heart came from the police themselves. During 1918 and 1919 they became increasingly disenchanted and were not only unhappy with their lot (they were paid the same as an agricultural labourer or an unskilled worker), but they were uneasy with the job of forcibly quelling labour unrest when called upon to do so. Their loyalty was shifting from the state to the people and it terrified the Prime Minister. On 31 August 1918 the police force struck for the day and 2,000 officers marched from Scotland Yard to Tower Hill to press demands for more pay and the reinstatement of a man dismissed for his 'political' activities. The government went into negotiation, but it would be some time before differences would be resolved and any degree of trust restored.

'Unless this mutiny of the guardians of order is quelled,' Lloyd George told the Conservative leader Andrew Bonar Law in private, 'the whole fabric of law may disappear. We will take any steps, however grave, to establish the authority of social order.' He further warned that unless those steps were taken there would be revolution in the country before 'twelve months are past'.

The grave measures that Lloyd George was probably contemplating included using the army to maintain law and order, but this was the same army that had been decimated and traumatised in the war that had just ended. Indeed there was a gathering school of thought that should the police be successful in their fight for trade union membership, then the military would follow suit. This was no idle musing as soldiers had already mutinied at Calais and Boulogne, demanding swift demobilisation, and the Grenadier Guards had openly declared that they would refuse any orders to disperse striking policemen.

In May of 1919 the Government refused to recognise a police trade union and introduced a new Police Bill that would ban officers from becoming trade union members, but sweetened its stand by offering a substantial pay rise and back pay, which split the ranks. The prospect of losing secure employment and accrued pension horrified many serving officers, especially at a time when they saw all around them people struggling for work. The Government offer and the improved wages killed off the unionisation initiative, but bad feeling abounded, and this was the fragile state of affairs between Government and the police force that faced Lloyd George when the Sergeant Green affair was brought to his attention in June 1919. (Two months later when hundreds of officers did still strike they were dismissed, lost all their pension rights and were banished to the economic wilderness. No Epsom police officers chose to take part in the industrial action.)

In fact, the murder of Sergeant Green had the potential to ignite three of the most vexing issues facing Prime Minister Lloyd George that summer. If the state did not secure justice for Sergeant Green, then he risked the explosive ire of a disenchanted and angry police force. If the state were heavy handed in its treatment of the Canadian soldiers, then in the short term further and more serious riots would be likely and the lawlessness could spread to British soldiers and ex-soldiers. If the state allowed the legal process to take its proper and normal course then serious damage could be done to Anglo-Canadian relations at the highest level.

This last factor was uppermost in the statesman's mind. The war had strengthened his belief in the importance of the Commonwealth and Empire to Britain and he was keenly aware of the great debt owed to countries such as Canada, Australia, New Zealand, South Africa and India for their loyalty to Britain in its time of need. He was also aware of their growing moods of independence in these dominions and introspection about the heavy sacrifices they had just made for a little island thousands of miles away from them in a war they did not start and one that barely concerned them.

'The strength and the power of every land has been drained,' Lloyd George said. 'All have bled at every vein, and this restlessness we see everywhere is the fever of anaemia.'

With this in mind it was Lloyd George's idea to organise a Royal Tour by Edward, Prince of Wales, son of King George V. The popular prince's task was to visit these countries, starting with Canada, to extend Britain's grateful sentiments and strengthen the bonds that still existed, but were fraying. The Prince was an obvious choice to undertake Lloyd George's vision. He was a soldier who had served with the Grenadier Guards and while in France had been attached to the Canadian Corps.

In *A King's Story: The Memoirs of H.R.H. the Duke of Windsor K.G.*, published in 1951, Edward himself describes the motivations for the Royal Tour of the Dominions starting in August 1919 and the following extract illuminates the thinking of the time and why Sergeant Green's murder may have shot up the political agenda and was dealt with so quickly and decisively:

> At the same time the Prime Minister, David Lloyd George, who still had almost dictatorial powers, also had ideas for my employment in the Empire beyond the seas. The last contingents of the Dominion and Colonial troops, which had fought in Europe and the Middle East, were on their way home; and he was anxious that, before the ardour of wartime comradeship had wholly cooled, I should set forth at once on a series of tours to thank the various countries of the British Commonwealth, on my father's behalf, for their contributions to the war. Everywhere the vaunted bonds of Empire showed signs of weakening. India was seething. In Canada, the resistance of the French Canadians to wartime conscription had left an ugly lesion among the people. Australia resounded to radical talk and labour troubles. South Africa had its racial differences. Lloyd George, acutely sensitive to the stirrings of the popular

mind, realised that the common people everywhere were fatigued by war and puzzled and disturbed by the new economic forces that were tearing away the foundations of their lives. As he once explained to me, the appearance of the popular Prince of Wales in far corners of the Empire might do more to calm the discord than half a dozen solemn Imperial Conferences.

My father quickly approved the project. These overseas excursions, he reasoned, would in any case provide me with a comprehensive view of the different peoples and conditions of his vast realm while affording his subjects the opportunity of seeing their next King. The Canadian Government having already approached him with the proposal that I should visit Canada that coming summer, it was decided I should do so in August 1919.

The tour was a major civil service undertaking and planning began in earnest in January of 1919 with a target sailing date of 5 August 1919. Buckingham Palace, the Admiralty, the War Office, the Home Office, Scotland Yard and the various embassies and High Commissions would all have had to be co-ordinated and involved. Decisions were being taken at speed on who Edward would meet and who he wouldn't and on what he would say and what he would not.

When Lloyd George was told about the murder of Sergeant Green at Epsom, probably by Winston Churchill, his Secretary of State for War, sometime on 19 or 20 June, he was likely to have been mortified. The appearance of the 'popular Prince of Wales' in Canada in only a few weeks' time, when his country was possibly executing one or more of their soldiers after they had sacrificed so much, did not bear contemplation. Regardless of the rights and wrongs of the situation Lloyd George feared that the Canadian people would not tolerate the state killing of any of their subjects after losing so many men in his country's defence. They would want to know why the hell those men were still in England seven months after the end of the war.

207

The Prince may get jeered, or worse. The great and the good of Canada may refuse to shake his hand.

Not only could it unravel the strategy so clearly described by Edward, Prince of Wales, but there was a real risk that this not only could become a major political issue between the United Kingdom and Canada but could lead to Canada leaving the Commonwealth. If Canada did, who knows how other countries would react? Sensational, it may appear, but the killing of a country bobby by some rampant soldiers had the capacity to ignite and accelerate the disintegration of the mighty British Empire.

Faced with these myriad undesirable scenarios that the handling of Sergeant Green's death could trigger, Lloyd George would have had no doubt that intervention and operation from the highest level (himself) was the safest way forward. Britain's lauded legal system could not be allowed to take its natural course, but at the same time police sensibilities would have to be catered for. He was used to acting unilaterally, making uncomfortable decisions and acting on them, and circumventing the machinery of government. This political style had stood him in good stead over the last three years and he would have quickly formulated in his mind the outcomes the country desired over the Epsom Riot. He would have communicated these informally to his trusted cabal of advisers and lieutenants and left it to them to chart the best course to achieve those outcomes. He had managed the war, and he was now determined to manage the peace. He would not allow the death of a small-town policeman, however tragic, to jeopardise that. He would not have hesitated in his belief as what needed to be done and he expected his people to execute it thoroughly. As he famously once said, 'There is nothing so fatal to character as half-finished tasks.'

Prime Minister Lloyd George, with his 'almost dictatorial powers', would have called the key players to meet him, to present his strategy, and these visitors would certainly have included Winston Churchill as Secretary of State for War, Sir Nevil Macready, Commissioner of the Metropolitan Police and Edward Shortt, the Home Secretary. It is possible that Lord Stamfordham, Private Secretary to the King and heavily involved in Edward's upcoming tour, was also involved, being the conduit between the Royal Family, the politicians and often the press. The Canadian High Commissioner would likely have been party to the discussions too.

Working backwards from what actually happened it appears to me that Lloyd George's desired outcomes were as follows:

1   The legal process surrounding the death was to be accelerated and tightly managed.
2   No charges of murder were to be brought under any circumstances.
3   The word 'murder' was not even to enter the equation.
4   No one Canadian was to become the focus of the prosecution.
5   Some 'guilty parties' were to be charged, tried and sentenced and sentences served in the quickest possible time. Ideally the 'guilty parties' were to be back in their home country within a few months, not years.
6   Bearing all this in mind, the legal system was not to be seen to have been compromised or manipulated and the police and the public generally were to feel that justice had been done.
7   Public opinion was not to be stoked and the media controlled in the handling of the story.
8   Thomas Green's sacrifice and memory was to be respected and acknowledged, but he was not to be allowed to become

a focus or national hero in the eyes of the media and the public, which would risk scrutiny of the case.

A tall order by anybody's standards, but remarkably achieved.

The cumulative effect of all of the evidence and unanswered questions that point to a covering up and an engineering of the events surrounding Sergeant Green's death is powerful. What happened to Frederick Bruns only strengthens the case. If the aftermath of Sergeant Green's killing was tightly managed and manipulated, as it most certainly was, then Frederick Bruns' mysterious death was positively buried. Even if there are logical answers to some of the following unanswered questions and others are red herrings, they cannot *all* be explained as such. In my mind the key questions are these:

The Riot

Why did the army not respond to the pleas for help from the police on the morning of 18 June 1919, when the risk of further disorder was very high?

Why was Sir Nevil Macready's complaint of 'culpable negligence' against the army not acted on and why did Sir Nevil choose not to pursue the matter?

What happened to the 'searching investigation' promised by Winston Churchill?

Who was the man who was 'very seriously injured' that the Canadian authorities referred to in their first statement on the riot? Was he one of the men picked out and arrested? If not, what happened to him?

The Investigation

Did Allan MacMaster really say 'We are not *manslaughterers*'? Or did whoever took the statement insert this instead of 'murderers' – his more believable response?

Why did Inspector Ferrier not interview Eddie Lapointe for some days after discovering that he may have had vital information about the murder of Sergeant Green?

When Eddie Lapointe's eventual statement did not tally with that of William Lloyd why was further pressure not applied to both men to establish the truth?

Why were statements not taken from the members of the Beauchamp/Maidment household, who had Canadian soldiers in their house saying they had just killed a policeman?

Why were these same witnesses not asked to try and identify these men at the camp, as they had obviously seen them very clearly and would have been motivated to do so?

Why was Charles Polhill not asked to try and identify the Canadian soldiers who carried Thomas Green into his house, and were there for some time, as they could have shed more light on events?

Why was no serious pressure applied to the Canadian officer Major James Ross, who was there or thereabouts during the riot, to identify or confirm Sergeant Green's assailant(s)?

In the report submitted by Regional Superintendent Boxhall he asks that Inspector Ferrier be officially commended for his handling of a case that 'bristled with difficulties'. To what difficulties is he referring?

Why were Private McDonald and Driver Veinot not interviewed or called as witnesses? They were the reason for the riot. They were sprung from the police cells. They were most certainly present and not spoken to.

The Inquest

At the first inquest, why were proceedings rushed so as a death certificate could be quickly issued and Sergeant Green buried? The coroner himself stated this to explain why the inquest was being held, even though police investigation was ongoing. This first inquest was held whilst Sergeant Green was still lying in the Infirmary.

The Trial

Why were Gervase Poirier's and Herbert Tait's stories about becoming accidentally involved in the riot so readily believed?

Why were such a limited amount of police witnesses called to testify at the trial? Over a dozen police officers were fighting the Canadians – they and others would have been witness to what went on inside the police station too, yet only Inspector Pawley and PC Rose were called.

Why was Sergeant Shuttleworth not called? He thought he could identify one rioter and was with the dying Sergeant Green in Polhill's house.

What was defence counsel getting at when he said, 'the proper steps were never taken to find the real miscreants'?

Why was the fact that some of the defendants were suffering from venereal diseases not deemed relevant or revealed at trial?

Why was Justice Darling's comment that all the men had seen action and may not understand our rules allowed to go unchecked?

Why did the media not protest at the lax sentences and time served by the men convicted of the rioting that led to Sergeant Green's death?

Why did the Home Secretary announce release dates in the future for the Canadian prisoners when some of them were already back in Canada, or on their way back there?

Frederick Bruns

Why was the inquest held on a Saturday and only forty-eight hours after the discovery of the body?

Why was the case handled by Surrey Constabulary when it was Metropolitan Police officers (Kersey and Rose) who attended the scene?

Who was Mabel May, how did the investigators know she existed and how did they find her?

Why were ticket collectors at Ashtead not consulted to ask whether Bruns did alight from the train and whether he was accompanied or not?

Who was the policeman that Private Frank Durrance was talking to when on guard duty? Why wasn't he traced and called to the inquest?

Who was the soldier that Durrance saw coming through the hedge? Why did he say he 'was a friend from the hospital' rather than give military name and number? Why was there no attempt to identify him and bring him to the inquest?

What was the incised wound running from the tip of Bruns' nose up to his forehead that concerned Dr Potts so?

When the jury enquired about an adjournment so the corporal of the guard and the mysterious soldier could be brought before the court why was not it granted, even if only for the former?

What were Bruns' parents told?

Were the American authorities notified about the suspicious death of one of their citizens?

Where did the details of this inquest go? Why are records missing from the Surrey Coroner's Office and Surrey Archives?

The Confession

What was Allan MacMaster referring to in his 1929 confession when he said he was pardoned by Edward, Prince of Wales?

There is no official record of this, but it is an oddly specific thing to say, even if his memory was not perfect.

Why did Scotland Yard not want to pursue MacMaster's confession at all?

When Allan MacMaster confessed to the murder of Sergeant Green in 1929 why were Thomas Green's next of kin not informed?

The Aftermath

What was Sergeant Blaydon's information on the 'conduct of some officers' he wished to discuss with Sir Nevil Macready, and only him? Could it have been connected to the Frederick Bruns case?

Why did Sir Nevil Macready stipulate that any correspondence on the Epsom Riot any time in the future should be directed only to him?

Why do Allan MacMaster's official discharge papers have 'Misconduct' blacked out and replaced by 'Demobilisation'?

Why did Sergeant Green not receive a posthumous award for gallantry, as most Met officers killed on duty have?

Why does the inscription on Sergeant Green's tombstone not mention his being killed, and how and by whom? Instead it refers vaguely 'to finding death in the path of duty'.

Why did Thomas Green's daughters Lily and Nellie choose to emigrate and go to Canada of all places, and so soon after their father's murder?

Why has this case – the only instance where a policeman has been killed defending his own police station on the British mainland *ever* – received such little publicity over the last ninety years?

Why did Epsom wait ninety years before officially acknowledging the town's station sergeant as a hero, with a plaque?

Why does the Epsom Riot case not warrant a mention in the memoirs or biographies of Justice Darling, Sir Richard Muir, David Lloyd George, Sir Winston Churchill, Lord Rosebery or Inspector Ferrier, or in the *Chronicles of the 20th Century*?

Why did Sir Nevil Macready downgrade the murder in his *Report of the Commissioner of the Police of the Metropolis for the year 1919*, as seen below?

> It is satisfactory to note that regrettable incidents, which oc-
> curred from time to time during the War, arising out of the
> arrests of soldiers by the Police, have practically died out, and
> Police authority has been reasserted throughout the Metropolis.
> A serious case of the kind which came to notice was the unfor-
> tunate riot at Epsom on the 17th June, 1919, when Canadian
> soldiers attacked the police station, with the result that a police
> constable lost his life.

According to Macready the riot was *unfortunate*. Nobody was *killed* or *murdered* and a police *constable* not a station sergeant lost his life. Sound familiar?

Finally, when Edward Shortland first developed his conspiracy theory in relation to Sergeant Green's death he put it to Sir Robert Mark, the famous and well-regarded Metropolitan Police Commissioner between 1972 and 1977. Mark was not familiar with the case, but listened intently to the background, and when asked by Shortland if he thought a cover up had taken place he said firmly, 'Of course. It had to be like that.'

A further item of evidence emerged during the research of this book that I believe underpins the whole high-level conspiracy theory. Allan MacMaster, in his confession, claimed he had been pardoned by Edward, Prince of Wales, but this was the only reference such a pardon anywhere in all the viewed published sources. It certainly was not announced to the press if it had taken place. Why would a pardon be granted? No new evidence had emerged or been presented to suggest these men were not guilty of rioting. An appeal had just failed, remember. And if for some reason there was a pardon, why would it be granted by Edward and not the King? On first impressions, then, one could imagine that this statement was plucked from somewhere by a drunken and possibly delusional MacMaster.

On contacting the Royal Archives in 2009 I was told that they could find no record of Edward, Prince of Wales or any member of the Royal Family granting a pardon to any Canadian soldiers. But – and this is a crucial but – they *did* find an index reference in King George V's private secretary's diary to correspondence between his office and General Sir Richard Turner, Chief of the Canadian General Staff, entitled 'Canadian Riot at Epsom Police Station'. Unfortunately, but almost predictably, all actual correspondence relating to this index reference has been lost. That is a shame. Nevertheless, here is a link between the Canadian riot and the Royal Family. Here is proof that there was a connection between the Crown and the imprisoned soldiers. We don't know definitively what that connection was, but there *was* a connection when there was no reason why there should have been. The correspondence was dated just before Edward's tour was to commence. The link between the tour, the King and Edward, Prince of Wales was Prime Minister Lloyd George. And there we have the chain.

It is likely that MacMaster was almost correct and had some limited knowledge of the machinations that were going on around the case. Lloyd George most likely instructed Edward (with the King's blessing) to inform the Canadian Government when he arrived in Canada that the prisoners would be released within a matter of weeks. It was a pardon by any other name and was probably among a selection of goodwill offerings that the Prince had at his disposal. Something happened along these lines, as what other legal or procedural trigger was there for the men to be released before half of their sentence was served?

One can imagine the scene as MacMaster landed back on Canadian soil. Signing his discharge papers, he spots the stamp DISHONOURABLY DISCHARGED and says, 'Oh no you don't. I've been pardoned, I have. By no less than the Prince of Wales, you know. You can scrub that off for a start.'

Puzzled officials set off a trail of phone calls up the military tree until, inexplicably to them, they are told to scrub it out and stamp DEMOBILISED instead.

'You should avoid any intimacy'

As I researched and wrote this book I became convinced that there was a cover-up locally, as well as nationally, and of a different nature. I felt from the beginning that it was curious that there was no real explanation as to what the fight in The Rifleman that sparked the riot was about. Granted, brawls between the Canadians and the Epsom men had been frequent, and this week in particular happening almost every night, but seeing that this punch-up was so pivotal, so important to what happened next, it is odd that a journalist would not have endeavoured to find out more. Some papers reported that the initial row was over an Epsom man insulting a Canadian sergeant and his wife and this was repeated in many places. Others said it was a fight between two Canadians with no mention of a woman. Elsewhere it was merely another brawl between the 'Imperials and the Canadians', with no specific spark.

On close inspection, one of Inspector Pawley's statements (held at The National Archives in Kew) tantalisingly touches on something else. Easy to miss is the line where he recalls: 'Private McDonald said – I will fucking kill him – referring to the man Williams.'

The inference from this is that the initial fisticuffs were between McDonald and 'the man Williams', who was most likely an Epsom man. The way Pawley refers to Williams is as if the reader should know who he is, yet there is no other mention of him anywhere else. Could there have been a deliberate decision to leave Williams out of the statements of the arresting officers (and Pawley didn't quite manage it completely), and if so, why?

My belief is that there is a strong possibility that Williams is the man referred to in the introduction of this book – the man mentioned by the elderly gentleman to me in The Marquis of Granby in the 1980s. He said, 'but I knew the man who started it', and that he had stormed into The Rifleman and whacked the Canadian soldier he believed had been playing around with his wife or girlfriend whilst he had been risking life, limb and sanity in the trenches of France. The reason to leave the motive for the fight and Williams' name out of the statements (and therefore records) could have been to protect the honour and good name of the lady concerned. Remember how the Epsom police had taken it upon themselves to become the moral guardians of the town's womenfolk when the Australians first turned up in Epsom in 1915? If Williams had been named, that would have inevitably led reporters to him and the reason for his ire. Those reasons, in turn, could have led to a whole new can of worms being opened – a can of worms that was capable of igniting further trouble in the town and offending the nation's moralistic sensibilities.

The animosity felt by the returning Tommies towards the Canadians was clearly a talking point and a serious issue. Magistrate Dorset spoke for many when he asked PC Percy Taylor why there was so much trouble between the two sets of men. Taylor could not offer any explanation except the slightly biased claim that the Canadians were 'bent on trouble'.

Sergeant Blaydon, you may recall, said with understatement that there was a bit of feeling between the Imperials and the Canadians. I suspect he knew what that feeling was, but could hardly have said something along the lines of, 'Well sir, the Epsom men have come home from overseas to find that the Canadians have been carrying on with their wives, girlfriends and sisters … and they don't like it.'

I am sure that the issue was even more serious than the Epsom men's understandable wrath at the amorous relation-ships that had been formed between the Canadians and the Epsom womenfolk. It stands to reason that some of these women, at least, would have been infected with venereal disease and it was this unpalatable fact, which could not be spoken, revealed or discussed, that was eating away at some of the returning Tommies. This is not a fanciful theory aired for the sake of sensationalism, but one that is a logical conclusion to draw from the available facts.

Venereal disease had been a blight on armies for centuries, but in the immediate prude and blinkered post-Victorian era it was a disease that bestowed great shame and secrecy on its sufferer ... soldier or civilian. Even before a soldier was sent overseas he was likely to come into contact with prostitutes, for wherever there was a garrison town there would be prostitutes and brothels, and using them became almost a rite of passage for many young men. In this period of our history it is generally acknowledged that more young men lost their virginities to prostitutes than those who didn't.

The scale of the problem in the First World War has seldom been fully acknowledged or discussed, but Lord Kitchener was certainly tuned into the potential risk when he had printed up the millions of guidelines issued to all soldiers at the start of the war and ordered to be kept in their pay book:

You are ordered abroad as a soldier of the King to help our French comrades against the invasion of a common Enemy.

Remember that the honour of the British Army depends on your individual conduct.

You are sure to meet with a welcome and to be trusted; your conduct must justify that welcome and trust. Your duty cannot be done unless your health is sound.

So keep constantly on your guard against any excesses.

In this new experience you may find temptations both in wine and women. You must entirely resist both temptations, and, while treating all women with perfect courtesy, you should avoid any intimacy.

221

Do your duty bravely.
Fear God.
Honour the King.

Kitchener,
Field-Marshal.

The evidence shows that a significant percentage of those rookie soldiers duly ignored Kitchener's orders. Twenty-four per thousand of British troops would be admitted to hospital suffering from venereal disease at some point during the war. The ratio was considerably higher among Australian and New Zealand soldiers, with an incredible 130 soldiers per 1,000. However, the Canadian soldiers had the worst rate of them all, with an eye-watering 160 per 1,000, or 16 per cent of all serving troops. The British Army reported 416,891 hospital admissions for venereal disease during the war, and a stay in hospital averaged some 50 days for a soldier with syphilis. This resulted in a massive debilitating effect on an army's strength and the commanders did whatever they could to stop the men consorting with prostitutes and passing infections on. Medical officers were constantly warning, threatening and persuading the troops about their sexual behaviour, but it was a losing battle, as wherever there were soldiers there would be prostitutes. Vigilant medical officers were known to line the men up and get them to drop their trousers and shorts and walk along the line lifting their penises with a stick and looking beneath for tell-tale sores.

Men suffering with syphilis or gonorrhoea were obliged to declare it and, when they did, having the disease was classified as a self-inflicted wound and their pay was duly docked. If they were married men this meant that pay allotted to their wives also suffered and they would have some explaining to do. Failing to declare venereal disease was an offence under military law and carried a penalty of up to two years' imprisonment with hard labour. Even so, soldiers were reluctant to declare being infected because not only would they suffer financial penalties and humiliating and painful treatments (such as communal disinfecting and urethral injections), but they would endure acute embarrassment and shame.

Indeed, some historians state that the blues uniform worn by many of the convalescents at Woodcote Hospital was to indicate that the man who wore them was a venereal disease case and as such could be identified by the public. It is suggested that they were not allowed out of the hospital to socialise to the same extent as their khaki-clad comrades. As we have seen, this was not strictly the case at Epsom. We know that some of the men in khaki had venereal disease and some of the men in blues did not. We also know that soldiers in blues were often out and about in town. What is pretty clear too, whatever the code, was that the Epsom population at large was not aware of such mores and had no idea of the scale of venereal disease in their midst.

Philip Gibbs, a respected war correspondent for the *Daily Telegraph*, wrote the following passage in 1920:

Another evil of the abnormal life of war sowed the seeds of insanity in the brains of men not strong enough to resist it. Sexually they were starved. For months they lived out of the sight and presence of women. But they came back into villages or towns where they were tempted by any poor slut who winked at them and infected them with illness. Men went to hospital with venereal disease in appalling numbers. Boys were ruined and poisoned for life. Future generations will pay the price of war not only in poverty and by the loss of the unborn children of the boys who died, but by an enfeebled stock and the heritage of insanity.

223

> The Prime Minister said one day, 'The world is suffering from shell-shock.' That was true. But it suffered also from the symptoms of all that illness which comes from syphilis, whose breeding-ground is war.

The ratio of Canadian soldiers infected with venereal disease at Woodcote camp would have been far higher still than sixteen per cent, as this was one of the hospitals where men suffering from gonorrhoea or syphilis would be sent. Historian Desmond Morton believes that an average of one in nine Canadian soldiers overseas was infected. Of the eight soldiers charged in connection with the Epsom Riot, four of them were sufferers, and an estimate of fifty per cent of the patients in Woodcote camp having some form of sexually transmitted disease would not be extreme. Even if it were only 30 per cent, this would constitute some 1,200 men. Interestingly, Sir Nevil Macready, when appraising the Home Office of the situation just after the riot, said that the Woodcote Hospital was 'mainly for venereal cases'.

A leader in *The Times* on 20 June 1919 that discussed 'The Epsom Outbreak' and its causes was the only media to refer to the sexual disease element in the whole affair and then in the most cryptic terms that only those familiar with the detail would grasp:

> On the other hand, we are bound to say that we have heard an account of troops responsible for the Epsom outbreak which puts quite a different complexion on it. According to this account, they are convalescents whom the Canadian Government refuse to repatriate until they are cured of the ills from which they are suffering. We do not know what truth there may be in this version, but the Canadian authorities had much better know what is being said. They may be sure that it will not dim British recognition of the military deeds of the

Canadian forces, which are among the imperishable memories of the war.

If there was any truth in this information that had come to *The Times*' attention (and it was then the newspaper of record and not disposed to scurrilous speculation or mischief-making) then there is the scenario that by the time of the riot nearly *all* of the convalescents at Woodcote Park were suffering from a venereal disease.

In the following day's newspaper George McL Brown of the Canadian Pacific Railway Company responded to the editorial in a long letter. He made a strong case for the extenuating circumstances faced by the Canadians with the delays they were experiencing in getting demobilised, especially in comparison to British and American troops. He also made the point that Canadian troops, unlike British Tommies, had not had the luxury of leave and time with their families in four years. In his final paragraph he rejected the contention about disease playing a part. It was an extraordinary public debate about an unmentionable illness that indeed was never mentioned:

'I have made some enquiry through official channels,' wrote Mr Brown:

> as to the suggestion contained in the final paragraph of your leading article, and am assured that the implication is without foundation – that the soldiers who took part in the deplorable Epsom incident were not of that unfortunate number suffering from ills to which you refer, which in any event they did not bring with them from Canada.

The official channels that gave Brown his assurance were either ignorant or lying. Of the men who were initially arrested half of them *were* being treated for a sexually transmitted disease. But he was right about one thing – the soldiers did not bring the disease with them from Canada.

The commander of the venereal disease hospital at Witley made the following comments about the 'venereals', which, bearing in mind that many were moved on to Woodcote Park after the Witley riot, are prescient:

> Those who have not dealt with Venereal patients in large numbers find it difficult to understand their mental attitude. They feel they are repulsive to themselves and to others. Where confined they suffer from great depression and become exceedingly sensitive. This leads easily to disorderly outbreaks, which tend to relieve the monotony and to satisfy the grudge the soldier always feels towards the authorities when his pay is restricted and his normal liberty interfered with.

So, we have a town of some 20,000 people, half of whom would have been women. Perhaps a quarter of these 10,000 women would have been of a similar age to the young Canadian soldiers. Most of the eligible and attached local men for these young women would have been absent, but in their place were up to 4,000 'exotic' males with self-confidence, spending money and some glamour. A quarter of those men, at least, were infected with venereal disease. It is a fact that many relationships were formed between the Epsom women and the Canadians – witness the scenes at Epsom Railway Station when a contingent of soldiers returned to the Front. It defies common sense to believe, therefore, that no Epsom women became infected by the men. If, say, just 20 per cent of those 2,500 available women had liaisons with Canadians, that would total 500 women. If 20 per cent of them became infected that would translate to 100 women. If a third of them were married or in relationships before the war that would have meant thirty partnerships doomed, forever broken or under extreme pressure due to the toxic secret of syphilis residing inside the four walls with them. The real figure is likely to have been far higher.

The local press records some of the instances of these fatally damaged relationships that made the courts. In March 1919 an Epsom man divorced his wife and recounted how when he returned from the Front he had to actually go to the Woodcote camp to try and persuade his spouse to come home. A month or so later another case detailed a lady who was refused entry to the camp whilst holding a baby and pleading to see her 'husband'. She was later taken into custody at Epsom after she was found sleeping in Rosebery Park with the baby. Another poor woman, Martha McCormack, was found lying in a wood in Ashtead. She was a widow, and instead of helping her, the police charged her with the theft of the blanket with which she was keeping herself warm. The blanket was marked Woodcote Park Convalescent Hospital.

The newspaper correspondents were in no doubt where the blame lay: in reporting the case in June of 1919 of Edward Tuck, who divorced his wife because of her liaison with a Lieutenant Lewis of the Canadian forces, they headlined the article WICKED WIFE. Some humour was to be had in these desperate circumstances and one report that would have brought a smile to most, except those directly involved, was the divorce hearing of Ethel Thorpe and her husband Wilfred. Ethel was divorcing Wilfred for his alleged infidelity and the key to her case was a letter she received from him when he was at the Front. When she opened the envelope, the letter was headed 'Dear Rosie ...'

Gonorrhoea and syphilis were well established in civilian society too at this time, but had nowhere near the visibility that military venereal disease did. Syphilis, especially, was the great shame and the great unmentioned and as such has eluded official statistics and history to a large extent. Its symptoms

227

often mimicked those of other diseases and complaints and it is these other diseases that doctors often recorded on medical files and death certificates. Just as sexual intercourse does not confine itself to only certain strata of society, neither did syphilis, although contact with prostitutes was the largest common denominator. A Royal Commission on Venereal Diseases was set up in 1913 and concluded that ten per cent of the population would contract or had suffered from syphilis. Yet few people ever knew anyone that had it – spouses deceived spouses, patients deceived doctors and sufferers deceived themselves. There were no mentions in newspaper and magazines or public information campaigns. This was an era where the populace did not acknowledge having sex, let alone a disease that could emanate from it.

To make matters worse, there was no cure. That did not come along until Alexander Fleming discovered that penicillin had curative properties for sexual infections a few decades later. Earlier treatments included the ingestion of arsenic and mercury and deep disinfecting of the reproductive organs. Sometimes, with syphilis, after the initial outbreak the condition could lay dormant for years, but in other instances would progress into the nervous system and brain and cause death. It is now believed that such notables as Napoleon Bonaparte, Adolf Hitler, Vincent Van Gogh and Al Capone all had the disease, plus poor old Christopher Columbus, who in addition has had blame heaped on him from bringing the virus into Europe in the first place.

One can only imagine the private trauma of an Epsom wife awaiting her husband's return from the war knowing she was carrying syphilis. What does she do? Tell him when he gets home? Refuse him sex until she believes she is clear? Break the relationship up to avoid the truth being discovered? Commit suicide? The first option, however frightening and difficult, would likely be the most common, and it could have been those cruelly enlightened husbands dealing with that most hurtful revelation that were careering around Epsom with a burning hatred for the Canadians, unable to reveal even to their closest friends exactly why, and leading and whipping up the aggression.

Of course, British Tommies were not immune from availing themselves of prostitutes behind the lines in France, and the infection of British troops was a massive problem too. The difference was that, unlike the Canadians in Epsom, they were not all bunched together (as carriers) in one place and for a length of time. Nevertheless, there would be infected men coming home from war laden with dread and despair over facing their wives with their disease. Some would have been in the surreal situation of returning to partners who were nursing exactly the same fears. They would have steered a wide berth of each other, each one not knowing why, but at the same time, temporarily at least, relieved.

Bearing all this in mind, the comments made to me by the elderly gentleman in The Marquis of Granby nearly thirty years ago start to make sense.

'Of course, there was a lot more to it,' he had said, and by way of explanation added, 'well, the Canadians, you know, bit careless … you know …'

The man Williams could have been one of those embittered husbands nursing this dark secret that was torturing his mind when he burst through The Rifleman doors and struck Private John Harding Allan McDonald. We simply do not know, but the chances are that someone living does. There would have been some Epsom people who would have known the full story – the hidden truth – behind the fight in The Rifleman and not all of them would have kept it to themselves. Local secrets may have been passed down from one generation to the next and the airing of this theory in this book may prompt an elderly resident or ex-resident of Epsom to solve the mystery for us. One thing we do know though, from military records, is that Private John McDonald was without a shadow of a doubt a carrier of syphilis about town.

EPILOGUE

The Girls

It was not three years since their father's death, or four months following their mother's, when Lily and Nellie, aged twenty-one and twenty respectively, boarded the Canadian Pacific liner *Corsican* on a voyage to their new life. It was one of the last trips the grand liner would make, as only a few months later it was wrecked off Cape Race near Newfoundland. The sisters declared $250 each to the immigration authorities when they arrived in April 1922 and put down the home of Mrs Charles H Stock, a friend, as their destination in Toronto. As their next of kin they named their mother's brother William Bowers Card, now living in the High Street, Addlestone, Surrey. What drove their decision to get up and go, especially to Canada, is a matter of conjecture. Bearing in mind that their mother had only been dead weeks when they left it is likely that it was something that the girls had been planning between them and their mother encouraging. Epsom held fresh and painful memories and they were young enough to start new lives without being treated with well-intentioned sympathy and pity as the girls whose father was murdered by the Canadians. Yet one would have expected, bearing in mind that their father had died at the hands of murderous Canadians, that this would not be their first-choice destination. However, they did have family out there, and perhaps that overruled any bitterness they held. Thomas's brothers William and Edgar (the former Met policeman) had emigrated earlier and were now well established.

It may also have been that despite what happened to their father one or both of the girls were, like many of the young women of Epsom, enamoured of the Canadians as a race. They may have even been courted by some. Lily, as I have suggested, may have been the 'Lil' mentioned by James Connors as being his sweetheart. And if she was and thought she was sailing to the land he spoke of so romantically, she would have had no idea that he had died pitifully in a London hospital and was never able to return home.

In Epsom there was a persistent rumour and belief that the Green girls' emigration to Canada was part of a bigger picture and I was told this as 'fact' on several occasions down the years. It was repeated to me in 2009 by a neighbour in Lower Court Road who had lived there for eighty-five years and whose parents were close to Thomas, Lilian and the girls. The story was that the Canadian government paid for and arranged their new life in Canada as recompense for its countrymen killing their father. It was a rumour that moved Lily to write from Canada to the *Epsom & Ewell Herald* in 1966 and refute. Why she felt compelled to do so forty-three years after the event is a mystery. She wrote that the reason they went to Canada was simply that they had family and friends there and wanted to go, and there was no more to it. Gordon Kirkham, grandson of Thomas Green and son of Nellie, told the author that he does not believe there was any help received from the Canadian government in his mother's and aunt's migration and the subject was never discussed with him.

Lily and Nellie set up home together in Toronto City and in 1923 were working together as sales assistants in Simpson's, a large department store. Once they gained their confidence the girls pursued their own careers and Nellie, among other things, worked for a milliner at John C Green & Company and later she became a manageress for the Women's Bakery store in New Toronto. In October of their first full year as Canadians Nellie married Richard Kirkham and Lily was a witness at the wedding. Richard was an émigré too, having arrived a decade earlier from Lancashire. They set up home in Third Avenue, New Toronto, which lay along the Lake Ontario shoreline. Richard worked for the Canadian National Railways and the couple raised two children, Gordon and Hazel.

Gordon Kirkham is alive and well and living in Victoria, British Columbia. He never met his grandfather, but felt he knew him well from the fond recollections of his mother and aunt. Their grief about his tragic demise has been transmitted to him. He relayed to the author an early story that his mother told him that gives us a taste of Thomas Green's character: the young Nellie had been in school (probably in Putney) when she was struck very hard across the knuckles by a teacher with a ruler. It left a mark and when at home that evening she tried to cover one hand with another at the dinner table to conceal the wheal. Her father asked her to move her hand and seeing the red patch asked how she it had come about. The next day when Nellie was at her desk in school she was confounded to see her father's large, uniformed frame appear at the classroom door. He walked in and admonished the teacher in front of all the children. 'Do that again and you'll be dealing with me,' he said wagging his finger.

Lily later married Sylvester Weeks, who had been born in America but was living in Canada. However, before she had wed, Lily and Nellie and her family had returned to England in 1933 with the intention of resettling. Only a year later the pull to return to Canada was too strong, or England was not how they remembered it. The country was going through straitened economic times and they decided that Canada, after all, offered the best prospects for their children. They sailed again, the Kirkhams with Lily in tow, on the *Ausonia* from Southampton. This time they settled in Canada for good.

Lily Weeks née Green did return to Epsom just one more time. She had always remembered her father's colleagues and continued to send them a card every Christmas long after they had all retired and the police station itself had moved to a modern building in nearby Church Street in 1963. The building that her father died defending was further battered when a flying bomb fell across the road, taking the station's roof with it, in 1944, and finally shut in 1963. In 1969 Lily was invited to England to mark the fiftieth anniversary of her father's death by Inspector Ebon and she attended a ceremony at the graveside. No doubt she would have visited the old house at Lower Court Road and any old friends that were still living and resident in Epsom.

Back in Canada there would have been few reminders for the girls of their father's death and the Epsom Riot, even though the Canadians' general First World War experience figured highly in the historical culture. Had one of them borrowed respected historian Desmond Morton's book *When Your Number's Up* from the library they would have been surprised to learn that 'at Epsom on June 24 [sic], an elderly British police sergeant died of a heart attack when Canadian convalescents attacked his station'.

In November 1993 Nellie, who had long been a widow and was now in her tenth decade, entered the Central Park Lodge nursing home in Toronto to see out her final months. In July of the following year she was joined by her older sister Lilian. Nellie's son Gordon remembers bringing them together again in the same room and how their conversation turned very quickly to their mother and father and the happy days in

234

Epsom. He watched them join hands and laugh and cry as they recalled their dad, Thomas Green – the man and father – and his tragic, premature death.

Sir Edwin Alderson died in 1927.

PC John Barltrop retired from the force in 1925 and died in Hungerford, Berkshire in 1967. Of all the officers that defended the station in 1919 he was the last to die.

PC George Barton was pensioned in 1925 and retired to the coast at Bexhill-on-Sea in Sussex, dying there in 1945.

PC Thomas Bewick retired in 1931 and moved to Whimple, Devon. He too died in 1945.

Major Dr Percy James Sandy Bird returned to Canada in late 1919. He died in 1940, aged sixty-three.

Sir Rowland Blades remained MP for Epsom until 1928. In 1926–1927 he served as Lord Mayor of London. In 1922 he was created Baronet and in 1927 was appointed Knight Grand Cross of the British Empire. In 1928 he was raised to the peerage as Baron Ebbisham (the old name for Epsom – Baron Epsom was already held by Lord Rosebery). He died in 1953.

Sergeant Fred Blaydon took his pension in October 1919 around the time Sir Nevil Macready was refusing to meet him. He could have stayed on a couple more years had he so wished. He died in 1932.

Private Shelby Bowen's hard labour didn't do him too much damage: he died in New York in 1971, aged eighty-nine.

William Bowers Card, Thomas Green's brother-in-law and the uncle that Lily and Nellie Green listed as their next of kin when they emigrated, became a master baker in Brighton. A young son, Ronald, died after falling 'whilst balancing'. William died in Brighton in 1949, aged eighty-two.

Superintendent Alfred Boxhall was a policeman on the rise. His records chart continual promotions and commendations. Tragically, he died prematurely in 1923 from diabetes, pleurisy and cardiac failure.

General Sir Julian Byng was knighted in 1921 and became George V's representative in Canada. Later, back in England, he served as Metropolitan Police Commissioner. In 1928 he was created Viscount Byng of Vimy. He died in 1935.

Winston Churchill became Prime Minister twice and led the country to victory in the Second World War. He died in 1965 at the age of ninety.

James Chuter Ede was elected to Parliament as the MP for Mitcham in 1923. He later held the seat of Tyneside and South Shields until 1964. He was Home Secretary in the 1945 Labour Government of Clement Attlee and Leader of the House of Commons in 1951. In 1964 he was created a life peer and took the title Baron Chuter Ede of Epsom. He died in 1965, aged eighty-three.

Major George Cornwallis-West committed suicide in 1951. He was seventy-seven years old and had been suffering from Parkinson's disease.

Justice Darling presided over his last trial in 1922. He sentenced Herbert Rowse Armstrong to the gallows, the only solicitor to be hanged in Britain. In 1924 he was raised to the peerage as Baron Darling of Langham, Essex. He died in 1936 at age eighty-six.

Sergeant Peter Durham was pensioned in 1926 and died in 1950 in Headington, Oxfordshire.

Edward, Prince of Wales became King Edward VIII in 1936, but abdicated in the same year because he wished to marry Wallis Simpson, a divorcee. He became Governor of the Bahamas and receded from public life, dying aged seventy-seven in 1972.

Epsom Canadian soldiers returned to Epsom in the Second World War. There were few recorded incidents of hostilities between them and the local population, even though many relationships were formed with Epsom women. A significant number left England for Canada as 'war brides' in 1945 and 1946. It is estimated that between 25,000 and 30,000 illegitimate children were born to Canadian fathers in England between 1939 and 1946.

Inspector John Kenneth Ferrier took retirement from the police force in 1924 and died in 1947, aged seventy-one. When he retired in 1924 one newspaper paid tribute to his efforts at Hurst Park racecourse, where he had directed operations against 'welshers' [swindlers], card tricksters and other undesirables. During his retirement he published a book, *Crooks and Crime* – no mention is made of the Epsom case.

PC Alfred Galloway suffered a personal tragedy in 1923 when his son, Justin, died from meningitis at just fourteen years old. Dr Thornely certified the death at 4 Miles Road, Epsom. By this time he had been retired from the police for two years. He died in Barry, Glamorganshire in 1948.

Edgar Green's first wife, Nellie, died and he remarried a Lilian in Canada. Thomas Green's younger brother died in 1958 in Toronto, Canada aged eighty-three.

William Green, Thomas Green's older brother, died in London, Ontario at ninety-one years old in 1950.

Colonel Dr Frederick Guest returned to Canada in September 1919 to his wife, Alice, and their children. He died in 1947 aged seventy-nine.

PC Harold Hinton's daughters Ethel and Elsie attended a ceremony in Epsom in 1994 to mark the seventy-fifth anniversary of the Epsom Riot and they remarked that their father never recovered from the injuries and trauma received in June 1919. The family donated his presentation gold watch to the Bow Street Police Museum.

PC Spencer George Hook remained in Epsom after his retirement from the police in 1928 and became the caretaker of the Congregational Hall. He was a member of the Comrades Club and died in 1940.

Colonel Sam Hughes died in 1921.

Herbert Jones, the Epsom-born jockey who collided with Emily Davison in 1913 Derby, went on to lose three brothers in the First World War. He said he always haunted 'by that woman's face' and in 1951 he placed his head in an oven and gassed himself.

Sergeant William Kersey took retirement shortly after the riot. He was pensioned in December 1919 and died in Ilford, Essex in 1939.

Nellie Kirkham née Green died on Sunday 24 July 1994 at Central Park Lodge, a residential home in Toronto, only a few days after that poignant reunion with her sister, Lilian. She was ninety-three years of age. She is buried in Park Lawn Cemetery, Toronto.

Major Edgar Mortimore Lafone was awarded an OBE on 3 June 3 1924 and retired from the police force in 1926 due to failing eyesight. He died in 1938. At his funeral one friend said of him: 'Human nature with all its confusions and contradictions was an open book to him.' Coincidentally, his son Michael married into General Sir Julian Byng's family.

David Lloyd George was ousted as Prime Minister by Andrew Bonar Law in 1922, but remained active in politics as Liberal leader. In 1936 he met Adolf Hitler in an attempt to thwart his European ambitions. His verdict on the man was: 'A magnetic dynamic personality with a single-minded purpose, a resolute will, and a dauntless heart.' He (and Hitler) died in 1945.

Private John Harding Allan McDonald died at Camp Hill Military Hospital, Halifax, Nova Scotia on 11 December 1961.

Sir Nevil Macready was credited with helping bring about the IRA truce in Ireland in 1921. In 1924 he published his memoirs, *Annals of an Active Life*. He died in 1946.

Private Robert McAllan died in 1939 aged sixty-five.

Private Allan James MacMaster died in 1939 aged fifty.

PC Albert Monk continued to serve as a constable until 1930 and enjoyed a long retirement, dying in 1957 in Carshalton, Surrey.

Sir Richard Muir died suddenly at fifty-seven in 1924. It was said that he never recovered from the death of his son in 1918.

PC Arthur Orchard was pensioned very quickly after the riot in October 1919 and continued to live in Middle Lane, Epsom until his death in 1946.

Inspector Charlie Pawley retired from the force in 1921. He died in Epsom in 1937.

Freda Pawley, daughter of Inspector Pawley and present at the riot, later worked for the Co-op in East Street, Epsom as a book-keeper until her retirement in 1964. She married Andrew Philp in 1965 and died in 1999. She was certainly the last surviving witness to the Epsom Riot.

Harry Pawley, son of Inspector Pawley and also present at the riot, lived out his days in Epsom, sharing a house for many years at Chase End with his sister Freda. In 1972 Harry presented his mother's watch, gifted her after the riot, to the

Bow Street Police Museum. He suffered with his war injuries and eventually went blind, dying in the 1970s.

Kate Pawley, wife of Inspector Pawley, died in 1945.

Charles Polhill, the butcher in whose house Sergeant Green lay dying, died only two years later in 1921.

Private Gervais Poirier emigrated from Canada to the USA, arriving in New York City in 1926. He died in Weehawken, New Jersey in 1974. He worked as a fireman.

PC James Thomas Rose retired from the police force in 1936, being the last man who defended the Epsom station in 1919 to remain serving. He replaced Sergeant Greenfield as the Coroner's Office policeman. He was a tug-of-war champion and active in Epsom socially until his death in 1962.

Lord Rosebery lived until 1929, despite some years of very poor health. He was eighty-two years old when he died and left the equivalent of £60 million in his will. At his own request, his family played the 'Eton Boating Song' on the gramophone as he slipped away.

Major James Ross stayed in England after the war, living at 26 Priory Road, Bedford Park, London. He died in 1955.

Sergeant James Shirley was pensioned in 1923 while still an acting sergeant and retired to Pagham, near Bognor, dying there in 1946.

PC Ernest Short retired in 1925 and died in Wyeths Road, Epsom in 1954.

Edward Shortt left politics in 1922 and turned his attention to banning films in his role as the President of the British Board of Film Censors. He died in 1935.

Sergeant Herbert Shuttleworth was pensioned in 1922 and died in 1935.

PC Daniel Stanford retired from the police in 1927 and died in Melbourn, Hertfordshire in 1962.

Gunner Herbert Tait died in the Westminster Hospital, London, Ontario in 1964.

PC Percy Taylor took retirement and pension in December 1919 following the riot and retired to Shoreham-on-Sea where he passed away in 1951.

Robert Todd emigrated to the United States in the late 1920s and naturalised as an American in Michigan in 1938.

Sir Richard Turner died in 1961 aged ninety.

Driver Alexander Veinot was returned to Canada in August 1919. He had been charged by the military for disorderly conduct and obstructing the police in the execution of their duty and awarded fourteen days' Field Punishment No 2. When he died in 1973 in Nova Scotia he was remembered at his funeral as a veteran of the two world wars.

PC Joe Weeding was pensioned in 1927 and died in 1963 when he was still living in Epsom.

Gilbert White, Surrey coroner, died in 1925.

Lilian Weeks née Green died on 5 June 1995 at ninety-four years of age. Like her sister Nellie she was still resident at the Central Park Lodge residential home in Toronto. She was cremated.

Sir Ernest Wild, prosecutor at the trial, died in 1934 aged sixty-five.

INTERVIEW
with
TIM RICHARDSON

Tim Richardson, a retired Metropolitan police officer, is the man responsible for rescuing Sergeant Green and his story from obscurity. He campaigned and lobbied for Thomas Green's sacrifice to be commemorated both within the police force and the town of Epsom.

How did you become aware of the case of Sergeant Green?

As a young boy living in Tadworth, close to Epsom, I read about the case of Sergeant Green in a local newspaper and was immediately curious. The story was about some family members of the police involved in the Epsom Riot donating their commemorative watches to the Bow Street Museum in about 1969. Maybe it was the time of the fiftieth anniversary. The killing of Sergeant Green seemed to me such a high-profile murder – I was amazed I had never heard about it before.

What happened next?

I left school and joined the RAF. When I came out I became a police officer within the Met and in 1982 I was posted to Epsom. When I got there I saw an old picture on the wall of the officers involved in the riot and my interest in the case was reignited. I also discovered that Sergeant Green's daughters were alive, residing in Canada, and each Christmas sent a card to the station.

Was there a general awareness in the station about the case?

Not really. The case was already then over sixty years old. Again, I did not do anything there and then because I was transferred away to other areas. In 1993 I was returned to Epsom and it struck me that the seventy-fifth anniversary of the riot was coming up. I made a proposal to the Chief Superintendent at Epsom that we mark the occasion with a memorial service and he passed it upwards to Scotland Yard who approved the plan. I then put an appeal in the local paper for anybody with any connections to the riot, or the officers, to contact me.

This time it was just not curiosity. I had a foot firmly in both camps. I was a policeman and understood only too well the extraordinary sacrifice made by Tom Green and the ordeal and challenge that all the other officers must have faced that night. Also, I had a developing interest in the First World War and had lost two great uncles who served as infantrymen in the Canadian Army during the Battle of the Somme.

Did anybody present at the riot come forward? Was there anybody left alive?

There was. Sadly, no officers – that would have been amazing, but I went to meet a delightful old lady named Freda Philp, and she was Inspector Pawley's daughter! She had been present at the riot and remembered it, and Sergeant Green, vividly. It was an amazing moment in my life to be sat there chatting with a lady who had experienced the whole thing. She was living in sheltered accommodation in St Martin's Avenue and by her bed was a box of photographs and she handed them to me.

247

They had been damaged by condensation, but they were fantastic. Pictures of her father, the funeral, evidence photographs and the like. To me, it was like opening a treasure trove.

Did the memorial service go ahead?

Yes, it was a huge success. Freda was the guest of honour, but we also found PC Hinton's two daughters. One was named Ethel Aboe and lived at Swail House. Again the reality of it all was brought home when she told me how her father was damaged mentally by the riot. I felt for him and when I look at his face in one of the pictures of the medal-giving ceremony, I can see his anguish. We had a memorial service at Thomas's grave and Freda laid a wreath, it was very moving. I had been up at the cemetery the previous day and touched up the lettering on Sergeant Green's stone. Afterwards we went back to Epsom Police Station and had a tea party. A lovely man called Michael Welton who was a minister at the Wesleyan Church in Epsom, and the police chaplain, carried out the service (he tragically died just two days before the plaque unveiling in 2009). We also had a plaque mounted at the station and that remains there to this day.

Was that the end of it?

On the contrary – it was the beginning. I learned more and more about the case and became gradually, and unofficially, the point of contact for anybody who had an interest in the Epsom Riot of 1919. A lady called Maggie Bird, who was the Chief Archivist at the Met, like me felt that the whole affair was important and she was invaluable in uncovering and gathering information. Maggie has, very sadly, recently died and will be sorely missed. I was asked to give a talk in London in 1995 to the Friends of the Met Museum and later Scotland Yard. Since then I have done many talks, including Epsom Police Station and The Imperial War Museum. As I do this, even now, I learn more.

Do you have any examples?

Yes, only a couple of years ago I was giving a talk at Leatherhead. There was an elderly man in the front row and I picked up a vibe from him almost immediately. His body language was aggressive and he appeared angry. He interjected at length and the Chairman had to intervene. After I finished I approached him to try and understand why he felt so strongly. He said that he was a Second World War veteran and accused me of not representing fairly 'both sides'. He thought I had no appreciation of how badly the Canadians were treated in Epsom. He said his father was at Woodcote camp, he did not state whether he was a Canadian, but I assume he was, and that the police were guilty of victimisation. He claimed that there was a sergeant in Epsom who had it in for the Canadians because his own daughter had been made pregnant by one of the men. I was taken aback and did not take this man's name or dig further, but we parted amicably. In the light of what Martin has uncovered in this book about James Connors and a girlfriend called Lil, who *could* have been Thomas Green's daughter, it is an intriguing claim. Relying on hearsay and unsubstantiated evidence goes against all my police training, I must add, but it is intriguing, nevertheless.

I have heard you tell a story about PC Rose. How did that come about?

Around 1982 I was walking my beat along Albert Road in Epsom. Walking my beat – that makes me sound ancient! An elderly man approached and I said good morning. We stopped and chatted and I must have brought up the subject of the riot. He had known James Rose and recounted the following story.

Rose was one of the officers that Inspector Pawley sent home after the first bit of trouble outside the police station, but was recalled when things started turning nasty. He lived just around the corner in The Parade and put on his uniform and stepped out into the street. He could hear the din and approached Ashley Road cautiously, but as he peered around the corner some Canadian soldiers at the back of the siege spotted him and gave chase. Rose felt he was running for his life as he charged back down The Parade. Fortunately, it was dark, and Rose knew his terrain better than his pursuers. He veered into an unlit footpath that led up to the Catholic church, near The Rising Sun pub, knowing there was a wall that jutted out into the path. Rose swerved around it, but the soldiers crashed into the structure at great speed, falling over on the floor and one another, allowing the PC to escape and gain entry into the police station by the rear entrance.

After he told me this I sought out the alley and sure enough the protruding wall was there. It still is.

You met Thomas Green's great grandson. How did occur?

It was in the nineties and I had a call from Epsom Police Station saying someone had turned up they thought I should meet. It was Ian Kirkham, grandson of Thomas's daughter Nellie. He was visiting from Canada and was keen to visit the places he had heard about all of his life. I was able to take him around in my Land Rover and we, of course, visited the grave and the scene of the riot and The Rifleman pub. We went to 92

Lower Court Road and Ian took some photographs. I knocked on the door and told the lady who lived in the old house our business and she said she had vaguely heard of the case, but had no idea that Sergeant Green had lived in her house. She then announced that her home was haunted and relayed a time when her young son was ill. She was sitting by his bedside and she had seen an elderly man across the landing. He was balding with a large moustache. She said she was not at all frightened and felt the 'ghost' to be thoroughly benign. Ian and I drove off feeling quite peculiar.

Why do you think the case of Sergeant Green remained under the radar for so long?

I don't know. I can't honestly answer that. I was never sure about the conspiracy theories surrounding the case, but have to say that when one looks at the cumulative evidence, the unanswered questions, then it is hard not to draw the conclusion that something went on. I suppose I don't give it a terrible amount of thought. From the start I have been interested in the human side of it all. It may sound twee, but I felt for Thomas Green and passionately believed that his sacrifice should be properly recognised and that his rightful place in police history should be staked. Also these things are never black and white and I think it is right that this important part of First World War, police and social history finds its true context.

Well, I think you have successfully done that. Thank you.

I hope I have helped. Thank you.

During the course of my research and writing this book I have tried to discover what happened to the second most important character in this sad story. Other than Allan MacMaster turning himself in at a police station and confessing to the murder of Thomas Green ten years after the event, little was known about him after his return to Canada. That confession confirmed that MacMaster did, at least, have a conscience about the man he murdered. Glenn Wright managed to access some army records from where we learned of his childhood illnesses and epilepsy, which hinted at underlying forces behind his violence. Archives held at Kew confirmed he was suffering with syphilis, which often induced madness and psychotic episodes. A note at The National Archives said he died in 1939. A couple of people close to the case thought he had become a drinker and a tramp, but were not sure where this came from.

I discovered via online sources that MacMaster had married Cassie Macaskill in 1921 and that she died in 1925, most probably in childbirth. This marriage is believed to have produced two children. It has recently come to light that MacMaster married again, only months after he was widowed, to a Susan Jasson, who was around nineteen years old – nearly half his age. He was living in Timmins, Ontario and making a living as a miner. And there, despite making contact with local papers, genealogists and all manner of people called MacMaster, I was forced to leave it.

Literally days before this book was due to be printed an email from an Allan MacMaster pinged up on my screen, accelerating my heartbeat for a few seconds. It was like this elusive man was crossing the divide between life and death and the

252

centuries, wanting to be heard. This Allan MacMaster was a young Nova Scotian politician who I must have emailed months earlier in my trawl of MacMasters. He said he believed my MacMaster was a second or third cousin of his and volunteered the following information about him before I ever told him about the reasons for my interest. He was born in Judique, he said. His father was a blacksmith. He served in the Great War and suffered an injury to his head, which caused him to have a metal plate fitted. This and his war experiences resulted in depression and mental illness in later life. In the end he committed suicide. And he was an exquisite fiddle player. I know all this, said Allan, because I am named after him.

Allan's father is a revered and celebrated violinist and fiddle-player in Canada. His name is Buddy MacMaster and his niece Natalie MacMaster has also experienced great success following the family musical tradition. They all descended from the Scottish MacMaster brothers who settled in Judique, Cape Breton around the turn of the eighteenth century. Buddy actually knew Allan, his son explained, and the following Sunday I settled down to a transatlantic telephone conversation with eighty-six-year-old Buddy. Now I was getting close to Allan MacMaster, talking to someone who had talked to him.

'He was my cousin,' Buddy explained in a soft, calming voice. 'I was born in Timmins, Ontario in 1924 and before we moved back to Judique in 1929 Allan was a regular visitor to our house and we saw him occasionally when he visited home after that. Allan was a big, powerful man, but played the fiddle beautifully, which may have been incongruous for such a solid man. It certainly made an impression on me and contributed to my determination to become a fiddler. He worked down the mines and around 1928 or 1929 there was an accident at the mine and Allan saved a man's life by hanging on to him after he almost fell down a pit. It took extraordinary strength to do that and I remember people talking about it for a long time afterwards. There was a sadness about Allan and people said that he was scarred by his war experiences. I had no idea about the Epsom Riot and had never heard it mentioned.

253

Unfortunately, when he drank, it triggered a mental illness in him and I think he got himself in situations from time to time. Tragically, I heard he did himself in, but I don't know the details. He had a son called John, I do know that, and John came to see me at one my concerts in the 1940s or 1950s but we lost touch. To me Allan MacMaster was always gentle and kind and a hero, after him saving the man's life, and that is why I named my boy after him.'

Buddy's recollections certainly add light and shade to the memory of Allan MacMaster, but they also raise some questions. Did he have a metal plate inserted into his head? And if so, was it as a result of injuries sustained in the Epsom Riot? There is no mention of this particular injury or procedure on his army records. Was he operated on after his return to Canada? Was it the guilt he undoubtedly felt over the murder of Sergeant Green that drove him to kill himself twenty years later? Did he decide that if nobody else would punish him for taking that policeman's life he had to do it himself? Was his last thought of Thomas Green before making that final act?

TIMELINE

1914

September   First Epsom men leave to fight in First World War

November   Construction of Woodcote camp begins on Royal Automobile Club land on edge of Epsom

1915

February   Woodcote Park opens as a hospital to Colonial soldiers

1916

January   Two Australian soldiers convicted of assaulting Epsom police officers

1917

June   Canadian private accused of the rape of an Epsom woman

1918

                 Various incidents and assaults by Canadians on Epsom police

August   Police strike

November   First World War ends

1919

January   First case of returning Epsom soldier clashing with Canadians

March   Rioting by Canadian soldiers at the Rhyl camp in North Wales: several fatalities

June   Street fighting between Canadian soldiers and Epsom men almost nightly

	Canadian soldiers riot at Witley camp, Guildford, Surrey
	Colonel Guest of Woodcote camp requests more military police
17 June, 9.00pm	Fight breaks out in The Rifleman between Canadian soldiers and locals
9.15pm	Canadians Private McDonald and Driver Veinot are arrested and escorted to Epsom Police Station
10.15pm	First group of Canadian soldiers gather around Police Station, but are dispersed into Rosebery Park
10.30pm	Woodcote camp are contacted and asked to fetch prisoners. The police are told there is unrest in the camp
10.35pm	Returning Canadian soldiers alert the camp to the events in the town and efforts are made to rouse everyone
10.45pm	Inspector Pawley calls for reinforcements from off-duty staff
10. 55pm	An angry mob led by soldier Allan MacMaster leaves the camp for the police station
11.00pm	A messenger calls at Sergeant Green's house and asks him to attend the station
11.05pm	The approaching Canadian soldiers vandalise The Ladas public house
11.10pm	The Canadians pour through Rosebery Park and gather rowdily outside the Police Station
	Sergeant Green enters the police station through the back entrance

11.20pm	Canadian officer Major Ross converses with Inspector Pawley and goes inside to effect the release of the prisoners
11.25pm	The mob decides that Ross's non-reappearance means he too has been arrested – they begin to shower the station with masonry and stones and start to storm the building
11.35pm	Windows are smashed and the Canadians flood the courtyard
	The handful of police make their first charge and temporarily drive back the rioters
11.45pm	Following fierce fighting the Epsom police retreat back into the station. They cover the doors and the windows to prevent the mob gaining entry into the building
11.50pm	Soldiers are now at the side of the building where the cells are located
11.55pm	Sergeant Green says to Inspector Pawley 'We will have to charge them'
	Leaving windows and door covered Green leads the charge at the side of the building
18 June, 12.00am	Fierce fighting ensues. Canadians are wielding sticks and posts. Police have truncheons. Sergeant Green has a poker
12.10am	Green is felled by a blow from a post delivered by Private James Connors, but manages to get back to his feet
	Canadian soldiers are swarming around the police cells and Private Allan MacMaster has torn away an iron cell bar

12.12am	MacMaster strikes Sergeant Green over the head with iron bar
12.15am	The two prisoners are freed by the rioters and the worst of the fighting subsides
	A group of soldiers pick up Sergeant Green's prostrate body and rush him across the road to the house of Charles Polhill
	The mob retreat across Rosebery Park bathing and cleaning their wounds in the park ponds on their way
	The soldiers attempt to administer first aid to Sergeant Green in Charles Polhill's hallway
12.30am	The soldiers leave Mr Polhill's and he walks over to the becalmed Police Station to inform them of Sergeant Green's presence
12.30am	Two soldiers ask for a drink at Mrs Beauchamp's lodging house and say they have killed a policeman
12.45am	Divisional Superintendent Boxhall and other police reinforcements arrive
12.30am	Police surgeon Dr Thornely arrives at Mr Polhill's to attend to Sergeant Green. He says he is still alive, but orders him to be taken to Epsom Infirmary
2.00am	Calls are made by Divisional Police to army for support to be sent to Epsom
7.15am	Sergeant Green dies at Epsom Infirmary
9.00am	Colonel Guest addresses the men at Woodcote camp, informing them of Sergeant Green's death

9.30am	Leader of Epsom Council telegrams War Office asking for a military presence in town to prevent further disturbances
	Application made at Epsom Court for all pubs and clubs to be closed in the borough. Application granted
10.00am	Major Lafone, Chief Constable of 'V' Division and Inspector Ferrier from Scotland Yard arrive at Epsom Police Station
11.00am	Inspector Ferrier, PC Rose and others visit Woodcote camp.
	PC Rose identifies Private James Connors and William Lloyd as being involved in the riot. They are arrested
12.00pm	Canadian HQ in London issue a statement saying that complete order prevails at Woodcote camp
2.00pm	First inquest on Thomas Green is opened at the Epsom Infirmary
	Winston Churchill, Secretary of State for War, sends a letter of condolence and support via local MP, Sir Rowland Blades
	Metropolitan Police Commissioner Sir Nevil Macready telegrams Winston Churchill over the 'culpable inaction' of the military for not turning up in Epsom
3.00pm	Magistrates rescind closing order for public houses when it is learnt that Canadians are confined to camp
	Soldiers showing injuries from the riot are moved from Woodcote camp to military hospital in Orpington
7.00pm	Ferrier questions injured men at Orpington

19 June	Sir Rowland Blades MP has an audience with Winston Churchill and others over the Epsom Riot at War Office
	A further seven soldiers are arrested at Orpington and sent to Bow Street Police Station for questioning
	William Lloyd's statement refers to a colleague witnessing the murder of Sergeant Green and names Eddie Lapointe as that witness
	Sir Richard Turner, Chief of Staff for Canadian troops in England, visits Epsom Police Station. Later he issues an appeal to all Canadians for calm and to avoid mutinous behaviour
20 June	Allan MacMaster, James Connors, Robert McAllan, Frank Wilkie, David Yerex, Herbert Tait, Gervase Poirier and Alphonse Masse are charged at Bow Street with manslaughter
	William Lloyd is released as he proves he was elsewhere
	Local newspapers carry an appeal from police, Council and themselves to locals not to carry out revenge attacks on Canadians
	Leader article in Times alleges widespread venereal disease at Woodcote Park
23 June, 10.00am	Inspector Ferrier interviews Eddie Lapointe for the first and final time. He does not tell the same story he told William Lloyd and says he did not see the murder
11.00am	Metropolitan police officers arrive into Epsom to attend Sergeant Green's funeral

2.00pm	Funeral procession begins from Lower Court Road, Epsom
2.30pm	Cortege arrives at Wesleyan Chapel on Ashley Road
3.00pm	Sergeant Green is interred at Ashley Road cemetery
25 June	Inquest resumes at Epsom Court House
26 June	Private Frederick Bruns' body is found in a quarry on the edge of Woodcote Park
27 June	Eight soldiers are charged at Bow Street Magistrates Court with being involved in the manslaughter of Sergeant Green
28 June	Bow Street Magisterial hearing concludes. Poirier and Tait are discharged and the other five are committed to trial
	Inquest of Frederick Bruns begins and concludes and records an open verdict
30 June	Green inquest reconvened at Epsom Court. They find that a sixth man, Robert Todd, the bugler on the day of the riot, should stand trial too
19 July	Epsom celebrates the Peace, officially
22 July	The full criminal trial begins of the six soldiers at Guildford Assizes
23 July	The trial ends. McAllan and Todd are acquitted. The others are sent to prison for twelve months
August	Edward, Prince of Wales commences Royal Tour of Canada and other dominions
September	An appeal on behalf of the four imprisoned men is rejected
14 November	The prisoners are released from civil prison into the custody of the Canadians

1 December	Edward, Prince of Wales arrives back from Canadian tour
4 December	The Home Secretary informs Parliament that the prisoners will be released into Canadian custody on December 15, even though they are already released
10 December	PC Harry Hinton resigns from police force. Injuries and trauma from the riot have overwhelmed him

1920

3 January	Allan MacMaster back in Canada and is discharged from army
14 January	Lord Rosebery presents surviving Epsom policemen with gallantry medals
19 May	James Connors dies of tuberculosis in Bermondsey Hospital
11 June	Sergeant Green's memorial stone is unveiled at Epsom Cemetery

1921

30 November	Lilian Green, Sergeant Green's widow, dies

1922

April	Lily and Nellie Green, Sergeant Green's daughters, emigrate
	Allan MacMaster marries Cassie McCaskill

1925

January	Cassie MacMaster dies in childbirth

1929

July	Allan MacMaster confesses to the murder of Sergeant Green

BIBLIOGRAPHY

Addy, Barbara, *The Public Houses of Epsom Past and Present* (Epsom & Ewell History & Archaeology Society, 2003)

Berry, Patricia, *Epsom: The Twentieth Century* (Sutton, 2003)

Brown, Kevin, *The Pox: The Life and Near Death of a Very Social Disease* (Sutton, 2006)

Crewe, ROA Crewe-Milnes, First Marquess of, *Lord Rosebery* (John Murray/1931

Eacott, Bill, *The Wootton Family: Australia to Epsom* (2003)

Edwards, J Hugh, *David Lloyd George: The Man and the Statesman* (Waverley, 1930)

Essen, RI, *Epsom's Military Camp* (Pullingers, 1991)

Felstead, ST, *Sir Richard Muir: A Memoir of a Public Prosecutor* (John Lane, 1927)

Ferris, Bob, *The Murder of Station Sergeant Green* (online at www.epsomandewellhistoryexplorer.org.uk/GreenBooklet.pdf)

Fido, Martin and Skinner, Keith, *The Official Encyclopedia of Scotland Yard* (Virgin, 1999)

Gibbs, Philip, *Now It Can Be Told* (Harper, 1920)

Hayden, Deborah, *Pox: Genius, Madness and the Mysteries of Syphilis* (Basic, 2003)

History of the Royal Fusiliers 'UPS' University and Public Schools Brigade (Formation and Training) (*The Times*, 1917)

Holmes, Richard, *Tommy: The British Soldier on the Western Front 1914–1918* (HarperPerennial, 2004)

Home, Gordon, *Epsom, its History and its Surroundings* (SR, 1971)

James, Robert Rhodes, *Rosebery: A Biography of Archibald Philip, Fifth Earl of Rosebery* (Weidenfeld & Nicolson, 1963)

Langley Vale: Memories of a Surrey Village (Langley Vale Women's Institute, 2001)

London Police – Their Stories: 80 Years at the Sharp End (Merlin Unwin, 1998)

MacInnes, Sheldon, *Buddy MacMaster: The Judique Fiddler* (Pottersfield Press, 2007)

Mantle, Craig Leslie, *The Apathetic and the Defiant: Case Studies of Canadian Mutiny and Disobedience, 1812 to 1919* (Dundurn, 2007)

Mathieson, William D, *My Grandfather's War: Canadians Remember the First World War, 1914–1918* (Macmillan Canada, 1981)

Morton, Desmond, *Fight or Pay: Soldiers' Families in the Great War* (UBC Press, 2004)

——, *When Your Number's Up The Canadian Soldier in the First World War* (Random House of Canada, 1993)

Orchard, Vincent, *The Derby Stakes: A Complete History from 1900 to 1953* (Hutchinson, 1954)

Putkowski, Julian, *The Kinmel Park Camp Riots 1919* (Flintshire Historical Society, 1989)

Raymond, ET, *The Man of Promise: Lord Rosebery – A Critical Study* (Fisher Unwin, 1923)

Shortland, Edward, *The Murder of Station Sergeant Thomas Green at Epsom Police Station 17th June, 1919*

Sleight, John, *One-Way Ticket to Epsom: A Journalist's Enquiry into the Heroic Story of Emily Wilding Davison* (Bridge Studios, 1988)

Walsh, Milly and Callan, John, *We're Not Dead Yet: The First World War Diary of Bert Cooke* (Vanwell, 2004)

Wilson, AN, *After the Victorians: The World Our Parents Knew* (Arrow, 2006)

Windsor, Edward, Duke of, *A King's Story: The Memoirs of HRH The Duke of Windsor* (Cassell, 1951)

264

INDEX

268

281

ACKNOWLEDGEMENTS

The following people's help was invaluable in the researching and writing of this book. Gordon Kirkham, grandson of Thomas Green, who shared his memories and knowledge of his grandfather, mother and aunt. Edward Shortland, who applied his detecting instincts to the case and has been dogged in pulling back the veils of secrecy that have surrounded the entire affair, and joining up some elusive dots. Jeremy Harte and David Brooks of Bourne Hall Museum, Ewell – they have done much to keep Thomas Green's memory alive over the years and kindly allowed me unfettered access to their archives. Tim Richardson, who more than anyone has been Thomas's champion among the living, educating all and sundry about what happened in June 1919 and why. Glenn Ross, an expert on the Canadian experience in the First World War, who discovered the human stories behind the Canadian soldiers and gave me much more advice and information. I am indebted to Les Turner who helped research Thomas Green's military days and Billingshurst Local History Society for information on the Green family and their ancestors. Trevor White's booklet *War-Time in a Surrey Town* was very useful and informative. Alan Moss and Keith Skinner provided deep research on the police officers involved and Bill Owen local knowledge and supporting information.